Knowledge and Practice in E and Organisations

Knowledge and Practice in Business and Organisations contributes to scholarly understanding of knowledge and practice, mapping the conceptual terrain, providing a critical review of debates in the field and setting out key theoretical perspectives. Knowledge and practice are explored in a range of organisational and policy settings through six context-specific discussions. The collection helps shape the field, identify areas for future research enquiry, and suggest implications for practitioners.

The range of sites of enquiry represented in the book (e.g., craft working, accounting, public sector organisations, creative industries, healthcare, and so on) make the book distinctive, enabling the reader to connect debates and ideas from across a range of sectors and disciplines. The book charts different currents of debate that have hitherto tended to remain unconnected. In one accessible volume, this book provides an excellent introduction to a set of concepts that have animated scholarly conversations across a range of disciplines and provides cases and examples of practices from beyond any one particular sector. Aimed at researchers and academics in the field, this book is a valuable resource, helping define and progress scholarly debate.

Kevin Orr is Professor of Management and Head of the School of Management at the University of St Andrews, UK, specialising in aspects of managing, leading and organising in public sector organisations.

Sandra Nutley is Professor of Public Policy and Management and Co-Director of the Research Unit for Research Utilisation (RURU), University of St Andrews, UK.

Shona Russell is Lecturer in Knowledge and Practice at the School of Management, University of St Andrews, UK.

Rod Bain is a PhD candidate at the School of Management, University of St Andrews, UK specialising in cultural and political aspects of sustainability, and community owned organisations.

Bonnie Hacking is Enterprise Adviser in the University of St Andrews Careers Centre, a Director of Enterprise Educators UK and a member of the Knowledge and Practice group, School of Management, University of St Andrews, UK.

Clare Moran is Policy Fellowships Coordinator, Centre for Science and Policy, University of Cambridge, UK. She is affiliated to the Research Unit for Research Utilisation, University of St Andrews, UK.

Routledge Advances in Organizational Learning and Knowledge Management

Series Editor: Patricia Ordóñez de Pablos, University of Oviedo, Spain

Knowledge and Practice in Business and Organisations

Edited by
Kevin Orr, Sandra Nutley, Shona Russell,
Rod Bain, Bonnie Hacking and
Clare Moran

Routledge
Taylor & Francis Group

NEW YORK AND LONDON

First published 2016
by Routledge
711 Third Avenue, New York, NY 10017

and by Routledge
2 Park Square, Milton Park, Abingdon, Oxon OX14 4RN

First issued in paperback 2018

*Routledge is an imprint of the Taylor & Francis Group,
an informa business*

Library of Congress Cataloging-in-Publication Data
Names: Orr, Kevin Martin.
Title: Knowledge and practice in business and organisations / edited by
    Kevin Orr, Sandra Nutley, Shona Russell, Rod Bain, Bonnie Hacking,
    and Clare Moran.
Description: New York, NY : Routledge, 2016. | Series: Routledge
    advances in organizational learning and knowledge management ; 2 |
    Includes bibliographical references and index.
Identifiers: LCCN 2015043996| ISBN 9781138940857 (cloth : alk. paper) |
    ISBN 9781315674025 (ebook)
Subjects: LCSH: Organizational learning. | Knowledge management. |
    Knowledge, Sociology of. | Organizational sociology.
Classification: LCC HD58.82 .K5775 2016 | DDC 658.4/038—dc23
LC record available at http://lccn.loc.gov/2015043996

ISBN 13: 978-1-138-61725-4 (pbk)
ISBN 13: 978-1-138-94085-7 (hbk)

Typeset in Sabon
by Apex CoVantage, LLC

Contents

PART B
Context-Specific Discussions of the Relationship between Knowledge and Practice

PART C
Integrating the Insights on Knowledge and Practice and Their Implications for Action

Boxes, Figures and Tables

BOXES

FIGURES

TABLES

Foreword

Why should busy practitioners and serious academics pay attention to knowledge, practice and their relationships? Why should they read a book like this one? Surely these scholarly matters are for philosophers only. Or are they? Read on.

A person you care about is ill. You consult two physicians. One is a young doctor who knows everything that has been recently written about the condition and has done research on the topic. The other is an old, wise practitioner who has been practising for years. Who should you trust? You go home and on the telly they are talking about the latest scandal. A manager is offering her sincere apologies, which are followed by the reassurance that lessons will be learned. How can organisations learn lessons? Others are calling for an independent enquiry. Who is right? Can people parachuted in from some big consultancy understand what has gone wrong? And what should they do with all the knowledge they gather? How will the lessons change the practice? The dean of a university (this may well be your dean if you are an academic) is talking about impact: "We are going to produce impactful research and generate value for the nation by creating highly skilled jobs". This makes sense. But what is this impact everybody is talking about? Do you hire more professors of practice—although they are not researchers but expert practitioners? And what are they supposed to do? How do you produce impact from research? And what is a highly skilled job? Is a junior biologist filling test tubes all day more skilled than a nurse or a shoemaker?

Matters of knowledge and practice are not the exclusive purview of philosophers after all. The relationships between knowledge and practice, how knowledge is understood, talked about and considered, impinge on a number of aspects of our professional activities and personal lives. The matter is indeed complex. But you would not expect something that is so critical to be so simple. And this is why you should read this book.

The editors of the volume have in fact done a superb job in assembling a number of agile and readable chapters that provide a clear and concise guide through this rugged conceptual terrain. In this book you will not find answers to the questions above—or at least not all. This is because most of the time there are no right answers. What you will find, however, are many of the conceptual tools you need to clarify what are the issues at stake, untangle the complexity and get a firm idea of what are the concrete implications of taking one view or another.

The book does not try to hide that different ways of understanding exist about contentious issues such as what counts as knowledge, who are knowledge workers, why all forms of knowing are not attributed the same value, or how knowledge can be actioned in practice. Indeed, one of the aims of the book is to map this fragmented landscape so that readers can learn how to navigate it—and the many tables in this text are an invaluable resource. This does not mean, however, that the book does not take a position in the debate. Although the authors do not talk in unison, something that you would not expect from such a large gathering of eminent scholars, they all share an interest in the relations between knowing and doing as well as a preference for addressing the issue from a specific angle—that of practice.

For many of the authors in this book, in fact, understanding how knowledge matters for practice requires nothing less than a Copernican revolution. Rather than thinking of action as the result of the application of a quasi-substance called knowledge, they suggest that we look at action itself as necessarily knowledgeable: acting knowingly. Knowing and doing become therefore inseparable. Some striking consequences follow from this. For example: theory, formalised knowledge, and abstract forms that summarise the knowing of others become resources for acting knowingly rather than 'things' that make us act in one way or another. Theory is critical but the traditional hierarchy between the two is reversed and other forms of knowledgeability—knowing with the body, knowing with the senses and affectivity—are given rights of citizens. Thinking in terms of resources of knowledgeability also draws attention to artefacts. These are the things that others made using their own knowledge and that we build on to act knowingly. The hierarchy of knowledges (theory first, practice after) is not so much denied as it is questioned: why do we give so much emphasis to abstract knowledge? Who is gaining from this way of looking at the world?

From a radical practice perspective, what counts as acceptably acting knowingly is tied to the historical and social conditions of where and when such acting knowingly is accomplished. You would not expect doctors today to act in the same way that their predecessors three or four centuries ago did: what counts as competent action is subject to historical change and tied to a specific community of knowers. It follows that knowing is inherently socially produced, socially shared and socially legitimated. Knowing is also social in another way. In order to learn how to act knowingly and how to put theories, models and other resources of knowledgeability to work, we must engage with others and learn the ropes through first-hand participation. Nobody learns how to play tennis from a manual. But the same applies also to becoming a barrister and even a mathematician: there are right and wrong ways to demonstrate a theorem.

This Copernican revolution has very profound practical implications. If knowledge is social, then amassing large amounts of lessons learned into a storage unit and waiting for people to come and collect them may not be the best way to foster knowledgeability. A better solution would be to leverage the social relationships that naturally bind people who are involved in the same activity and build on their aspiration to be as good as they can in what they do. Similarly, knowledge cannot be moved unchanged and intact from one location to another as we would transfer a box. To become useful, knowledge has to be interpreted in the light of the local situation and fit local perceived needs. Disseminating 'content', no matter how good, may not work. A better idea would be to find a translator or boundary-spanner who can bridge the gaps and facilitate the assimilation process. Or to avoid distinguishing between producers and consumers in the first place—using instead a co-production approach. The list could continue, but the chapters of the book, and especially those in Sections B and C, do an excellent job of exploring and illustrating the implications of this way of turning the issue of theory and practice on its head. It should be added that practice also remains central for those authors who are not ready to take such a radical turn, and prefer instead to stay on firmer and more traditional grounds. In this sense, the book is permeated by a pragmatist view: knowledge has little to do with observing the world from a spectatorial position. Knowledge is always triggered by some real need or desire to move from doubt to belief in the world. Its ultimate validity can only be judged in terms of its concrete consequences and what difference it makes in our lives.

One of the most notable features of this book is that some of the principles espoused in the volume were actually applied reflexively in the production of the book itself. The book emerged from a collaborative process which included face-to-face conversations, round tables, writing workshops, and feedback and review sessions between seasoned academics and promising young scholars. The writing activity was therefore based on co-production and collaboration among members of the same community of knowing—the same principles that the authors espouse in the text. This is a rare feat in academe, where the rule is 'do what I say but not what I do'. Judging from the results, the process seems to have worked quite well! Enjoy, and good reading.

Davide Nicolini

Acknowledgements

Writing this book has been a highly collaborative effort and there are many friends and colleagues we'd like to thank for their part in bringing the edited collection to fruition. As editors we take this chance to express our thanks to all the authors who have contributed to the book. These include faculty members and PhD students in the School of Management at the University of St Andrews, but also research partners from other universities and from other worlds of practice. We are excited about the intellect and commitment of our PhD students who have provided important voices in the development of the project and who feature as co-authors in many of the chapters. We hope that this experience of collaborative research and the writing process will help fuel their future endeavours. At the outset of this process two of the editors, Sandra and Shona, were co-convenors of the Knowledge and Practice group in the School. We would like to thank two successor conveners—Shiona Chillas and Alina Baluch—for their roles in continuing to create a vibrant and collegial space in which we come together to explore and nurture ideas. It is also a pleasure to acknowledge the 'hidden' role played by other members of the group who acted as critical readers and who gave thoughtful feedback on drafts of work as well as positive encouragement throughout the process. These include Jan Bebbington, Judith Hughes, Alison Powell, Sandra Romenska and Juliette Summers. We know the book has been enriched by the contributions of several external commentators— Tim Allen, Mike Bennett, Stanley Blue, Clive Grace, Duncan Maclellan, Julie Miao and Elizabeth Shove—who straddle academic and different practitioner communities. We are fortunate to be in a position to work with such insightful partners. It's been an added thrill to include artwork produced by one of the authors, Louisa Preston. We are also proud that Davide Nicolini has provided the foreword to the book as we recognise the influence he continues to have in the field. Finally, thank you to David Varley, Brianna Ascher and all the editorial team at Routledge for their immediate faith in, and unwavering support for, the project and for their help in enabling our progress to the stage where, through this book, we can share ideas, cultivated in a remote part of Scotland, with the wider world.

The Editors

Contributors

CONTRIBUTORS AFFILIATED PRINCIPALLY TO THE SCHOOL OF MANAGEMENT, UNIVERSITY OF ST ANDREWS

(Further biographical details are available via the School's website: www. st-andrews.ac.uk/management/)

Cinla Akinci is Lecturer in Management, specialising in intuition in decision-making and organisational learning.

Rod Bain is a PhD candidate, specialising in cultural and political aspects of sustainability, and community owned organisations.

Alina Baluch is Lecturer in Management, specialising in employment relations, and performance in voluntary and public organisations.

Anna Brown is a PhD candidate, specialising in embodied knowing explored through the processes of becoming and being a maker (of ceramics).

Shiona Chillas is Lecturer in Management, specialising in work and employment issues.

Huw Davies is Professor of Health Care Policy and Management, Co-Director of the Research Unit for Research Utilisation (RURU) and Associate Director of the Social Dimensions of Health Institute (SDHI).

John Ferguson is Professor of Accounting, specialising in accountability, ethics and governance.

Gail Greig is Lecturer in Management, specialising in collective knowing and learning through practice-based theorising, including activity theory.

Paul Hibbert is Professor of Management and Dean of the Faculty of Arts and Divinity.

Tobias Jung is Senior Lecturer in Management, specialising in philanthropy, non-profit organisations and evidence-based policy and practice.

Charles Lovatt is Senior Teaching Fellow in Entrepreneurship, Innovation and Creativity.

Samuel Mansell is Lecturer in Business Ethics and Pro-Dean of the Faculty of Arts and Divinity.

Duncan Maclennan is Professor of Strategic Urban Management and Finance.

Christopher Mueller is a PhD candidate, specialising in practice, knowing and power.

Sandra Nutley is Professor of Public Policy and Management, and Co-Director of the Research Unit for Research Utilisation (RURU).

Kevin Orr is Professor of Management and Head of School, specialising in aspects of managing, leading and organising in public sector organisations.

Louisa Preston is a joint PhD candidate with the School of Arts and Humanities, University of Stirling, specialising in the impact of digital technologies on arts and cultural organisations.

Toma Pustelnikovaite is a PhD candidate, specialising in labour migration and knowledge work.

Shona Russell is Lecturer in Knowledge and Practice, specialising in environmental policy and sustainability issues.

Lorna Stevenson is Reader in Accounting, Co-Head of School, and Co-Director of the Centre for Social and Environmental Accounting Research.

Tricia Tooman is a PhD candidate, specialising in how professional teams in healthcare learn and change.

Lucy Wishart completed her doctorate on Understanding the Governmentality of Zero Waste Scotland, and remains an active member of the Knowledge and Practice group.

CONTRIBUTORS AFFILIATED PRINCIPALLY WITH OTHER ORGANISATIONS

Tim Allen is Director and Owner, PRA Consultancy Services Limited; Co-Director and Co-Owner, UK Research and Consultancy Services Limited; and Visiting Fellow at Cranfield University.

Nic Beech is Vice-Principal at the University of Dundee, and Honorary Professor at the School of Management, University of St Andrews.

Mike Bennett is Director of Public Intelligence; Co-Owner of UK Research and Consultancy Services Limited; and Honorary Fellow at the School of Management, University of St Andrews.

Stanley Blue is Lecturer in Sociology at Lancaster University.

Louise Crawford is Professor of Accounting at Aberdeen Business School, Robert Gordon University.

Emilia Ferraro is a Lecturer in the Department of Geography and Sustainable Development, University of St Andrews.

Clive Grace is Co-Director and Co-Owner, UK Research and Consultancy Services Limited, and an Honorary Research Fellow at Cardiff Business School.

Christian Grahle joined Google as a Business Development Manager after completing his doctorate at the School of Management, University of St Andrews.

Bonnie Hacking is Enterprise Adviser in the University of St Andrews Careers Centre, a Director of Enterprise Educators UK, and a member of the Knowledge and Practice group, School of Management, University of St Andrews.

Jenny Harrow is Professor of Management at Cass Business School, and Co-Director of the Research Centre on Charitable Giving and Philanthropy.

Tian Miao (Julie) is Lecturer in Urban Planning and Development, University of Glasgow.

Clare Moran is Policy Fellowships Coordinator, Centre for Science and Policy, University of Cambridge. She is affiliated to the Research Unit for Research Utilisation at the School of Management, University of St Andrews.

Davide Nicolini is Professor of Organisation Studies at Warwick Business School, and co-directs the Innovation, Knowledge and Organisational Networks Research Unit (IKON).

Jo Rycroft-Malone is Professor of Implementation and Health Services Research, Pro-Vice Chancellor Research and Impact, University of Bangor.

Elizabeth Shove is Professor of Sociology at Lancaster University, and co-directs the DEMAND (Dynamics of Energy, Mobility and Demand) Centre.

Joyce Wilkinson is Lecturer in Health Sciences, University of Stirling and is affiliated to the Research Unit for Research Utilisation at the School of Management, University of St Andrews, where she completed her doctorate.

Figure 0.1 Where are we going?

1 Introducing the Aims, Background and Content of This Book

Kevin Orr, Rod Bain, Bonnie Hacking,
Clare Moran, Sandra Nutley and Shona Russell

How is what we know shaped by what we do, and how is what we do shaped by what we know?

The central aim of this book is to contribute to scholarly understanding of knowledge and practice in organisational and policy settings, through a blend of conceptual and empirical discussion. It offers a guide for readers interested in considering questions such as how we know what we know, what the relationship between knowledge and practice is, and what ways of knowing our everyday ways of 'doing things' rely on. In addressing such questions, the book provides an introduction to concepts and debates that have animated scholarly conversations across a range of disciplines. These include debates on whether knowledge is best understood as a product or a process; whether some forms of knowledge and ways of knowing should be valued more highly than others; whether practices should be understood simply as what people do, or more widely as what they say, too; and whether practices are part of everyday life or the very substance of that life. To illustrate these debates and understand how they have played out in different settings and enquiries, the book includes cases and examples of knowledge and practice relationships from a variety of sectors and enquiry approaches.

The first part of the book guides readers to and through the relevant conceptual terrain and provides critical reviews of debates in the field. It sets out key theoretical perspectives on knowledge, on practice and on their interrelationships. The second part of the book then offers context-specific discussions of knowledge and practice. The range of contexts explored (e.g., craft working, accounting, public sector organisations, creative industries, healthcare, and so on) enables readers to connect debates and ideas from across a variety of sectors. They can examine knowing and practicing in settings that are often overlooked by books on management and organisation studies. The third part of the book integrates the insights on knowledge and practice from earlier chapters and reflects on their implications for action. The book ends with a provisional conceptual map of the emerging knowledge and practice terrain, some reflections on the process of producing this book, and suggestions for future directions of enquiry and action.

The process of planning and producing this book was distinctive in its collective and collaborative nature, and we next discuss this process and its implications for the approach taken. We then introduce some of the different ways in which the core concepts of knowledge and practice are defined and used in the book. This is followed by a more detailed explanation of the scope, structure and content of the book. Finally, we suggest different ways of reading and using the book.

ACCOUNTING FOR OUR OWN PRACTICE: WHO WE ARE, AND WHY AND HOW WE WROTE THIS BOOK

The book emerged as an idea from discussions among members of the Knowledge and Practice research group in the School of Management at the University of St Andrews. This is one of five thematic research groups at the School that seeks to foster individual and collective scholarship around particular research themes rather than traditional functional specialisms (which in business and management schools tend to include various combinations of accounting, finance, human resources, international business, marketing, operations management, organisation studies, services management, and strategy). The thematic groups are connected by the School's overall commitment to the concept of 'responsible enterprise' and to engaging with a breadth of sites of organising and practising. The Knowledge and Practice group has around 40 members who stretch beyond the boundaries of the School, including colleagues from other disciplines within the university, and other institutions.

Many members of the Knowledge and Practice group currently work, most of their time, in an academic setting, but our ideas are steeped in long-standing and ongoing engagement with practitioners and policymakers from other settings—dialogues that are highly generative, and a central part of our own practices and approaches to knowledge creation and practice development. Moreover, many of us have worked for extended periods in other public, private or third sector settings.

Members of the group share an interest in knowledge and practice, but the nature of their interests, the contexts in which they explore these interests, and their approach to studying or acting to improve knowledge and practice links differ. As members heard more about the work of others, they felt there was much that could be learned by documenting, sharing and comparing these differences. The idea of doing this via writing a book on knowledge and practice became a focal point for mobilisation, something that colleagues committed to with enthusiasm. We were soon immersed in an 18-month schedule of writing retreats, workshops and seminars to develop chapters and carry out editorial and review responsibilities. This was a coalition of the willing and the interested, and for long, if not unbroken, stretches there was a great deal of passion too. The group included PhD students, emerging and mid-career researchers, professors, long-standing members of the School, and colleagues who had more recently joined. It encompassed experienced academic writers and those newer to the game, including those on the cusp of their first publications. Some were closer to debates about knowledge and its use, while others were more committed to enquiries about practice. Approaches also varied in terms of the explanatory, critical or normative goals of group members. It was often quite the carnival.

One ambition for the book was outward looking: it was conceived as an intellectual project that could draw together and represent group interests in a way that contributes to international scholarly discourse about knowledge and practice. Another driver for the enterprise was a local goal. We had faith that the process of producing the book—in particular, developing its coverage, authorship and intellectual approach through generative dialogue and discussion—could be used to nurture scholarship and a sense of community within the Knowledge and Practice group itself.

In relation to the second goal, much has already been achieved. For example, a strong sense of collective responsibility for the overall shape and content of the book developed amongst many members of the group. They were not just concerned about their own chapter. For this reason, when we use phrases such as 'our approach' here and in the concluding chapter, we are referring not just to the editorial team but also to the wider group of authors, and to those PhD students and faculty who acted as engaged and critical readers.

THE PLURALISTIC APPROACH OF THE BOOK

Our early conversations established that we wished to discount the unlikely prospect of producing a unifying text that would dissolve intellectual differences between the authors (or arrive at a corporate stance—'the St Andrews school' of knowledge and practice). Instead, one of our governing instincts was that we could produce a book which benefited from the diversity of approaches to the subject matter. Members of the collective had different starting points in relation to career stage and history, area of research, epistemological position, methodological preference and so on. We had to navigate differences between us in terms of explanatory, normative and critical stances, and attitudes to—and experience of—applied research and engaged scholarship. We hope that ultimately readers find this diversity enriches the conversations in the book.

We regard universities, and our own School of Management, as inclusive sites for intellectual enquiry, which should welcome a range of theoretical and methodological orientations. It therefore seemed inappropriate to privilege one theory over another, not least as it risked colleagues finding themselves on the wrong side of a particular intellectual dividing line. We felt the project would be diminished by this loss of voice and alternative perspective. There is much to be gained from engaging with different ways of thinking about knowledge and practice, whether that is, for example, through power and politics, practice theory, or identity work lenses. We were struck by the opportunity for collective learning to occur through the process of pooling individual knowledge and airing the diversity of perspectives on knowledge and practice. Developing the book offered us the chance to embrace the dialogue that followed from sharing drafts and engaging in discussion at workshop meetings and awaydays. We discussed connections and divergences, and how they could be represented. The content of many chapters evolved substantially due to a growing awareness of the pluralism that animates the group and the book.

DEFINING KNOWLEDGE AND PRACTICE

In the light of all we have said thus far, it should come as no surprise that we have not used a narrow definition of either knowledge or practice in defining the scope and focus of the contributions in this book. The many ways of understanding both these terms are explored in Chapters 2 and 3 respectively. Subsequent chapters in the book go on to exemplify differences in interpretation and use.

In terms of knowledge, we are interested broadly in what we know, how we know it, and in ways of knowing. In some parts of the literature, knowledge is treated more as an object (to be found) and at other times the word 'knowing' is preferred because it is viewed as a process (to be engaged with). As discussed in Chapter 2, these differences matter because they shape the knowledge in (or knowledge into) practice 'problem' that is at the heart of this book.

In relation to practice, we are curious about what people (individually and collectively) do and say in work-related contexts. We are also interested in how these doings and sayings are produced and reproduced. Some contributors talk in terms of practice settings, the sites in which activities take place and ideas are applied in producing products and services. Others view practices as the very substance of social and organisational life.

Epistemology clashes amongst academics—the varying assumptions about the nature of knowledge, its roots, its relationship with practice—add further complexity to these conversations. Are knowledge and practice separate or intertwined? How can we understand the interrelationship and the direction of influence between the two? Knowledge and practice are popularly described as two separate entities—we see this in the oft-posed question of how to put knowledge into practice, or invitations to think through the practical implications of a theory, or allegations against academics that they generate impractical knowledge, and so on. For some, therefore, practising and doing are quite separate from knowledge and knowing. However, for others, in particular those adopting a practice theory perspective, the social world consists of practices and knowing is a social process collectively accomplished, and therefore the two—knowing and practising—are mutually implicated. In this book, we see authors who are committed to practice theory and its assumptions about the inseparability of knowledge and practice, those who are closer to describing a somewhat more dualistic relationship in which the key challenge is the mobilisation of knowledge into practice, and still others who emphasise the significance of politics, power and identity in different sites of knowledge and practice.

The different perspectives on knowledge and practice have implications for how we describe individuals and their roles. The language of knowers and doers is often implicit in many discussions of knowledge and practice, especially when knowledge is seen to emanate from research. This casts researchers as the knowers, and practitioners or policymakers as the doers. On the whole, we prefer to think in terms of academic practitioners and other practitioners, both of whom are knowers too.

SCOPE AND COVERAGE OF THE BOOK

The contexts covered in the book embrace a rich array of practice settings offering a wide spectrum of settings within which to consider knowledge and practice issues. The selection reflects the orientations, knowledge and engagements of the individuals who came together to write the book. Our School's commitment to 'responsible enterprise' signals our belief that knowledge and practice takes place in a wide variety of organisational spaces and eschews the notion that the only sites worthy of attention are those where profits are made or a bottom line achieved. The choice of context-specific chapters therefore communicates the belief that what happens in these spaces matters, and will interest and engage the general reader as much as the sectoral specialist. Our examples are drawn from the UK but they relate to global debates and international conversations about knowledge and practice.

STRUCTURE AND CONTENT OF THIS BOOK

The book is structured around three main parts—A, B and C—and each fulfils a particular role in the overall story. These three parts and chapters contained therein are explained and summarised below to help guide readers through the book, and provide further insight into the issues discussed and the settings explored.

Part A: Mapping the Conceptual Landscape

The five conceptual chapters act as critically engaged reviews of the major ideas and perspectives on knowledge and practice that are to be found in the social science literature. They are written in order to introduce, in an accessible way, a set of intellectual resources and reference points relevant to the subsequent explorations and commentaries in the book. In keeping with the overall approach of the book, the chapters avoid outlining 'one best way' of theorising knowledge, practice and related concepts. They instead map the lines of debates, looking across different fields and disciplines in order to provide an appreciation of the scope and depth of scholarly enquiry about knowing and practising.

In Chapter 2, 'Understanding Knowledge and Knowing', Tricia Tooman, Cinla Akinci and Huw Davies help us begin our journey by guiding us through the increasingly complex conceptual terrain in which a consensual definition of knowledge continues to be elusive, and perhaps illusory. Their review of literatures they describe as ontologically, epistemologically and methodologically 'eclectic' shows how terms used to account for knowledge and knowing are used in divergent and often incompatible ways. The authors provide an authoritative treatment of the suite of ideas about knowledge and knowing that play through the wider literature and the subsequent chapters of the book. The contribution of the chapter is to set out the assumptions that underpin these diverse and distinctive approaches to knowledge, and in doing so it sets the conceptual scene for the chapters that follow.

In Chapter 3, 'Understanding Practice(s) and Practising', Rod Bain and Christopher Mueller provide an overview of key theoretical perspectives on practice. They consider and explain the 'turn to practice' that has taken place in social science, a shift that has occurred in social theory, empirical social science, and management and organisation studies. Perhaps confusingly, this turn has led to a myriad of ways of theorising and engaging with practice and so the contribution of the chapter is to map these ideas and approaches in ways which provide a foundation for different readings of the book. The chapter examines theories seeking to conceptualise practice, and the lines of debate between these different theories. It also discusses empirical work that has sought to access practice. It acts as a companion to Chapter 2 and engages with the question of how we might think about the relationship between knowledge and practice, or knowing and doing. Its consideration of issues such as researchers' positions and theoretical commitments help an engagement with the approaches taken by other contributors to this volume, not least in the empirical chapters which make up Part B of the book.

Chapter 4, 'Power, Knowledge and Practice', introduces a further conceptual dimension to the book. Christopher Mueller, Alina Baluch and Kevin Orr explore connections between theories of knowledge and of practice and their assumptions about power relations in the social world. They highlight power as an everyday phenomenon that mediates, and is mediated by, processes of knowing and doing. The chapter maps different ways in which power has been theorised in social science and applies these understandings to the ideas about both knowledge and practice set out in Chapters 2 and 3. The contribution of the chapter is to identify the benefits of viewing the three concepts—knowledge, power and practice—in conjunction with each other. It sets out the implications of understanding that power is implicated in both knowing and doing, and so begins a thread of thinking that runs through later chapters.

Chapter 5, 'Perspectives on Knowledge Work', explores the rise of literatures on knowledge work and knowledge workers, emerging from scholarship on post-industrial society, knowledge creating companies, communities of practice and organisational knowledge. Toma Pustelnikovaite and Shiona Chillas discuss the spectrum of conceptualisations of knowledge work—considering whether, for example, it is a separate category of work, or all work is knowledge work. A contribution of the chapter is to explain how at the centre of these discussions is a debate about what knowledge is valuable, to whom and why. The authors track the reconfiguration of the social order from artisanal empirical knowledge to the rise of higher-educated specialist workers, and the shift in many spheres of the economy from manual to mental labour. Following on from Chapter 4, their critical analysis accentuates the political and power dynamics in this arena—how, for example, knowledge work can be de-knowledged by managerial interventions which drive down its economic value, or the bargaining power or status of those knowledge workers in relation to competing professions or groups.

In Chapter 6, 'Identity, Knowledge and Practice', Nic Beech, Gail Greig and Louisa Preston explore how we might understand and research the links between practice and identity, and what this implies for our understanding of knowledge. "What do we do?" and "who are we?" are related questions—aspects of identity are drawn upon to carry out many work activities, and in turn the performance of these activities form part of our identity. The contribution of the chapter is to connect a particular perspective on practice, activity theory, with debates about identity to show how the tools and resources of social life are used in a knowing way. The legitimacy of workers in carrying out particular activities rests upon their professional or occupational identities. The authors also suggest the way in which each of us move into and out of different groups and communities as part of our everyday identity work. These moves may challenge, for example, academic-practitioner distinctions. The authors conclude by suggesting some methodological routes for taking these insights further.

Part B: Context-Specific Discussions of the Relationship between Knowledge and Practice

The six chapters in this part of the book explore the relationship between knowledge and practice in different contexts, and provide an in-depth understanding of knowledge and practice issues in these settings. As well as delivering on our belief that a richness of understanding can be achieved through an engagement with a diversity of arenas, the authors also utilise a range of intellectual and theoretical perspectives to shape their enquiries and accounts. Taken together, the chapters provide an empirical basis for the book's explorations of knowledge and practice. They ground the conceptual discussion of the early chapters in an array of interesting and lively practice settings.

In Chapter 7, 'Sensing Bodies: The Aesthetics of Knowing and Practising', Anna Brown, Gail Greig and Emilia Ferraro present an account of knowledge and practice in craftwork. Set in the context of Brown's pottery studio and her journey of becoming a maker, the authors show us how practice is a process of becoming knowledgeable. In particular, they discuss how knowing and doing emerges from the senses. Individuals are always bound in with others and with the materiality of the social world. We glimpse instances where Brown apprehends new ways of listening, seeing and hearing, and we learn how in so doing her knowing, practising and way of being in the world changes. In this way, we see that knowledge alters our very ways of being. The chapter shows the value of reflecting on the nuances of micro-practices in this non-mainstream setting. It sheds light on the richness of the journey involved in committing to a particular profession.

Chapter 8, 'Everyday Creative Development Practices in Advertising', also focuses on a creative context: that of the advertising industry, where creative practices interact with commercial imperatives, project management and client expectations. Christian Grahle and Paul Hibbert show us a multidimensional creative development process in which different actors co-create ideas, strategies, services and products. We see in the account how advertising practitioners work with their clients to share knowledge to better understand and address problems. Partly this process involves developing a 'gut feeling' but it also entails exchanging ideas with the client and testing these out with groups of consumers. Thereafter comes the involvement of directors to interpret and realise the vision, mediated by project managers and cost controllers who apply other sources of knowledge and may have other priorities for action. The contribution of the chapter is to show how we can understand the everyday creative development process as comprised of five stages and to show how these come to be blended and organised in that setting.

Chapter 9, 'Mind the Gap! Exploring Academics' and Professional Practitioners' Views of Accounting Knowledge', focuses on knowledge and practice in the accounting profession. In their critical exploration of this setting, Lorna Stevenson, Louise Crawford and John Ferguson portray a sector characterised by jurisdictional disputes, for example between qualified accounting practitioners and higher education researchers, and between the bodies representing these two groups. The authors explain the long-standing legitimation struggles between different bodies; at stake is who can lay claim to legitimate accounting knowledge that will drive and govern the profession. Research-based accounting knowledge, on offer from universities, struggles to assert itself in the face of knowledge that appears to come more directly from the domain of practicing accountants. The account offers a sharp sense of competition between different providers of knowledge to members of the profession. The chapter conveys the different perspectives amongst stakeholders in relation to the value of the practical or the abstract, or of theory and practice. In this arena at least, a particular scepticism seems to be reserved for academic knowledge. The chapter culminates with a consideration of the strategic implications of these divisions for accounting education in universities and for the relevance of accounting research for everyday professional practice.

Chapter 10, 'Negotiating Knowledge through Boundary Organisations in Environmental Policy', is the first of two chapters focused on public sector contexts. Clare Moran, Shona Russell and Lucy Wishart explore how knowledge is negotiated through boundary organisations operating at the interstices of science, policy communities and industry. The authors focus in depth on two such boundary organisations, Zero Waste Scotland (ZWS) and the Centre for Research and Expertise on Water (CREW). They examine the processes for stakeholder consultation and how these bodies organise around collaborative enquiry and practice development. Their account highlights that boundary organisations are placed in potentially confusing spaces, where roles and responsibilities can become blurred and ambiguous. The authors show how those enacting boundary-spanning roles are involved in challenging processes of negotiating with other stakeholders and other knowledge workers who may have contending, and shifting, priorities. Their account sets out the contingencies and dilemmas at large in this milieu. Practitioners must work across different language communities, decode the politics of particular issues and contexts, untangle complexity, and build trust between different actors. The authors highlight the politics of the interfaces between research, policy and practice, describing the multilateral, and often asymmetrical, power relationships among participants, professions and institutions. The chapter provides an illustration of how the question of what—and whose—knowledge counts in decision-making is inexorably political.

In Chapter 11, 'Organising to Connect Academic Knowledge and Practice in Healthcare', Joyce Wilkinson and Jo Rycroft-Malone discuss their in-depth study of a high-profile 'knowledge into practice' partnership between higher education institutions and the National Health Service in the UK. The Collaborations for Leadership in Applied Health Research (CLARHCs) scheme represents a major initiative to realise the potential of collaboration for generating and applying research knowledge in ways that benefit patients and service users. However, the chapter highlights the complexity, and politics, of that collaborative context. The multitude of professions involved—each with its own interests, perspectives and orientations towards healthcare practice—hold to different views about what constitutes legitimate knowledge. The authors draw attention to the significance of boundaries—organisational, professional or epistemic—and therefore to the importance of boundary spanning actors who can nurture and develop collaborative practices. The CLAHRCs case offers wider learning for others, and the authors identify some implications for practitioners pursuing cross-boundary or collaborative approaches to knowledge and practice.

Chapter 12, 'Philanthropy: Knowledge, Practice and Blind Hope', takes a critical look at philanthropic foundations and explores the nexus between philanthropy, knowledge and practice. To set the scene, Tobias Jung and Jenny Harrow provide an overview of the setting and how philanthropists' ambitions and visions for knowledge have developed since the early twentieth century. They examine philanthropic bodies' own knowledge and in particular their predominant approaches to learning, lesson drawing, and knowledge mobilisation and the values and assumptions that underlie these practices. The authors show how a defining goal of many philanthropic bodies has been the identification, diagnosis and tackling of societal problems through actionable knowledge. Philanthropic organisations provide a rich case study of the interplay between knowledge and practice given their roles as 'patron, provider, mediator and stimulant' of knowledge. The authors assess the extent to which organisations that purport to engage with public issues do so by engaging the public. They also consider whether these organisations assess and learn from their efforts at promoting change, and whether, and how, these bodies (which wield such influence) articulate with democratic institutions or other mechanisms of public accountability. Through their examination of the relationships between philanthropic bodies and other actors in civil society, the authors again return our focus to boundaries and power imbalances.

Part C: Integrating Insights on Knowledge and Practice, and Their Implications for Action

The first two chapters in this part of the book offer different ways of integrating and extending the insights on knowledge and practice that emerge from the context-specific chapters in Part B. In doing so, they draw on and add to the concepts introduced in Part A of the book. The authors of these chapters comment briefly on the implications of these insights for action. The final chapter in this part of the book brings together five shorter contributions from authors whose interests interconnect with those of the Knowledge and Practice group at St Andrews. These contributors offer further insights on the implications of the ideas in the book for different areas of activity, including management education and consultancy.

In Chapter 13, 'Knowledge Mobilisation: Creating, Sharing and Using Knowledge', Sandra Nutley and Huw Davies provide an overview of different ways of viewing the process of knowledge mobilisation and strategies aimed at improving knowledge in use. They offer five lenses drawn from different fields of social science—literatures on individual learning, organisational learning, knowledge management, innovation diffusion, and the mobilisation of research knowledge. They focus on two main questions: how is knowledge conceptualised in each of the fields, and how has the process of knowledge creation, sharing and use been modelled? Having identified the insights of each field, the authors consider the implications of these contributions for developing strategies to improve knowledge mobilisation. They consider each of the context-specific chapters and cases in light of these five fields, and connect Chapter 7 (sensing bodies) with ideas about individual learning, Chapter 8 (advertising) with the field of organisational learning, Chapter 10 (environmental policy) with innovation diffusion, and Chapter 11 (healthcare) with mobilising research-based knowledge.

In Chapter 14, 'Co-producing Knowledge and Practice', Kevin Orr and Tobias Jung consider the extent to which the lens of co-production assists us in making sense of the debates and discussions that play through the settings provided in the context-specific chapters. Co-production has been a subject of growing interest amongst scholars, policymakers and practitioners, reflecting wider injunctions around collaboration and partnership working. The authors map the array of social science perspectives on co-production, and distil the key themes into a framework that is used to interrogate the context-specific accounts provided in Part B. Their review highlights recurring issues, including boundaries, legitimacy and agency. To explore how these issues run through the chapters within the book, they examine how co-production features in the different contextual accounts of knowledge and practice, and identify the insights that each chapter can offer to an understanding of co-production and vice versa. Finally they consider the strengths and limitations of applying a co-production lens in each case and assess its utility as an integrating concept.

Chapter 15, 'Further Voices, Future Actions', offers five reflective contributions. They are written by authors whose own practice straddles universities and other arenas. In the first of these, Stanley Blue and Elizabeth Shove argue for an account of knowledge and know-how that is rooted in practice. They suggest how knowledges, being part of practices, are always in processes of development and decline. Tim Allen and Clive Grace then reflect on the lessons from their involvement in initiatives to improve knowledge and practice in local government. They set out the challenges and some possible solutions. This is followed by Duncan Maclennan, Julie Miao and Clare Moran, who draw on their participation in debates about the future of cities to outline ways of rethinking knowledge and practice connections in cities, under the banner of 'smart cities'. In the fourth contribution, Mike Bennett reflects on how the relationship between consultancy knowledge and practice is approached in the different organisations. He offers insights into the everyday realities of seeking to co-produce knowledge in this context. Finally, Samuel Mansell and Charles Lovatt discuss the implications of the ideas in the book for ethical practice in management education. They remind us of the need for critical reflection throughout the educational process. Together these further voices provide additional layers of analysis and perspective.

Concluding the Book

In Chapter 16, 'Concluding Reflections: Exploring and Mapping the Knowledge and Practice Terrain', the editors provide some closing thoughts, based on a 'look across' the book and what lies beyond it. We revisit our diverse points of departure and examine what has unfolded through the chapters and the underpinning writing process. We consider our provisional points of arrival: our emerging map of the knowledge and practice terrain, some of its fault lines, and our experience of travelling between and across its boundaries and domains. Finally, we consider directions of future travel (for ourselves and others) and sketch some domains and lines of enquiry that could be explored. We also suggest some ideas and values to take on future journeys, and some things we may try to leave behind.

WAYS OF USING THIS BOOK AND READING BEYOND IT

We hope and trust the book will be of interest to a variety of readers: academics, students, practitioners and policymakers working in other settings, and the casual reader of books about organisational life. Our collective experience gives us a keen awareness of the number of people working in non-academic settings who are interested in connecting with research and indeed in shaping scholarship and co-producing ideas. This book may provide a stimulus for future engagements or a basis for future conversations between different individuals and groups.

The introduction to a book is partly concerned with offering diverse readers a sense of direction. The above discussion of the structure and content of the book should have gone some way to achieving this. There are also signals, signposts and connections within each chapter to ideas and debates explored in other chapters.

There are, of course, multiple ways in which different readers might approach the book. For those interested in the overarching concepts and in engaging with authors' treatment of core ideas about knowledge and practice, the chapters in Part A provide a set of interlinked conversations about these central issues. These chapters set out the scope and contours of scholarship in this area in ways that are then picked up and developed by the authors of later chapters in the book.

For readers with particular interest in specific fields, another possible way to approach the book is to zoom in on the settings of most immediate appeal in Part B. For example, your interests might be clustered around knowledge and practice in public sector settings. If so, you may be drawn to the context-specific explorations of health services and environmental policymaking, as well as perhaps the reflections on knowledge and practice in local government and cities. For those inclined to move straight to those sections with which perhaps they feel the closest immediate connection, we hope the linkages authors make to other chapters will act as invitations to read across more than one setting, or entice you to engage with the conceptual chapters in Part A of the book.

You may want to cut to the chase and consider our conclusions and their implications for action. In this case you will be drawn to the final chapters of the book. Again, we hope that links made to earlier chapters, the foundations for our conclusions and conceptual map, will encourage you to explore the underpinning ideas, debates and examples provided in those chapters. Finally, we hope the book will motivate you to read beyond it. For this reason, the authors of each of the main chapters offer a few suggestions for further reading.

Part A

Mapping the Conceptual Landscape

2 Understanding Knowledge and Knowing

Tricia Tooman, Cinla Akinci and Huw Davies

INTRODUCTION

Talk of knowledge is commonplace, yet the nature of knowledge remains elusive, evading universal and consensual definition (Easterby-Smith & Lyles 2011). While the natural sciences (such as chemistry, biology and physics) and their diverse fields of application (such as industry, medicine and engineering) seem to have converged in their understanding about what counts as knowledge (focusing on concrete and measurable phenomena), nothing like such agreement is seen on what constitutes knowledge in and about the social world. In the social sciences (such as anthropology, sociology, political science, human geography and even economics), what counts as knowledge is complex, challenging and contested. Indeed, in a growing and increasingly complex literature on knowledge and knowing, similar terms are used in differing, divergent and sometimes incompatible ways (Alvesson & Kärreman 2001; Tsoukas & Vladimirou 2001).

Some of the challenges in 'knowing' the social world and in creating 'knowledge' about that world arise from differences in views about the underlying nature of the phenomena being studied or described (that is, their ontology). Conceptualisations here may range from relatively positivist orientations (seeing the world as made up of concrete actors and actions) to more constructivist positions (for example, seeing phenomena as the product of human interactions and discourse). In addition, there are wide and different perspectives on how one can come to know this world (issues of both epistemology and methodology): from abstractions of the world emphasising measurement and statistical analysis, to views looking for meaning in action and dialogue. No exploration of the nature of knowledge and knowing can develop separate from some consideration of these issues: the multiplicity of perspectives available necessarily subverts the task of providing universal and consensual explanations.

The aim of this chapter is to introduce some of the key conceptualisations of knowledge, with a particular emphasis on the understanding of complex human actions in social environments. Our intention is to expose and explore the implied assumptions about the nature of knowledge buried in various conceptualisations of the term. In doing so, we will assume a degree of ontological, epistemological and methodological eclecticism: that is, a diversity of underpinnings about the nature of the social world and how we may come to know it.

At the centre of these debates about what it means 'to know something' are differing viewpoints on whether knowledge is an object (to be found) or a process (to be engaged with) (Cook & Brown 1999). That is, can we see knowledge as explicit and codifiable, something that is portable and transmissible from person to person and across contexts? Or is it better to think in terms of a process of knowing, not readily separable from the knower, and embedded in specific contexts? The answers to these questions shape our understanding of the knowledge in (or knowledge into) practice 'problem' that is at the heart of this book, and so should shape the strategies employed for expanding knowledge for practice.

To explore what we mean by 'knowledge and knowing', this chapter will address four main challenges. First, we consider the nature of knowledge and the extent to which knowledge can be seen as separate from the knower. Second, we explore where knowledge comes from, distinguishing between formal ways of knowing using structured methods (sometimes called 'science' or 'analysis') and more informal and personal ways of knowing (sometimes called 'intuition'). Third, we lay out some of the assumptions that are revealed by differing approaches to knowledge. Finally, we begin to touch on the implications of diverse views about the nature of knowledge for practice improvement, ideas that are developed further in subsequent chapters.

WHAT IS KNOWLEDGE?

Knowledge is a "loose, ambiguous, and rich" concept that defies simplistic categories (Alvesson & Kärreman 2001). We find a wide array of terms, types and descriptors in the literature. Some scholars make a case for the development of a shared definition (Tsoukas & Vladimirou 2001); however, there is considerable debate as to whether agreeing upon specific definitions would be possible or even useful (Nutley *et al.* 2007; Oborn *et al.* 2010). To explore such diverse perspectives, in this section we discuss four main issues: (1) whether complex social knowledge exists separate from the knower; (2) the differing kinds of knowledge available to us; (3) the role of explicit *versus* tacit knowledge; and (4) the interweaving of different strands of knowledge and ways of knowing within and across individuals.

Knowledge: Object or Practice

It is common to see terms like knowledge and information used interchangeably with labels such as data, research or evidence, exemplifying a view of knowledge as an object that is readily detachable from a knower; something that can be decontextualised, that is generalisable, and so is transmissible intact to other contexts. Tsoukas (1997) argues against the temptation to equate knowledge and information. To do so, he points out, is 'information reductionism' where knowledge is narrowed down to a thing. Some propose a progression of terms beginning with data, information, knowledge and onward to wisdom, based on the increasing role of human intervention and judgement (Tsoukas & Vladimirou 2001; Greenhalgh 2010); as Burke (2000) puts it: from 'raw' to 'cooked'. These scholars say that knowledge is not a variant of information but rather involves the ability to make judgements, draw distinctions, and imbue information with meaning within a particular time and place. Furthermore, in this view knowledge is anchored, or situated, and dependent on both the knowers and the context (Lave & Wenger 1991). What is known, the one who knows it, and the context of action are bound together. As a result, if knowledge is more than a flow of information and is connected to practice in a particular context, it is more aptly identified as knowledge-in-practice, or *knowing* (Gourlay 2006).

Kinds of Knowledge and Knowing

The complex character of knowledge is also evident from the many forms and dimensions portrayed in the literature. One example usefully delineates three domains of knowing: the empirical, theoretical and experiential domains (Brechin & Sidell 2000). Empirical knowing is considered the most explicit, such as research-informed knowledge derived from direct and structured observation. Theoretical knowing suggests a conceptual reasoning process, sometimes intuitive, where various ways of approaching a problem are considered to constitute a plausible way of understanding what is observed. Lastly, experiential knowing involves craft and mastery that are hard-won through experience, often more evident in the doing than in any explicit articulation of knowledge.

In line with the three domains of knowing is the common distinction between content-based subject matter and skills-based capability: a demarcation between knowing *that* and knowing *how* (Ryle 1949). Knowing that is sometimes described as a cognitive (or embrained) form of knowing; whereas knowing how by contrast is seen as an embodied form of knowledge (see Chapter 3 Practice and Chapter 6 Identity). Such embodied knowing is most often physical, action-oriented and exhibited in the demonstration of skills, and thereby inseparable from the knower (Blackler 1995).

Know-how comes from "the tacit insights experience provides . . . and is critical in making [explicit] knowledge actionable and operational" (Brown & Duguid 1998:95). Whereas some view such knowing and doing as separate and sequential tasks, others view them as connected and intertwined (Star 2000). For example, to say that someone is fixing a car indicates both knowing *that* (i.e., a cognitive process of holding and accessing relevant facts about mechanical problems and their solutions), as well as operational knowing *how* (evidenced in specific skills and behaviours) (Cook & Brown 1999). Fixing a car in practice brings the potential for new knowledge, emerging insight, and refined skills, so increasing the capacity to both know that and know how. Many scholars focus on the link between *know that* and *know how* to say that knowing is only evidenced in what can be seen in practices (see Chapter 3 Practice).

Explicit and Tacit Knowledge

Given their prevalence in any discussion of knowledge, the distinction between explicit and tacit knowledge are worthy of further consideration. According to Polanyi (1962), tacit knowledge is associated with skilful performance and know-how. In his most famous example, Polanyi (1962) explains that in order to be able to ride a bicycle one needs to have the tacit knowledge of how to stay upright. This is knowledge that one possesses: not the activity of riding itself, but the knowledge used in riding. Whilst explicit knowledge can be used as an aid to acquire tacit knowledge (e.g., telling someone how to turn to avoid a fall), explicit knowledge alone cannot enable someone to ride a bicycle. To do so, one must spend time on a bicycle to acquire the tacit knowledge necessary for riding, ultimately achieving competence by becoming unaware of how it is done. What was once a conscious task becomes embodied: the body knows what to do.

Drawing on these ideas, Nonaka *et al.* (1998) proposed a multilay-ered model of 'knowledge creation'. According to this model, knowledge is created through a continuous and dynamic interaction between tacit knowledge and explicit knowledge in the creative activities of human beings, something termed 'knowledge conversion' (Nonaka *et al.* 2001). This conversion is a social process between individuals; it is not confined within any given individual. Hence knowledge is created through interactions between individuals with different types and contents of knowledge. According to Nonaka *et al.* (2001) this interaction is shaped through what they termed the SECI process (socialisation, externalisation, combination and internalisation); that is, through shifts from one mode of knowledge conversion to the next.

In this process, socialisation (from tacit knowledge to tacit knowledge) occurs through shared experiences, feelings, emotions and imitation. A classic example of socialisation is the learning of an apprentice; this occurs mainly by exposure, experience, observation, imitation and modelling. Externalisation (from tacit knowledge to explicit knowledge) is when tacit knowledge is made explicit and "knowledge becomes crystalized" (Nonaka *et al.* 2001:495), at which point it can be shared by others and can be made the basis for new knowledge. This relies on a social process of articulation. The successful conversion of tacit knowledge into explicit knowledge depends on the use of metaphors, analogies and models. Combination (from explicit knowledge to explicit knowledge) occurs when knowledge is exchanged and combined through such media as documents, meetings, telephone conversations and computerised communication networks. And finally, internalisation (from explicit knowledge to tacit knowledge) is closely related to learning-by-doing. Explicit knowledge that is internalised broadens, extends and reframes organisational members' tacit knowledge. It serves to develop shared mental models and technical know-how, and becomes a valuable asset. The tacit knowledge accumulated at an individual level is, in turn, shared with other individuals through socialisation, and it sets off a new spiral of knowledge creation. Essential components of this model are its iterative nature and the observation that any knowledge conversion process occurs within a specific context. (Nonaka *et al.* 2001).

The SECI model outlined above is not unproblematic, especially with regard to the notion of the conversion of tacit knowledge to explicit knowledge. Tsoukas (2003) asserted that Nonaka and Takeuchi's (1995) interpretation of tacit knowledge as 'knowledge-not-yet-articulated' (i.e., knowledge waiting for its translation or conversion into explicit knowledge) is to misunderstand: he suggests that this interpretation ignores the essential ineffability of much tacit knowledge, reducing it to merely what can be (eventually) articulated. To some, the important distinction between these terms (explicit; tacit) hinges on the *essentially* inarticulable nature of tacit knowledge: knowledge held deeply within the knower, heavily shaped by experience, more than a mere accumulation of bits of information, and not always conscious. Indeed, Polanyi contended that tacit and explicit knowledge work in tandem and represent two distinct dimensions of interdependent knowing (Brown & Duguid 2001).

The Interweaving of Different Levels and Strands of Knowledge

The level or unit of analysis is also germane to discussions about the nature of knowledge. Simply put, who acquires, produces and holds knowledge? From the time of the Enlightenment, knowledge has been generally understood in individualistic terms (Burke 2000; Tsoukas & Vladimirou 2001). Yet, the rise of organisational knowledge and learning has challenged this view (Easterby-Smith & Lyles 2011) by arguing that knowledge at a group or collective level is more than a sum of individual group members' information repositories. Collective knowledge constitutes shared meanings built upon the interaction of individuals and the development of organisational norms, systems and processes (Brown & Duguid 2001; Tsoukas & Vladimirou 2001).

Linked to the distinction between individual and collective knowledge are differing perspectives on whether learning and knowing are predominantly cognitive processes (located within an individual) or shared social and contextual processes. The former emphasise the merits of rational, logical, value-free forms of mental processing. Yet social learning theorists offer a different view, where individuals are connected and embedded in social environments (Fenstermacher 1994; Cook & Brown 1999), and where knowledge is built and sustained from social interaction. Directly or indirectly, in this view knowledge is seen as being built on the work of others, or via joint enterprise, and so is communal in nature. In contrast to an individual rational-thinker model, if knowledge is derived from social interaction and is context-dependent, then it is also inextricably linked to (shared) values and (collective) judgement: information only takes on meaning when groups come to a shared understanding of what is important and the implications for action (Wittgenstein's argument found in Greenhalgh 2010).

Dualism abounds in approaches to understanding knowledge and knowing. This is reflected in Cartesian-based distinctions between mind and body and in approaches that separate the social and material worlds (Schatzki 2003). Such divisions have led to explanations of learning and knowing that privilege mind over body and the social over the material world. This approach is criticised by those who argue that we need to focus on the interweaving or 'entanglement' of mind, body, people, objects and places when seeking to understand knowing and doing (Schatzki 2003; Gherardi 2006, and see Chapter 7—sensing bodies for an example).

The interwoven nature of knowledge and knowing is evident in an Aristotelian notion of knowledge (van de Ven & Johnson 2006; Nonaka *et al.* 2008; Abbasi 2011). The classical Aristotelian definition of knowledge entails three parts: *episteme* (systematic, often scientific, research-informed knowledge, or information), *techne* (skilful craftsmanship, artistry, stemming from hands-on aesthetic experience), and *phronesis* (wisdom, judgement, including culturally relevant morals and ethics). It is important to stress that in this view each strand does not constitute knowledge on its own, but rather 'knowledge' is a fusion of these three forms, and each form plays an essential role within knowing, doing and context-based understanding. Importantly, knowledge is not separate from the knower and the knower's social and physical place; rather 'knowledge' encompasses all of these, woven together and whole. Cook and Brown pick up on Aristotle's interwoven nature of knowledge; they argue that four categories of knowledge—explicit, tacit, individual and group—encompass "unique and irreducible"' forms of knowledge (Cook & Brown 1999:384). Each form of knowledge is distinct and serves particular roles as they are interwoven in the process of knowing.

In summary then, there are different views about the nature of knowledge, and many terms are used to describe knowledge and knowing. Some point to knowledge as separate from the person and the context; others hold to a dynamic interplay between different forms of knowledge within and between social beings. It is by understanding these divergent views that we begin to frame some of the challenges facing those who wish to address the knowing and practice conundrum.

HOW DO WE KNOW WHAT WE KNOW?

So far we have outlined various conceptualisations of knowledge, but significant issues remain: what are the sources of our knowledge? And how do we know what we know? Drawing from the conceptual foundation of dual-process theories (Stanovich & West 2000), we explore the idea that there are two different modes of information processing. The two systems have been labelled simply as System 1 and System 2. System 1 ('fast') is characterised as being contextually dependent, automatic, largely unconscious, associative, intuitive and implicit in nature. Being mostly grounded in prior learning and experience, it is relatively undemanding in terms of its use of conscious thinking. In contrast, System 2 ('slow') processing is contextually independent, analytic, rule-based, and explicit in nature. Such thinking makes greater demands on cognitive calculation than its System 1 counterpart.

Neither the experiential, intuitive (System 1) mode nor the rational, analytical (System 2) mode is superior to the other (Epstein 2008). Each has its strengths and limitations. The rational system is capable of solving abstract problems, planning, applying principles broadly across situations, and taking long-term considerations into account. The experiential system, on the other hand, is able to effortlessly direct behaviour in everyday life. The experiential system can solve problems that are beyond the capacity of the rational system because they require a holistic rather than analytic orientation, because they depend on lessons from lived experiences, or because they require creativity via associative connections.

While traditionally the emphasis has been on reason and rationality in attempting to explain human cognition and action (an emphasis on System 2 thinking), more recent work has highlighted the central role played by intuition, experience and the accumulation of tacit knowledge (System 1). These ways of knowing are less formal, less structured, less reproducible than rational reasoning, but are nonetheless powerful drivers of human action.

A variety of definitions of intuition have been offered (see Akinci & Sadler-Smith 2012 for a review). These include "analyses frozen into habit and the capacity for rapid response through recognition" (Simon 1987:63), so emphasising the experience-based nature of intuition; or "affectively charged judgements that arise through rapid, non-conscious, and holistic associations" (Dane & Pratt 2007:40), which emphasises the role of emotions and unconscious processes—"knowing without knowing how one knows" (Epstein 2008:29). Going further, Epstein (2008:29) asserted that intuition is "the accumulated tacit information that a person has acquired by automatically learning from experience", so excluding beliefs acquired in ways other than by personal experience.

It is helpful (although sometimes difficult) to draw a distinction between intuition and tacit knowledge. While intuitions may be acquired tacitly, they are different from tacit knowledge in that intuitions are essentially *judgements* that can be interpreted and communicated (Dane & Pratt 2007). So by one account (Epstein 1994) the experiential (intuitive) system represents events primarily concretely and imagistically; it is capable of generalisation and abstraction through the use of prototypes, metaphors, scripts and narratives. Whilst we are not able to identify the source of intuitions (how we know), we *are* able explicitly to communicate intuitions once we are aware of them (for example through metaphor). This contrasts with tacit knowledge that (some would argue) cannot be captured, translated or converted to explicit knowledge (Tsoukas 2003); true tacit knowledge remains essentially inarticulable but manifested in behaviour (Polanyi 1962).

Emotions (affect) play a central role in the processes of thinking, knowing and information processing. The experiential (intuitive) system is intimately associated with emotional experiences, including 'vibes', which refer to subtle feelings that people may not be aware of. Feelings may take the form of concrete exemplars and schemas inductively derived from emotionally significant, intense or repetitive past experiences (Epstein 1994). The recalled feelings influence the course of further processing and reactions.

To sum up, the message conveyed by the dual-process theories is that behaviour and conscious thought are guided by the joint operations of two systems (intuition and analysis), with their relative influence being determined by various factors, including sociocultural expectations, contextual mediators, personal cognition styles and the degree of emotional involvement.

Thus far we have reviewed a range of perspectives on the nature of knowledge and knowing, and the means by which this knowledge is acquired and influences our judgements and actions. Next we collate the assumptions that lie, often unstated, beneath these diverse perspectives.

WHAT ASSUMPTIONS UNDERLIE DIFFERENT VIEWS OF KNOWLEDGE?

The divergent accounts so far of the nature of knowledge and knowing contain within them divergent assumptions and so give rise to differing implications for how to set about the tasks of creating, sharing and using knowledge. Some of these assumptions are laid out in table 2.1 (below), under the two broad headings of knowledge as a *thing* and knowing as a *process*. Rather than dualist opposites, these descriptors can be taken as anchors for arguments of extent. For example, to the extent that knowledge is a thing to be found, then it is seen as primarily explicit, value-neutral, and individualistic; whereas construing knowing as a situated process of discovery emphasises the social and specific context, where collective and tacit forms of knowing are apparent.

Table 2.1 Assumptions and implications in understanding knowledge and knowing

Whether knowledge is . . .	
. . . an object, a product, a commodity . . .	*. . . a situated process of knowing . . .*
. . . suggests these assumptions and implications:	
Pre-existing knowledge	Emergent knowing
Objective	Subjective
Value-neutral	Value-laden
Discovered	Constructed
Certain	Uncertain
Static	Dynamic
Focused on data and information	Combining information, experience, judgement
Meaning is found	Meaning is interpreted
Explicit: know *that*	Tacit: know *how*
Content knowledge	Skills and judgement
Embrained	Embodied
Generic, generalisable, independent of context, decontextualised	Specific to a time and place, context-dependent, situated
Individual	Collective
Received, interpreted and understood by the individual	Co-constructed from and understood within the social context and system (Wittgenstein's 'all knowledge is collective')
Can be packaged and transferred	Cannot be packaged and transferred (Polanyi's 'all knowledge is personal')
Getting 'knowledge *into* practice'	Building shared 'knowing *in* practice'

Adapted from Brown & Duguid 1991;Blackler 1995; Tsoukas & Vladimirou 2001; Duguid 2005; Gourlay 2006; Greenhalgh 2010

A broad reading of knowledge and knowing permits diverse understandings and divergent implications. And in consequence, the actions we take to shape the knowledge/practice relationship will look rather different depending on how we resolve our view of knowledge/knowing (which is in itself a context-contingent task) (Ward *et al.* 2012). We next consider three main approaches to taking action that are based on different assumptions about knowledge/knowing.

WHAT ARE THE IMPLICATIONS FOR USING KNOWLEDGE AND IMPROVING PRACTICE?

If knowledge is seen as a flow of information, then knowledge creation, diffusion and use look very different from when knowledge is seen as a socially constructed, context-dependent fusion of know *what*, know *how* and know *why*. A clearer understanding of the philosophical underpinnings of different perspectives helps clarify why particular strategies have merit in constructing ways of improving knowledge sharing and use. These issues are picked up again in Chapter 13 (knowledge mobilisation), but here we introduce a three-fold typology of approaches to the knowledge/practice problem.

Strategies that aim to improve the connection between knowledge and practice can be grouped into three categories: linear approaches, relational approaches and systems approaches (Best & Holmes 2010). *Linear models* depend on generalisable, transmittable forms of knowledge, and focus on the direct transfer of the knowledge product moving from the creators to the users. The challenge of 'knowledge in practice' is framed as a 'knowledge *deficit* in practice' problem, and thus the solution is found by inserting the missing information that will lead to improved performance. Linear models tend to dominate knowledge-sharing practices partly because they are relatively easy to implement (Davies *et al.* 2015). *Relational models* focus on the linkages and interactions between people as the basis for knowledge creation and sharing that in turn affects practitioner behaviour. When knowledge in practice is viewed as a connectivity problem, the solution lies in bringing knowledge creators (e.g., researchers) and knowledge users (practitioners) together, where their interaction will transform one another's knowing, and result in improved knowing in practice. *Systems models* view knowledge as socially mediated and embedded within a myriad of actors and groups joined together as multifaceted, emergent, and interdependent components within a system. There is a mutual web of interdependence between people who make up the system and the system structures themselves (teams, organisations, cultures, etc.). It follows that people both shape and are in turn shaped by the system. The challenge of improving knowledge in practice revolves around developing complex adaptive systems, where knowing in practice remains a continuous work in progress.

How one conceptualises the nature of knowledge also has implications for learning, both individually and at the organisational level. If knowledge is an object, then individual learning is often construed as a linear, stepwise process of knowledge acquisition. This is demonstrated in Bloom's *et al.* (1956) six levels of learning, which are ordered from the knowledge of something to the ability to evaluate and offer a critique of it. Alternately, when knowledge is viewed as socially constructed, emergent and having meaning drawn from a particular context, then learning is both an individual and collective process of transformation (Merriam *et al.* 2007). This view shifts the focus from individual knowledge acquisition to how individuals and groups change, transform, and learn as a result of connecting and engaging over a shared task (Wenger 2000). In this way, learning is viewed as social, interactive, influenced by system structures and a lifelong process (Illeris 2002). Again these ideas are developed elsewhere, including in Chapters 7 (sensing bodies) and 13 (knowledge mobilisation).

CONCLUDING REMARKS

This teasing out of the diverse ways in which knowledge and knowing have been discussed reveals rich diversity and some sharp distinctions. Greater clarity about what we mean when we talk of knowledge and knowing has the potential to reveal the shaping assumptions being made. These in turn have many implications for how we conceptualise and intervene at the nexus of knowledge and practice, as subsequent chapters demonstrate.

SUGGESTED FURTHER READINGS

Cook, S.D.N. & Brown, J.S. (1999) Bridging epistemologies: The generative dance between organizational knowledge and organizational knowing. *Organization Science.* 10(4): 381–400.
  The authors articulate the limitations of viewing knowledge in simplistic, uniform ways and provide a model of 'Knowing as Action' that illustrates knowing as an interactive and interdependent relationship between individuals and groups.
Peter Burke's two-volume work *A social history of knowledge: From Gutenberg to Diderot* (2000) and *From the encyclopaedia to Wikipedia* (2012). Cambridge: Polity.
  Burke traces the evolution of knowledge from how it was understood prior to the Enlightenment through to modern day. The review is extensive yet readable, and provides worthwhile historical perspectives to these extensive contemporary debates.
Akinci, C., & Sadler-Smith, E. (2012) Intuition in management research: A historical review. *International Journal of Management Reviews.* 14(1): 104–122.
  This provides a critical review of intuition (versus analysis) research in management and other related fields over the past eight decades beginning from the first conception of intuition in organisational contexts in the 1930s. In this respect, it offers a comprehensive account of various theoretical conceptualisations encompassing expert intuition, affect, heuristics and biases, System 1/System 2, and the recognition-primed model, among others.

REFERENCES

Abbasi, K. (2011) Knowledge, lost in translation. *Journal of the Royal Society of Medicine.* 104(12): 487.
Akinci, C., & Sadler-Smith, E. (2012) Intuition in management research: A historical review. *International Journal of Management Reviews.* 14(1): 104–122.

Alvesson, M., & Kärreman, D. (2001) Odd couple: Making sense of the curious concept of knowledge management. *Journal of Management Studies.* 38(7): 995–1018.

Best, A., & Holmes, B.J. (2010) Systems thinking, knowledge & action: Towards better models & methods. *Evidence & Policy.* 6(2): 145–159.

Blackler, F. (1995) Knowledge, knowledge work & organizations: An overview & interpretation. *Organization Studies.* 16(6): 1021–1046.

Bloom, B.S., Engelhart, M.D., Furst, E.J., Hill, W.H., & Krathwohl, D.R. (1956) *Taxonomy of educational objectives: The classification of educational goals. Handbook 1: Cognitive domain.* New York: David McKay.

Brechin, A., & Sidell, M. (2000) Ways of knowing, in R. Gomm & C. Davies (eds.), *Using evidence in health & social care.* London: SAGE, pp. 3–25.

Brown, J.S., & Duguid, P. (1991) Organisational learning & communities of practice: Toward a unified view of working, learning, & innovating. *Organization Science.* 2(1): 40–57.

Brown, J.S., & Duguid, P. (1998) Organizing knowledge. *California Management Review.* 40(3): 90–111.

Brown, J.S., & Duguid, P. (2001) Knowledge & organization: A social-practice perspective. *Organization Science.* 12(2): 198–213.

Burke, P. (2000) *A social history of knowledge: From Gutenberg to Diderot.* Cambridge: Polity.

Cook, S.D.N., & Brown, J.S. (1999) Bridging epistemologies: The generative dance between organizational knowledge & organizational knowing. *Organization Science.* 10(4): 381–400.

Dane, E., & Pratt, M.G. (2007) Exploring intuition & its role in managerial decision making. *Academy of Management Review.* 32(1): 33–54.

Davies, H.T.O., Powell, A.E., & Nutley, S.M. (2015) Mobilising knowledge to improve UK health care: Learning from other countries & other sectors—A multi-method mapping study. *Health Services & Delivery Research.* 3(27).

Duguid, P. (2005) The art of knowing: Social and tacit dimensions of knowledge and the limits of the community of practice. *The Information Society.* 21(2): 109–118.

Easterby-Smith, M., & Lyles, M.A. (2011) The evolving field of organizational learning & knowledge management, in M. Easterby-Smith & M.A. Lyles (eds.), *Handbook of organizational learning & knowledge management.* 2nd Ed. Chichester: John Wiley & Sons, pp. 1–20.

Epstein, S. (1994) Integration of the cognitive & the psychodynamic unconscious. *American Psychologist.* 49(8): 709–724.

Epstein, S. (2008) Intuition from the perspective of cognitive-experiential self-theory, in H. Plessner, C. Betsch, & T. Betsch (eds.), *Intuition in judgement & decision making.* New York: Lawrence Erlbaum Associates, pp. 23–38.

Fenstermacher, G.D. (1994) The knower & the known: The nature of knowledge in research on teaching, in L. Darling-Hammond (ed.), *Review of research in education.* Washington, DC: American Educational Research Association, pp. 3–6.

Gherardi, S. (2006) *Organizational knowledge: The texture of workplace learning.* Oxford: Blackwell.

Gourlay, S. (2006) Conceptualizing knowledge creation: A critique of Nonaka's theory. *Journal of Management Studies.* 43(7): 1415–1436.

Greenhalgh, T. (2010) What is this knowledge that we seek to 'exchange'? *The Milbank Quarterly.* 88(4): 492–499.

Illeris, K. (2002) *Three dimensions of learning.* Leicester: NIACE.

Lave, J., & Wenger, E. (1991) *Situated learning: Legitimate peripheral participation.* New York: Cambridge University Press.

Merriam, S., Caffarella, R., & Baumgartner, L. (2007) *Learning in adulthood*. 3rd Ed. San Francisco: John Wiley & Sons.

Nonaka, I., Konno, N., & Toyama, R. (1998) Leading knowledge creation: A new framework for dynamic knowledge management. Paper presented at the 2nd Annual Knowledge Management Conference. Haas School of Business, University of California at Berkeley, September 22–24.

Nonaka, I., & Takeuchi, H. (1995) *The knowledge-creating company*. Oxford: Oxford University Press.

Nonaka, I., Toyama, R., & Byosiere, P. (2001) A theory of organizational knowledge creation: Understanding the dynamic process of creating knowledge, in M. Dierkes, A. Berthoin Antal, J. Child, & I. Nonaka (eds.), *Handbook of organizational learning & knowledge*. New York: Oxford University Press, pp. 491–517.

Nonaka, I., Toyama, R., & Hirata, T. (2008) *Managing flow*. Basingstoke: Palgrave Macmillan.

Nutley, S.M., Walter, I., & Davies, H.T.O. (2007) *Using evidence: How research can inform public services*. Bristol: Policy Press.

Oborn, E., Barrett, M., & Racko, G. (2010) *Knowledge translation in healthcare: A review of the literature*. Cambridge: Judge Business School.

Polanyi, M. (1962) *Personal knowledge*. Chicago: University of Chicago Press.

Ryle, G. (1949) *The concept of mind*. London: Hutchinson.

Schatzki, T.R. (2003) A new societist social ontology. *Philosophy of the Social Sciences*. 33(2): 174–202.

Simon, H.A. (1987) Making management decisions: The role of intuition & emotion. *Academy of Management Executive*. 1(1): 57–64.

Stanovich, K.E., & West, R.F. (2000) Individual differences in reasoning: Implications for the rationality debate? *Behavioural & Brain Sciences*. 23: 643–726.

Star, J.R. (2000) On the relationship between knowing & doing in procedural learning, in B. Fishman & S. O'Connor-Divelbiss (eds.), *Proceedings of the fourth international conference of the learning sciences*. Mahwah, NJ: Erlbaum, pp. 80–86.

Tsoukas, H. (1997) The tyranny of light: The temptations & the paradoxes of the information society. *Futures*. 29(9): 827–843.

Tsoukas, H. (2003) Do we really understand tacit knowledge?, in M. Easterby-Smith & M.A. Lyles (eds.), *The Blackwell handbook of organizational learning & knowledge management*. Oxford: Blackwell, pp. 410–427.

Tsoukas, H., & Vladimirou, E. (2001) What is organizational knowledge? *Journal of Management Studies*. 38(7): 973–993.

van de Ven, A., & Johnson, P.E. (2006) Knowledge for theory & practice. *Academy of Management Review*. 31(4): 802–821.

Ward, V., Smith, S., House, A., & Hamer, S. (2012) Exploring knowledge exchange: A useful framework for practice & policy. *Social Science & Medicine*. 74(3): 297–304.

Wenger, E. (2000) *Communities of practice: Learning, meaning, & identity*. Cambridge: Cambridge University Press.

3 Understanding Practice(s) and Practising

Rod Bain and Christopher Mueller

INTRODUCTION

What is practice—and what is it not? Practice is an expression used frequently by social scientists, but with a variety of meanings, from a common-sense understanding that it is *what people do,* to highly theorised accounts of practices as a means of understanding social life (Schatzki 2012). For some scholars, practice and doing are distinct from theory and knowing. For a growing number of other researchers, such separation is best resisted. Through its title, this book signals a clear interest in knowledge and practice in organisations. Yet, what does practice mean in the context of studying knowledge and practice in organisations, management and policy?

The idea that practice is *what people do* is reflected in the Oxford English Dictionary (OED), but even here we begin to see that the concept is potentially more complex than this. Practice (noun) and practising (verb) are defined in a number of ways by the OED (Oxford English Dictionary Online 2015), including:

- The carrying out or exercise of a profession
- The actual application or use of an idea, belief or method, as opposed to the theory or principles of it
- To pursue or be engaged in a particular occupation, profession, skill or art
- To carry out or perform (a particular activity, method or custom) habitually or regularly
- An established legal procedure, or the law and custom on which such procedure is based

These definitions suggest that practice involves people, their actions, and the repetition of those actions. Practice relates to human activities that may be repetitive, or performed regularly or habitually. These activities may also be customary, or perhaps traditional. However, these definitions also suggest a distinction—that practice may be understood as theory's other; doing something as opposed to pursuing abstract theoretical representations of complex human activities. In this view, practice and practising are understood dichotomously, as distinct from abstract or theoretical knowledge.

In recent years a 'practice turn' has been identified in social science, and not least in management and organisation studies (Schatzki *et al.* 2001; Gherardi 2013; Nicolini 2013). This turn is not a simple conceptual manoeuvre. Eikeland (2007) has identified at least three ways of turning to practice: firstly, by turning our theoretical gaze more intensely on the practice of others; secondly, by turning our back on theory; and thirdly, by turning our critical attention to our own research practices. With regard to each of these turns, there are many ways to understand practice, and still more ways to access it through empirical research. Different understandings of practice are related to different assumptions about the nature of the world, and what we can say about it. That is to say, a discussion of practices raises ontological and epistemological issues.

This chapter discusses the above issues and aims to provide a conceptual foundation for the discussion of practice in the remainder of the book. We begin with the long-standing distinction between practice and theory, and also discuss the separation of policy and practice, which is a variant of this. We then discuss the (re)turn to practice, which challenges the separation of practice from theory/policy. We continue with a discussion of how practice has been theorised within this return to practice, particularly focusing on an approach which assumes that the social world consists in practices (Schatzki 2002). Finally, we discuss the benefits offered by a practice theory approach to understanding the social world.

DISTINGUISHING PRACTICE FROM THEORY AND POLICY

The separation of doing from knowing, of practical knowledge from analytical or theoretical knowledge, has been a trope of Western thought since at least Plato and Aristotle. Plato was clear that philosophers, who engaged in the pursuit of truth, were superior to practitioners, who engaged in more material and mundane activities. Aristotle's contribution, however, is less clear-cut. Aristotle conceived a tripartite model of knowledge and knowing (*episteme, phronesis,* and *techne*) that paradoxically justifies a theory/practice distinction, while also supporting a more hybrid understanding of knowing and doing (Nicolini 2013; see also Chapter 2 Knowledge).

Descartes is a widely cited supporter of a theory/practice, or knowing/doing, dichotomy. A Cartesian world view, which has endured in Western thought since the Enlightenment, is characterised by the superiority of mind over body, and thought over action. This view is related to a number of other persistent binary relationships, including subject/object, human/non-human (including materiality and nature), and head/hands, where the second type is usually understood as inferior to the first. This view is associated with a positivist epistemology, and the privileging of objective knowledge and reason over other modes of knowing (Ferraro & Reid 2013). Allied to this, the word 'practice' has also come to describe a particular kind of knowledge— practice knowledge—(see Chapter 2 Knowledge), where performing an activity or carrying out a particular form of work produces understandings of that activity that may be distinct, and valued differently, from analytical or abstract representation of that form of working.

A distinction is often made between policy and practice. This is in line with the OED's second definition: that practice is the actual application of an idea, belief or method, as opposed to the principles of it. Those working in policy settings, including international, national, regional and local governments, may articulate desired policy directions, but policies are implemented—or not—by those working in practice settings (such as local service delivery organisations). Studies of policy implementation (Hill & Huppe 2014) have highlighted the importance of differentiating between policy intentions and how policies are enacted in practice. These studies focus on how policy intentions are mediated and transformed by the actions and inactions of practitioners working in front-line service delivery. Michael Lipsky (1971, 2010) referred to these practitioners as 'street-level bureaucrats' and found that they exercise considerable discretion in pressured situations.

The importance of understanding the differing perspectives, concerns and routines of those who work in practice settings, as opposed to policy roles, has been picked up by those concerned with improving the use of research-based knowledge in public service delivery (Davies *et al.* 2000; Nutley *et al.* 2007). From the 1990s onwards, there has been much interest in the use of research-based knowledge to improve both public policy and service delivery, often under the banner of promoting more evidence-based policy and practice. At times in these discussions, some fairly sharp distinctions have been drawn between knowledge (science), policy and practice. There have been laments about a knowing-doing gap, which is frequently considered to stem from the divergent nature and concerns of science, policy and practice. However, there is some acknowledgement—as evident in later chapters of this edited collection—that such a sharp distinction is not always so neat as it might at first appear (Nutley *et al.* 2007, see also Chapters 10 Environment, 11 Healthcare, and 13 Knowledge mobilisation).

(RE)TURNING TO PRACTICE THROUGH DISSOLVING CARTESIAN DUALISM

Although distinctions between practice and theory (or policy) may be accepted within some arenas of management studies, others are uncomfortable with such a contrast. A separation of practice from policy/theory is explicitly challenged by some theoretical accounts of practices and practising. The recent interest in practice is based around the insight that social phenomena such as "knowledge, meaning, human activity, science, power, language, social institutions, and historical transformation occur within and are aspects or components of the field of practices" (Schatzki *et al.* 2001:11). From this perspective, practice is indeed what people do, and also what they say, and therefore policymaking and implementing, working, managing and researching (and teaching) may all be understood as practices.

Practice has been of interest for social scientists since at least the 1970s, when Pierre Bourdieu's theory of practice was published (Bourdieu 1977; Ortner 1984). The surge of interest in practice echoes similar periods in which the attention of social scientists, including organisation and management scholars, has 'turned' towards hitherto neglected or unrecognised aspects of the social world. Other social scientific turns include, *inter alia*, those towards linguistics (Rorty 1992), culture (Chaney 1994; Ray & Sayer 1999; Nash 2001), affect and feelings (Clough & Halley 2007), and space (Warf & Arias 2008). The turn to practice has, for some, displaced earlier interests, including abstract structures, individual agency, culture, affect or space, in favour of everyday activity as a focus for research.

Although described as a 'practice turn' by Schatzki and colleagues (2001), other scholars suggest this conceptual movement actually represents a *return* to practice (Miettinen *et al.* 2009; Nicolini 2013). While the most recent theories of practice (e.g., Schatzki 2002) are underpinned by insights from Ludwig Wittgenstein and Martin Heidegger, and develop Pierre Bourdieu and Anthony Giddens's work, claims of a return are justified by the practical interest of earlier theorists including Karl Marx, Charles Pierce and John Dewey. Miettinen and colleagues (2009), and elsewhere Nicolini and Eikeland (Eikeland & Nicolini 2011; Nicolini 2013), identify these earlier theorists' interest in practice, which themselves were built on Aristotelian and Hegelian foundations.

This has not been a consolidated intellectual manoeuvre. There is "no unified practice approach" (Schatzki *et al.* 2001:11). Rather, it is a broad polysemic field. There may be a sharing of broad interest and the development of a distinct vocabulary, but there are also overlapping—and occasionally conflicting—principles (Schatzki *et al.* 2001; Rouse 2007; Miettinen *et al.* 2009; Eikeland & Nicolini 2011; Nicolini 2013). There are at least two ways that practice has been approached in the return to practice: firstly, through empirical research that focuses on revealing the detail of practices; and secondly, through the development of theoretical or philosophical accounts of practice (Rouse 2007; Miettinen *et al.* 2009; Eikeland & Nicolini 2011).

Empirical practice-based investigations in business and organisation studies have been used to understand a number of aspects of organisational life, including strategy-as-practice (e.g., Rasche & Chia 2009), the practices of organisational learning and knowledge management (e.g., Nicolini *et al.* 2003), leadership practices (e.g., Carroll *et al.* 2008), and technologies as practice (e.g., Orlikowski 2000).

While management and organisation studies has proven a particularly fertile field for practice-based scholarship, sociologists concerned with topics including sustainability, energy and consumption have also advanced the literature (e.g., Shove 2005, 2010; Shove & Walker 2014). Their work has helped to shed light on the social and material aspects of consumption and energy use, in contrast to earlier individualistic understandings of these topics. Moreover, they have also identified the potential of practice theories for addressing public policy problems (Shove *et al.* 2012; Blue *et al.* 2014).

Empirical work adopting a practice-based approach has tended to follow broadly ethnographic methods (Nicolini 2009). Studies have differed in the extent of their engagement with theories of practice. For some scholars practices are indeed what people do, and the study of the activities of everyday work and life uses a grounded approach. Anthropological and ethnomethodological perspectives in particular may seek to approach practices in the 'real' world, unmediated by *a priori* theoretical frameworks, in order to investigate social institutions and order. From this perspective, commitment to models, frameworks or theories risks obscuring aspects of the practices in focus, and there is no epistemological imperative for recourse to theories of practice (Miettinen *et al.* 2009).

For other scholars an engagement with philosophical accounts of practice offers a useful starting point for empirical investigation, not least because these theoretical frameworks can help define practices (as they are understood by certain philosophers), and establish ontological and epistemological assumptions consistent with a focus on practices understood as more than a microanalysis of what people do (Schatzki 2012). A practice theoretical lens, as discussed in the next section, offers an alternative to more established social theories. Consequently, this approach promises a number of potential benefits, including an opportunity to dissolve some of the long-standing problems within the philosophy of social science (Nicolini 2013).

THEORISING PRACTICE

The theoretical contributions to praxeological thought—the essential concept that social life is contingent, emergent and formed by practices—include those by Bourdieu, Giddens, Garfinkel, Butler, Latour, Taylor, Schatzki, Lave and Wenger, Engeström, and Shove, Pantzar and Walker (Reckwitz 2002; Nicolini 2013). Although not all of the named authors have explicitly formulated a theory of practice, they have enabled others to develop one (e.g., Schatzki 1996, 2002), and contributed significantly to our contemporary theoretical understanding of practice. These contributions are summarised in table 3.1.

Within the practice theoretical field, there is a diversity of scholarly traditions. Hence, it is appropriate to talk of 'family resemblances' (Nicolini 2013:9), recognising that there is no single theory of practice but rather a broad family of scholarly approaches with a shared interest in everyday practices. A number of commonalities exist across this wide intellectual

Table 3.1 Theoretical contributions to praxeological thought

Pierre Bourdieu (1977)	Habitus is Bourdieu's conceptual attempt to avoid the dichotomy between subjectivism and objectivism. Habitus accounts for reproduction of society (but neglects societal transformation and materiality).
Anthony Giddens (1984)	Giddens understood that "practices, ordered across space and time", are the basic concern of the social sciences (1984:2). Through the concept of structuration, Giddens sought to resolve the structure/agency dichotomy—rather than viewing structure/agency as a dualism, he argued it was a duality. Structure, in this view, is recursively created by the "situated activities of human agents" (1984:25), is not external to agents, and is both constraining and enabling.
Harold Garfinkel (1967)	Garfinkel's ethnomethodology is not a theory of practice, but is praxeologically oriented through an interest in the practices "involved in constituting knowledge in the world" (Nicolini 2013:134). Practices are seen as forming both the substance of everyday life, and the processual and contingent performance of those practices.
Judith Butler (1990)	Through her study of gender as a "constructed identity, a performative accomplishment" (1990:179), Butler's work has contributed insights into the performance, performativity and accomplishment of everyday life to praxeological thought.
Bruno Latour (1993)	Latour's science studies (1993) emphasise the performativity and contingency of scientific knowledge. However, although his actor network theory (ANT) embraces material artefacts and things, Latour is not a practice theorist and does not view practices as the unit of analysis (Nicolini 2013).
Charles Taylor (1993a, 1993b)	Taylor (like Schatzki) draws upon Wittgenstein and Heidegger to argue that humans are "self-interpreting animals" (Reckwitz 2002:244), and neither wholly rational nor wholly norm-driven.
Theodore Schatzki (e.g., 1996, 2002)	Schatzki has drawn upon and augmented Wittgenstein and Heidegger, arriving at a social ontology based around the primacy of practice.
Jean Lave & Etienne Wenger (1991)	Lave & Wenger's concept of 'legitimate peripheral participation' (1991) foregrounds the socially situated nature of learning. Learning and socialisation are important elements of practice theory.
Yrjo Engeström (2014)	Engeström builds on Lev Vygotsky's work. This includes Cultural and Historical Activity Theory (CHAT), and an understanding that activity is a potentially transformative practice (Nicolini 2013).
Elizabeth Shove, Mika Pantzar, & Gordon Walker (2012)	Shove and colleagues synthesise Schatzki and Reckwitz (and others) to develop a practice-theoretical approach to address public policy problems.

Adapted from Nicolini (2013) and Reckwitz (2002)

field. These include the idea that a practice is an "organized constellation of different people's activities" (Schatzki 2012:13). Practices are also viewed as social phenomena, because they involve more than one person, albeit not necessarily at the same time. It is commonly considered that practices are embodied (working against the Cartesian separation of head from hands); that materials (artefacts and non-human nature) are part of practices; and that knowledge is a mode of action and is bound up with the use of artefacts. Knowledge is thus considered to be more than merely verbal or textual representations of the world (Schatzki *et al.* 2001; Reckwitz 2002; Miettinen *et al.* 2009).

Activity and materiality are central to most contemporary definitions of practice. Schatzki, for instance, defines practices "as embodied, materially mediated arrays of human activity centrally organized around shared practical understanding" (2001:11). Similarly, Rasche and Chia (2009:721) define practices "as a nexus of routinized performances of the body". The emphasis on the body underlines a rejection of distinguishing mind and body that would depict us as a thinking subject that is detached from action (Rasche & Chia 2009). Activities and performance thus constitute *bodily doings* (e.g., taking notes, writing this chapter) and *sayings* (e.g., speech acts; language therefore is a bodily doing, too) (Schatzki 1996; Reckwitz 2002; Rasche & Chia 2009). Whilst activities, doing the practice, is a focal point in these definitions, practices for these scholars are more than just situated action. Many practice theorists argue that reducing practices to a microanalysis of *what people do* misses the potential of the practice lens (Chia & Holt 2006; Rasche & Chia 2009; Feldman & Orlikowski 2011; Shove *et al.* 2012; Gherardi 2013; Nicolini 2013). Such microanalysis ignores the recursive nature of practices and how practising contributes to or interferes with the ongoing production of organisational life.

Contemporary practice theory tends to conceive practices as a continuous and recursive process of production and reproduction of social order (Giddens 1984; Schatzki 2001; Gherardi 2006; Shove *et al.* 2012). This is described as "arrangements of people and the organisms, artefacts, and things through which they coexist" (Schatzki 2001:51). An illustration of this may be a classroom, a hospital or an organisation (Nicolini 2013). Practices can be understood to be the context of social activity; they are the 'site' of the social (Schatzki 2002, 2003, 2005). From this perspective, the social world consists in practices; this is a social ontology. Moreover, it is a non-hierarchical 'flat ontology' (Schatzki 2011:14), in which there are no distinct levels such as container and contained, or macro, meso and micro (Miettinen *et al.* 2009). Studies following these insights accept practices, not individuals or abstract structures, as the unit of analysis.

To illustrate these points, we offer a short cameo of university life through a practice lens. From a practice perspective, a university can be understood to consist, broadly speaking, in practices of (for example) education, research, knowledge dissemination, and management. These practices are performed by people (e.g., students, support staff, academics, visitors, managers), using artefacts and things (e.g., buildings, rooms, chairs, desks, pencils, notepaper, light bulbs, computers, lecterns, projectors, journals, books, WiFi, the internet, laboratory apparatuses).

Teaching and researching themselves consist in other practices, and if we 'zoom in' (Nicolini 2013) we find reading, talking, listening, understanding, critiquing, writing, collaborating, experimenting, gathering data, observing, analysing and so on. Everyone, from senior staff to first-year students, shares (to a varying extent) a repertoire of practices (of writing, reading, communicating, sharing jokes and food, and so on), and in this way the flat ontology, with no dichotomous micro/meso/macro distinctions, can be discerned. The people in a university generally know what to do in these settings, partly because the "practice of being a competent class student is inscribed in the habituated bodies of children" from a young age (Nicolini 2013:4). Similarly, the practices of participating in (for example) research seminars, conferences, job interviews, running experiments, and lecturing are inscribed on practitioners' bodies as they learn (perhaps through observation of peers, or formal training courses) how to perform these practices.

Apart from the focus on recurrent activities, some practice theorists pay particular attention to the often neglected notion of materiality (Reckwitz 2002; Røpke 2009; Schatzki 2010; Shove *et al.* 2012; Carlile *et al.* 2013; Nicolini 2013). For example, Carlile and colleagues (2013) are attentive to the inherent entanglements between humans and matter, which they describe as sociomateriality—a line of thinking developed in Chapter 7 (Sensing Bodies). Similarly, Schatzki seeks to "erase the boundary lines between society and materiality" (2010:124). He argues that humans and non-human nature, or materiality, are dimensions of one another (Schatzki 2010). Shove and colleagues (2012) show how a focus on the material elements of practices can shed light on how change occurs in society.

Returning to our illustrative cameo of university life, it is not trivial to acknowledge that pens, paper, computers, desks, books and so on are all important resources for practices of learning, teaching, academic research and management, or that vehicles are important for field trips. In this way, sociomaterial transformations are made visible: as innovations in material objects such as projectors, computers, the internet, online journals and e-books were embraced in universities, teaching, learning and researching practices were modified by these technologies, facilitating (for example) easier distance learning and research collaboration, or wider dissemination of research findings. In this way, practices evolve—and the social world changes—through our sociomaterial entanglement with the world, and the associated innovation and modification of artefacts and technologies.

The foregoing illustrative cameo has also served to begin demonstrating the distinct vocabulary of a practice approach. Although the practice theoretical lexicon may not be extensive compared to some social theories (Reckwitz 2002), it does embrace certain characteristics and specific words (Nicolini *et al.* 2003). The active and processual characteristic of a world seen through a practice lens is conveyed by verbs in the gerund, such as 'doings and sayings', teaching, learning or researching (Schatzki 1996:89; Nicolini *et al.* 2003). *Nexus* describes the web of activities, including doings, sayings, and material arrangements, that comprise practices (Schatzki 2012:18). *Material arrangements* describes the "bodies, artefacts, organisms, and things" that our practices "use, react to, and give meaning to", while arrangements also "induce, prefigure, and are essential to practices" (Schatzki 2014:19). Practices come together into *bundles* of practices that are in turn linked together into larger *constellations* of practices (Schatzki 2012). Through these lexical practices, practice theory displaces the agents, structures, texts and so on of more established social theories, and replaces them with bodies, movements, materials and practical knowledge (Reckwitz 2002).

THE BENEFITS OF ADOPTING A PRACTICE THEORY LENS

What are the benefits of the practice lens? An approach following a practice ontology along the lines sketched out in the previous section is radically different from many other social theories. An exploration of these differences illuminates some potential benefits of the approach. There are at least four ways in which a practice approach differs from other theories (Reckwitz 2002; Shove *et al.* 2012; Nicolini 2013) and each of these is discussed below.

Firstly, from this perspective, the social world is understood to consist in practices, activity and performance. The production and reproduction of practices are what make the social apparently durable. Consequently, practices are the unit of analysis rather than the usual dichotomous categories of, for example, individuals and organisations.

Secondly, practices involve bodily action, mental activity and material things. The body is not a mere instrument for action, because a practice is a routinised bodily action (Reckwitz 2002). By dissolving the Cartesian mind/body separation, a practice approach brings bodily doings and materiality into analytical focus (Gherardi 2009).

Thirdly, practice theory negotiates a path between the classical perspectives of the (semi-) rational decision maker *homo economicus* and the norm-following *homo sociologicus* (Reckwitz 2002). *Homo practicus* is a mind/body who carries (out) practices and enjoys space for creativity and innovation as required while performing practices (Shove *et al.* 2012; Nicolini 2013). The performance of practices is "neither mindless repetition nor complete invention" (Nicolini 2013:5). From this perspective, debates around structure and agency are reconfigured and possibly dissolved.

Fourthly, knowledge is understood differently. Knowing is a social phenomenon, and it is shared with others. It is "a form of mastery that is expressed in the capacity to carry out a social and material activity" (Nicolini

2013:5). Discourse is understood as a practice, but the social world is more than signs, texts and symbols.

The above summary of how a practice theory lens differs from other social theories indicates the way in which it can offer alternative insights into the processual constitution of organisations and institutions. It can offer fresh insights into how the social world changes and why it remains the same (Shove *et al.* 2012; Nicolini 2013). It is an approach that promises to dissolve some of the long-standing problems within social theory, such as the separation of mind from body, doing from knowing, and structure from agency.

CONCLUDING COMMENTS

This chapter has identified a number of different perspectives on the concept of practice, ranging from common-sense understandings to highly theorised accounts of social life. Sharp contrasts exist between these perspectives, particularly in ontological and epistemological terms. Subsequent chapters adopt a variety of these perspectives, and illustrate some of their implications for interventions in the knowledge and practice of organisational life and policymaking.

SUGGESTED FURTHER READINGS

Three good resources on practice theory (all within the practice ontology paradigm) include:

Schatzki, T.R. (2005) Peripheral vision: The sites of organizations. *Organization Studies.* 26(3): 465–484.
> This paper is a useful introduction to Schatzki's work, including his site ontology and its relation to other social theories.

Nicolini, D. (2013) *Practice theory, work, and organization: An introduction.* Oxford: Oxford University Press.
> A broad overview of different theoretical contributions to practice theory. Nicolini proposes a synthesis approach, which promises a useful integration of elements of many of these distinct approaches.

Shove, E., Pantzar, M., & Watson, M. (2012) *The dynamics of social practice: Everyday life and how it changes.* London: SAGE.
> An excellent review and operationalisation of practice theory, underlaid with a strong argument for the benefits of practice theory in social policy.

REFERENCES

Blue, S., Shove, E., Carmona, C., & Kelly, M.P. (2014) Theories of practice & public health: Understanding (un)healthy practices. *Critical Public Health.* 26(1): 36–50.

Bourdieu, P. (1977) *Outline of a theory of practice.* Cambridge: Cambridge University Press.

Butler, J. (1990) *Gender trouble*. London: Routledge.

Carlile, P.R., Nicolini, D., Langley, A., & Tsoukas, H. (2013) *How matter matters: Objects, artefacts, & materiality in organisation studies*. Oxford: Oxford University Press.

Carroll, B., Levy, L., & Richmond, D. (2008) Leadership as practice: Challenging the competency paradigm. *Leadership*. 4(4): 363–379.

Chaney, D. (1994) *The cultural turn: Scene-setting essays on contemporary social history*. London: Routledge.

Chia, R., & Holt, R. (2006) Strategy as practical coping: A Heideggerian perspective. *Organization Studies*. 27(5): 635–655.

Clough, P.T., & Halley, J. (2007) *The affective turn: Theorizing the social*. Durham NC: Duke University Press.

Davies, H.T.O., Nutley, S.M., & Smith, P.C. (2000) *What works? Evidence-based policy & practice in public services*. Bristol: Policy Press.

Eikeland, O. (2007) *Turning to practice—What does it mean, & why is it important?* Making the 'practical turn' practical: Collaboration across nationalities, professions, & varieties of action research, September 10, Oslo. Available: https://hioa.academia.edu/OlavEikeland. Accessed: May 4, 2015.

Eikeland, O., & Nicolini, D. (2011) Turning practically: Broadening the horizon. *Journal of Organizational Change Management*. 24(2): 164–174.

Engeström, Y. (2014) *Learning by expanding*. Cambridge: Cambridge University Press.

Feldman, M.S., & Orlikowski, W.J. (2011) Theorizing practice & practicing theory. *Organization Science*. 22(5): 1240–1253.

Ferraro, E., & Reid, L. (2013) On sustainability & materiality: Homo faber, a new approach. *Ecological Economics*. 96: 125–131.

Garfinkel, H. (1967) *Studies in ethnomethodology*. Englewood Cliffs, NJ: Prentice-Hall.

Gherardi, S. (2006) *Organizational knowledge: The texture of workplace learning*. Oxford: Blackwell.

Gherardi, S. (2009) Introduction: The critical power of the 'practice lens'. *Management Learning*. 40(2): 115–128.

Gherardi, S. (2013) *How to conduct a practice-based study: Problems & methods*. Cheltenham: Edward Elgar.

Giddens, A. (1984) *The constitution of society: Outline of the theory of structuration*. Cambridge: Polity Press.

Hill, M., & Huppe, P. (2014) *Implementing public policy: An introduction to the study of operational governance*. London: SAGE.

Latour, B. (1993) *We have never been modern*. Cambridge, MA: Harvard University Press.

Lave, J., & Wenger, E. (1991) *Situated learning: Legitimate peripheral participation*. Cambridge: Cambridge University Press.

Lipsky, M. (1971) Street-level bureaucracy & the analysis of urban reform. *Urban Affairs Quarterly*. 6: 391–409.

Lipsky, M. (2010) *Street-level bureaucracy: Dilemmas of the individual in public service*. New York: Russell Sage Foundation.

Miettinen, R., Samra-Fredericks, D., & Yanow, D. (2009) Re-turn to practice: An introductory essay. *Organization Studies*. 30(12): 1309–1327.

Nash, K. (2001) The 'cultural turn' in social theory: Towards a theory of cultural politics. *Sociology*. 35(1): 77–92.

Nicolini, D. (2009) Zooming in & zooming out: A package of method & theory to study work practices, in S. Ybema, D. Yanov, H. Wels, & F.H. Kamsteeg (eds.), *Organizational ethnography: Studying the complexity of everyday life*. London: SAGE, pp. 120–138.

Nicolini, D. (2013) *Practice theory, work, & organization: An introduction.* Oxford: Oxford University Press.

Nicolini, D., Gherardi, S., & Yanow, D. (2003) *Knowing in organizations: A practice-based approach.* New York: M.E. Sharpe.

Nutley, S.M., Walter, I., & Davies, H.T.O. (2007) *Using evidence: How research can inform public services.* Bristol: Policy Press.

Orlikowski, W.J. (2000) Using technology & constituting structures: A practice lens for studying technology in organizations. *Organization Science.* 11(4): 404–428.

Ortner, S.B. (1984) Theory in anthropology since the sixties. *Comparative Studies in Society & History.* 26(1): 126–166.

Oxford English Dictionary Online (2015) Oxford: Oxford University Press. Available: www.oed.com. Accessed: May 4, 2015.

Rasche, A., & Chia, R. (2009) Researching strategy practices: A genealogical social theory perspective. *Organization Studies.* 30(7): 713–734.

Ray, L.J., & Sayer, R.A. (1999) *Culture & economy after the cultural turn.* London: SAGE.

Reckwitz, A. (2002) Toward a theory of social practices: A development in culturalist theorizing. *European Journal of Social Theory.* 5(2): 243–263.

Røpke, I. (2009) Theories of practice—New inspiration for ecological economic studies on consumption. *Ecological Economics.* 68(10): 2490–2497.

Rorty, R. (1992) *The linguistic turn: Essays in philosophical method.* Chicago: University of Chicago Press.

Rouse, J. (2007) Practice theory, in S.P. Turner & M.W. Risjord (eds.), *Philosophy of anthropology & sociology.* Oxford: North-Holland, pp. 639–682.

Schatzki, T.R. (1996) *Social practices: A Wittgensteinian approach to human activity & the social.* Cambridge: Cambridge University Press.

Schatzki, T.R. (2001) Practice mind-ed orders, in T.R. Schatzki, K. Knorr Cetina, & E. von Savigny (eds.), *The practice turn in contemporary theory.* London: Routledge, pp. 50–63.

Schatzki, T.R. (2002) *The site of the social: A philosophical account of the constitution of social life & change.* Pennsylvania: Pennsylvania State University Press.

Schatzki, T.R. (2003) A new societist social ontology. *Philosophy of the Social Sciences.* 33(2): 174–202.

Schatzki, T.R. (2005) Peripheral vision: The sites of organizations. *Organization Studies.* 26(3): 465–484.

Schatzki, T.R. (2010) Materiality & social life. *Nature & Culture.* 5(2): 123–149.

Schatzki, T.R. (2011) *Where the action is (on large social phenomena such as sociotechnical regimes).* Sustainable Practices Research Group. Working Paper 1, Manchester.

Schatzki, T.R. (2012) A primer on practices, in J. Higgs, R. Barnett, S. Billett, M. Hutchings, & F. Trede (eds.), *Practice-based education: Perspectives & strategies.* Rotterdam: Sense Publishers, pp. 13–26.

Schatzki, T.R. (2014) Art bundles, in T. Zembylas (ed), *Artistic practices: Social interactions and cultural dynamics,* London: Routledge, pp. 17–31.

Schatzki, T.R., Knorr Cetina, K., & von Savigny, E. (2001) *The practice turn in contemporary theory.* London: Routledge.

Shove, E. (2005) Consumers, producers & practices: Understanding the invention & reinvention of Nordic walking. *Journal of Consumer Culture.* 5(1): 43–64.

Shove, E. (2010) Beyond the ABC: Climate change policy & theories of social change. *Environment & Planning A.* 42(6): 1273–1285.

Shove, E., Pantzar, M., & Watson, M. (2012) *The dynamics of social practice: Everyday life & how it changes.* London: SAGE.

Shove, E., & Walker, G. (2014) What is energy for? Social practice & energy demand. *Theory, Culture & Society.* 31(5): 41–58.

Taylor, C. (1993a) Engaged agency & background in Heidegger, in C. Guignon (ed.), *The Cambridge companion to Heidegger*. Cambridge: Cambridge University Press, pp. 317–336.

Taylor, C. (1993b) To follow a rule, in C. Calhoun, E. LiPuma, & M. Postone (eds.), *Bourdieu: Critical perspectives*. Cambridge: Polity Press, pp. 45–60.

Warf, B., & Arias, S. (2008) *The spatial turn: Interdisciplinary perspectives*. London: Routledge.

4 Power, Knowledge and Practice

Christopher Mueller, Alina Baluch and Kevin Orr

INTRODUCTION

Power relations are an integral part of our everyday lives. We have all exercised power, just as we have experienced it. Sometimes this occurs in the most mundane ways—we may have made colleagues work long hours by calling a snap meeting at five p.m., or been compelled by a deadline to spend weekends welded to a laptop. Power is often seen "as the capacity of individuals to exert their will over others" (Huzzard 2004:353)—and, if required, to do so against their will (Weber 1954; Hardy & Clegg 2006). In this way, for example, employees must submit to a controlling performance appraisal regime. Power can also be an enabling aspect of organisational life—for example, a team leader may create an environment of openness during a project meeting, encouraging colleagues to speak candidly; a decisive intervention in a process may free up time or create autonomy; or an individual may be given more decision-making power as part of their personal or professional development. Such examples have nothing grandiose about them; they do not involve heroic deeds or the majestic wielding of power. Instead, they highlight the commonplace nature of power relations: power is an everyday phenomenon.

Just as power is an integral part of our day-to-day interactions, it is at the same time deeply entwined with knowledge. Drawing on the examples above, employees must know how to conduct themselves in relation to the performance management norms of the organisation. Relations of power may also regulate access to knowledge, including one participant but excluding another. The team leader giving voice to colleagues during a meeting is inclusive and thus open towards knowledge arising through interactions in the team.

This chapter begins by providing an overview of the different ways power has been understood. We then consider the relationship between power and knowledge. Following this, we use a practice-theory lens to demonstrate the fruitfulness of viewing power, knowledge and practice in conjunction with each other. Finally, we offer some thoughts about the implications of these connections for practitioners.

UNDERSTANDINGS OF POWER

From Weber (1981) onwards, much of social science has addressed important questions around the exercise and distribution of power. Is power repressive or generative? Who has power or how is it distributed? Who benefits from its use and can it be exercised with responsibility? Is power generated by individuals or by economic and social relations? Are the powerful beyond accountability or influence? Can social life—or knowledge and practice—exist beyond power relations?

Theories of power have been developed by political scientists, sociologists and psychologists. Marx (1975) thought of power as stemming from the economic order of capitalism—who has control over capital, technology, materials information and know how. Weber (1978) focused on power relations in bureaucracies, where power and authority comes from hierarchical position. Providing a social psychological view of power, French and Raven (1959) identify five bases of social power: legitimate power (akin to Weber's ideas about power through hierarchy), referent power (through mutual loyalty or charisma), expert power (from technical knowledge or credentials), coercive power (forcing someone to act against their will), and reward power (the capacity to provide or withhold what others desire or value, such as money, affirmation, security or information).

Although power is a contested concept, it is helpful to view it as a 'family resemblance concept'—a constellation of concepts exhibiting overlapping similarities (Wittgenstein 1967; Haugaard & Clegg 2009; Haugaard 2010; Nicolini 2013). Like family members, different concepts of power are related to each other, but the family tree is twisted, knotted and complicated. The family members include, for example, the interconnected notions of 'power to' (e.g., Parsons 1967; Arendt 1970) and 'power over' (e.g., Weber 1978); power as domination (e.g., Lukes 2005), coercive or repressive (e.g., Dahl 1957); productive connotations of power (e.g., Foucault, Parsons), and resource-dependency views (e.g., Pfeffer 1981; Clegg et al. 2006:126); power and its relationship to truth (Foucault 1980); power and resistance (e.g., Foucault 1978); and episodic, dispositional and systemic power (e.g., Clegg 1989).

The family history of the different understandings of power can be traced across the three faces of power. Initially, it was largely assumed that there was a single face of power and that power could be defined in fairly straightforward terms. So, for Dahl (1957), A has power over B to the extent that A can get B to do something that B would not otherwise do. This account of power relations has instinctive appeal. It is clear and may resonate with our own experience of occasions when we feel compelled to act in ways that we feel are detrimental. However, this view of power makes a number of problematic assumptions. Power is seen in relation to its effects; power is possessed by individual actors and exercised through actions and behaviours; power is understood as power over (as domination); and power relations represent a zero sum—for some to win it is necessary for others to lose.

The second face of power highlights that power is exercised through setting the agenda for decision-making processes—delineating what is to be discussed or deliberated. In other words the capacity to shape agendas and control the boundaries of discussion represents a fundamental exercise of power, one which is not considered by the first face of power. If we are to understand power, we must look not just at how decisions get resolved, but also how the focus of decisions are bounded, framed and scoped in the first place (Bachrach & Baratz 1962). In this way we need to consider power in relation to both front stage decision-making and back stage agenda setting. This more expansive treatment of power encourages us to think about informal interactions, behind-the-scenes discussions, and the wider process of coalition building and exclusion, all of which enable particular groups or actors to prevail.

Lukes introduced a third face of power, one which moves our focus beyond situations in which conflict is observable, and towards the 'insidious exercise of power' in which people have their preferences shaped and their sense of grievance neutralised or their understanding of their own interests warped. In doing so, people ". . . accept their role in the existing order of things, either because they can see or imagine no alternative to it, or because they see it as natural or unchangeable, or because they value it as divinely ordained and beneficial . . ." (Lukes 1974:24). Lukes invites us to consider the struggles that underpin decision processes, how agendas are shaped and influenced, and the actions and inactions involved in the shaping of people's understanding of their own interests. The exercise of power is context shaping. It defines the choices and parameters of subsequent action. Lukes provided a landmark intervention in the debates about power, but his position suggests that power is only ever a pejorative concept, perhaps something that cannot be exercised responsibly.

The above debates indicate that power is inextricably connected to knowledge. Who or what is shaping the agenda is dependent on, for example, which actors have access to knowledge or the type of knowledge being privileged at the time. And just as power legitimises and shapes knowledge, knowledge facilitates the exercise of power (Heizmann 2011).

For Foucault (1977), power and knowledge are intimately connected (or co-determinate). Power through knowledge and knowledge through power produce 'reality'. Power and knowledge directly imply one another: "there is no power relation without the correlative constitution of a field of knowledge, nor any knowledge that does not presuppose and constitute at the same time power relations" (Foucault 1977: 927). There is no way of existing or practising outside relations of power; power is ubiquitous and all-encompassing. Though power-knowledge regimes may change or evolve, there is no possibility of liberation. We will return to a consideration of the implications of the inescapability of knowledge and power.

The remainder of this section concentrates on the definitions of power most prevalent in the literature on organisations, knowledge and practice. These are grouped according to whether power is viewed as a coercive capacity, as a productive capacity or as action (power by doing). This leads us to tease out three forms of power: episodic, dispositional and systemic.

Power As Coercive Capacity

In the first group of definitions (table 4.1), power is viewed as a coercive capacity (or dispositional power), manifesting itself in the ability to exercise power over someone. Such definitions of power carry negative connotations, creating a sense that the effects of power are to create deliberate constraints or wilful impositions.

Power As a Productive Capacity

In the second group of definitions (table 4.2), power is imbued with more positive associations, emphasising the capacity of power to produce benefits, gains or the achievement of goals. For example, Foucault (1980) is critical of repressive notions of power insofar as they imply power is concentrated in the sphere of certain individuals, who 'possess' power. For these writers,

Table 4.1   Power as a coercive capacity

Author(s)	Definition
Weber (1954:323)	Power is "the possibility of imposing one's own will upon the behavior of other persons".
Salancik and Pfeffer (1977:14)	Power is "the ability to get things done the way one wants them to be done".
Huzzard (2004:353)	Power is "the capacity of individuals to exert their will over others".
Lukes (2005:85)	"Power as domination is the ability to constrain the choices of others, coercing them or securing their compliance, by impeding them from living as their own nature and judgment dictate".

Table 4.2   Power as a productive capacity

Author(s)	Definition
Arendt (1970:44)	Power is the "capacity to act in concert".
Foucault (1978:94)	"Relations of power are . . . the immediate effects of (the) divisions, inequalities, and disequilibriums . . . they have a directly productive role, wherever they come into play".
Lukes (2005:63)	"Power refers to an ability or capacity of an agent or agents, which they may or may not exercise".
Giddens (1984:257)	Power is "the capacity to achieve outcomes".
Schatzki (2005:478)	"Power is one person's actions structuring other people's possible actions".

power is more than the force that simply says "no", nor is power part of a zero-sum game in which one actor 'wins' at the expense of the other.

Power As Doing

A third grouping of definitions (see table 4.3) emphasises the active exercise of power—how power is practised or carried off. We can discern power as being present in a range of verbs—such as managing, leading, supporting, changing, implementing, auditing, assessing, disengaging, disrupting, reforming and so on—which we might think of in organisational settings.

Emerging from the above definitional groupings is a somewhat contrasting view of power as an activity (episodic power) and power as capacity (dispositional power). Dahl (1957) is renowned for an *episodic* view of power. Accordingly we can only talk about power when its exercise has been witnessed. Episodic power may comprise notions such as power over, power to, as well as repressive or facilitative aspects of power. Dispositional power is seen as existing outside of action (Giddens 1984); it is something that a person has although he or she is not exercising it. In other words, an individual possesses power at any given point in time.

To these two forms of power (episodic and dispositional), we can add a third, *systemic power,* which is embedded in wider social and cultural systems, rather than vested in individual actors (Lukes 1974). It provides the backdrop for episodic power and is taken to 'structure' the possibilities for action. Such power operates through routines and ongoing taken-for-granted practices.

These forms of power—episodic, dispositional and systemic—do not exist in strict isolation from each other and the concept of family resemblance reminds us not to view power absolutely as one of the single notions discussed above. Instead, power can be both repressive and facilitative; at times power over is more apparent than power to, at other moments the two act in conjunction altogether. In the next section, we look at ways of understanding the relationship between power and knowledge.

Table 4.3 Power as doing

Author(s)	Definition
Dahl (1957)	A has power over B to the extent that A can get B to do something that B would not otherwise do.
Foucault (1977:26 & 27)	"Power is exercised rather than possessed; it is not the 'privilege', acquired or preserved, of the dominant class, but the overall effect of its strategic positions—an effect that is manifested and sometimes extended by the position of those who are dominated".

POWER AND KNOWLEDGE

As explored in Chapter 2, there is a range of perspectives and assumptions about the nature of knowledge—for example, about whether it is best understood as a process or an object, whether it is codifiable and transferable, or whether knowing is separable from the knower and embedded in the specificities of context. As explained in that chapter, there is a spectrum of terms available to describe or conceptualise knowledge, including the degree to which writers see knowledge as situated and thereby emphasise *knowledge in* practice or *knowing as* practice.

In table 4.4 we offer ten ways of thinking about knowledge, and we set alongside these some illustrative examples or explanations of each one. The final column of the table considers the way in which the particular way of conceptualising knowledge relates to questions or issues of power.

Considering knowledge in relation to these questions of power, we can see that the power relations at stake will likely differ depending on the way knowledge is conceptualised. For example, if knowledge is understood as situated, power relations will dictate the dominant social constructions in the setting. If, on the other hand, knowledge is understood as tacit, power will feature in who can gain access to the often personal, sensory and untold knowledge necessary for a certain way of practising. For our purposes, knowledge as knowing, situated and tacit each play a role in considering knowledge and power in conjunction with practice.

Table 4.4 Ten ways of thinking about knowledge

On knowledge	Examples	Questions of power
Knowledge as credentialing	Credentials such as degrees, professional awards, certificates and other bona fides. Or being able to display one's credentials through being able to speak the language of the group or frame the issue using appropriate language—of being knowledgeable.	Credentials increase autonomy, choices open to, and influence of the bearer. What credentials are valued and who can access these (e.g., who is able to go to university, or flourish at school) also reflects power relations.
Knowledge as privileging	Knowledge is available only on an approved or insider basis. Sensitive, confidential or classified information, or knowledge intentionally withheld from others for whatever reason.	Reinforces the status and influence of the knowledgeable. Disenfranchises and excludes others who cannot access such knowledge.

On knowledge	Examples	Questions of power
Knowledge as endangering	Famously, a little knowledge is a dangerous thing. Reflects scepticism that mobilising knowledge beyond its current sphere will have positive or productive consequences. Rather, in the wrong hands or to the newly enlightened it will be damaging.	Power rests in the capacity to withhold or restrict, or the ability to authorise its wider dissemination. Recognises the revolutionary, or at least disruptive, potential of knowledge.
Knowledge as instrumental	Self-consciously, deliberately and tactically deployed to achieve particular goals and purposes, from the mundane and episodic (how to bake a cake) to the grand and programmatic (how best to reconfigure welfare services, or improve the patient experience in healthcare).	Power is at play in relation to who sets the goals, whose interests do they serve and what is at stake, or what is taken for granted.
Knowledge as the taken for granted	Collectively held assumptions about how the world is, or normative views about the present and future, what is desirable and undesirable, or the right or wrong way of behaving, being or practising.	Norms and assumptions reflect dominant voices and webs of beliefs that have proved useful or viable to particular groups. Which groups and members do they advantage and disadvantage?
Knowledge as technical	Practically oriented and competence or skills based. Helps to carry out practices.	Knowledge is simply functional, and is value neutral and politics free. Helps to survive or thrive in the face of the pressures of social life, the economy, markets, career and the environment.
Knowledge as knowing	The verb—knowing—is preferred to the noun, knowledge, emphasising how knowledge is accomplished and generated rather than exists as an object to be possessed, acquired, guarded or transferred.	Ways of knowing, and the legitimacy of these, reflect power relations. It is intertwined with issues of capacity, agency and autonomy.

(Continued)

Table 4.4   (Continued)

On knowledge	Examples	Questions of power
Knowledge as situated	Knowledge resides in or is accomplished through social and cultural interaction. Knowledge is not the result or property of autonomous agents operating in isolation from each other. It is dependent on the knowers and the context.	Which, and whose, social constructions predominate in a given setting or time reflect issues of choice and voice and wider relations of power.
Knowledge as co-produced	Members of project groups coming together to generate knowledge; knowledge generated through interactive discussion in a classroom; academic and practitioner research collaborations.	Power and politics play through questions such as whose voices get privileged, who sets the agenda, whose interests are served, what constitutes a legitimate knowledge base and so on.
Knowledge as tacit	Polanyi gives the example of the knowledge necessary to the active accomplishment of riding a bike. Tacit knowledge might also be drawn upon in a range of social, cultural or professional settings where there are unwritten rules or norms.	Power is suggested by the issue of who is able to acquire tacit knowledge appropriate to the particularities in this range of settings. The knowledge necessary for the active accomplishment of, for example, being an accountant or a consultant. Polanyi's example of riding a bike is a relatively uncontroversial one; appropriate language, behaviour, dress code or way of practising may entail ambiguous and less accessible knowledge.

POWER AND PRACTICE

Taking a practice theory view of the relationship between power and practice in the following section, we now address how the study of power might benefit from adopting practices as the unit of analysis instead of concentrating on individuals and their characteristics or the relations between them. To this end, this section engages with a view of power as a "practical accomplishment embedded in practices" (Contu 2014:2). This is a position that chimes with practice theory (see Chapter 3 Practice), where the concept of practice refers to much more than merely what people do. Practices are viewed as the 'site' in which social relations and interactions take place.

In practice theory, practices are defined as an accumulation (or nexuses) of "organized human activities" (Schatzki 2005:471). In other words, practices consist of routinised, recurrent and socially recognisable doings and sayings, such as taking notes, writing emails, making phone calls, or speech acts (Nicolini 2009; Rasche & Chia 2009; Schatzki 2012). These may be performed individually or collectively. Either way, practices are largely social.

Practices are 'organised' by means of three distinct but interrelated components of practices (Schatzki 2002, 2005). First, practices are organised by understandings of how to do things, such as knowing how to fill out a form properly. Second, practices are governed by rules, which are explicitly formulated directives or instructions of how to do things, such as a smoking ban in office buildings. Finally, practices are governed and sustained by a norm-giving dimension (Gherardi 2013; Nicolini 2013) that establishes how a practice should be carried out, which establishes the parameters of what is a legitimate or illegitimate contribution to a practice (Schatzki 2002; Nicolini 2009).

In practice-based studies that examine power and its relations, an episodic conceptualisation of power involves a "conflict of individuals mobilising different resources and [a] clash over opposite wants" (Contu 2014:7). Yet, those adopting a more productive notion of *power to* view it as both "a producer and a product of the socio-technical relations in the local setting, and its connections to wider systems" (Mørk *et al.* 2010:577). This systemic view of power is also present with multiple actors situated in webs of power (Hardy & Thomas 2014) or power as an outcome of situations (Goss *et al.* 2011). If marginalised, these actors may have less dispositional power (e.g., lower status, tenure or professional background), but still have opportunities for episodic acts of power that, in turn, lead to shifts in power relations (Levina & Orlikowski 2009). These relations of power determine possibilities for action and are produced, reproduced and transformed by practices.

UNDERSTANDING POWER, KNOWLEDGE AND PRACTICE— A PRACTICE-POWER APPROACH

In this section, we contribute to ongoing conversations that understand power from the perspective of social practices (e.g., Levina & Orlikowski 2009; Heizmann 2011; Contu 2014). By asking how power operates if a practice theoretical view is taken, we integrate the notions of episodic, dispositional and systemic power. At the same time, since there can neither be practice nor power in the absence of knowledge, we will suggest how the concepts of power, knowledge and practice form a triangular relationship.

The analysis is shifted from who *has* power towards *how* it is exercised (McGabe 2009). Episodic power refers to the exercise of power in terms of agency. However, solely focusing on this kind of episodic act of practising power is problematic. Despite being a pointer towards an instance of power being executed in a particular situation, it lacks explanatory potential as to how and why an individual is able to do so in the first place. In addition to scrutinising an episode of power in the here and now, a 'strong programme' of practice research (see Nicolini 2013) also calls us to ask "why it is the way it is, and how it contributes to, or interferes with, the production of organizational life" (Nicolini 2013:12).

To address these questions, the notion of dispositional power is helpful. For example, a doctor has the capacity for episodic exercise because of the dispositional power conferred through medical and legal practices. There is thus a mutual relationship between episodic and dispositional power. Dispositional power can only exist *inside* of action—although it may not be exercised by a particular individual at a given point in time—because its exercise (i.e., episodic power) ties meaning to an actor's power dispositions (Haugaard 2010). A member of Parliament executing power by voting on a law perpetuates existing power dynamics inherent in political practices, and therefore perpetuates the practice itself.

As noted earlier, a practice needs to be recurrent in order to be socially recognisable. Organisations, for example, only exist as long as those practices that comprise them (such as holding meetings, dealing with customers, having internal reviews, etc.) are repeatedly performed (Schatzki 2006; Nicolini 2013). Paradoxically, a practice remains even if it is not being carried out at a given moment. A teacher is still a teacher even after leaving the classroom at the end of the day. If the practice is not carried out over longer periods of time, however, its structure (the ends of educating youth, or rules and norms governing in the school) and hence its activities (e.g., introducing new lessons, or handing out assignments) become unintelligible and meaningless. As a consequence, the practice ceases to exist altogether.

The same argument applies to the dispositional powers of a practice. Even if, for example, an accountant does not practice at a given point in time (e.g., at night), the practice and hence the accountant's dispositional power continues to exist because both remain intelligible and meaningful. It is thus not a question of whether a particular practitioner accomplishes dispositional power at a specific point in time (through episodic exercise), but whether the disposition remains meaningful in the absence of the accomplishment. We can only say dispositional power exists *outside* of action (Haugaard 2010) if we accept that it is not an abstract force but one that only exists through its enactment. Like agency and structure (Giddens 1984), they are in a recursive relationship that is made possible through practice.

The social system of power provides actors with unequally powerful dispositions, thereby establishing which actions are possible and which are not. This 'system of power' *is* an accumulation of interconnected practices (Lawrence 2008; Haugaard 2010). It is therefore practices themselves that operate as 'systemic power'. Practices, through their organising components of understandings, rules and normativity, ascribe meaning and 'horizons of legitimacies' to, and thus generate the conditions for, dispositional power (cf., Haugaard 2003, 2012; Nicolini 2009). In other words, practices establish whether the parties involved consider the dispositions of, for example, the doctor legitimate and meaningful.

Practices are naturally enabling and constraining (Schatzki 2002)—a practitioner may be enabled to do one thing, but constrained from doing another. Practices thus account for the capacity of actors to make things happen (Haugaard 2003). For example, depending on the crime committed, a country's legal practices enable a judge to give some sentences (e.g., a lifetime in prison), but simultaneously restrict the judge from giving others (e.g., the death penalty).

Since practices are both enabling and constraining, practices produce "a landscape of inequalities" (Nicolini 2011:616). Through practices actors naturally exhibit different status claims. Nicolini's study found that different practices exhibit distinctive "regimes of empowerment and legitimation regarding 'who can do what' and 'whose view counts'" (2011:613). This means that different status claims produce certain relations of power. In organisational practices, for example, 'old-timers' are normally more empowered than 'novices' just joining the community, and may enable or restrict access to other participants of organisational practices (Lave & Wenger 1991; Wenger 1998; Mork *et al.* 2010). Thus, whose view counts is a reflection of power relations influencing the use of voice in a particular context. Dispositional power, and therefore episodic as well, is derived from what is considered legitimate and appropriate, and therefore from relations of empowerment and disempowerment (Haugaard 2010).

Fundamental to our argument is the 'performative' nature of practices. If a practice is not performed, there is no practice. And to perform any kind of practice, knowledge is of the essence. It is hard to imagine how one may perform any practice—be it ruling in court, teaching students or playing a sport—without knowing *how to do it;* that is, how to practice. The contribution that the notion of practice makes to how we think about knowledge is that it is an activity performed together, rather than something people generally have (Gergen 1991; Gherardi 2006; Nicolini 2011).

Through being 'socialised' into a practice, one learns what it means to be a competent practitioner, how to perform the activities of which practising is comprised, where the boundaries of the practice are; that is, what is legitimate and appropriate and what is not (Lave & Wenger 1991). We tacitly learn the 'rules of the game', knowing how to be competent participants of particular practices (Jacobs & Coghlan 2005). As a teacher, how can you discipline students, what measures are deemed appropriate, and what goes too far? By partaking in a practice, by doing it, we automatically know. And since knowing something and doing something are two sides of the same coin, the activity of knowledge—knowing—is an integral part of our everyday life.

In summary, there are neither power relations without knowledge, nor can there be any knowledge without presupposing and constituting power relations (Foucault 1977). Power, it is proposed, produces knowledge; it is legitimised and shaped by power, while concurrently knowledge facilitates

Power

Figure 4.1   The triangular relationship between power, knowledge and practice

the exercise of power (Heizmann 2011:380). Similarly, power is central to our understanding of practices. Practices both enable and constrain relations of power. Through providing a normative structure, a horizon of possibilities and legitimacies, practices produce different positions of power and influence how power may be exercised. At the same time, exercising power according to the way it is prescribed by practices ultimately results in a reproduction of the practice at hand.

We suggest the need for adopting a practice-power approach, not only to attend to how power is produced by and reproduces practices, but also to consider how power may contribute to transforming practices. After all, there cannot be change in practices without expressions of power; that is, inclusion and exclusion, empowerment and disempowerment. Whilst practices can exhibit shared *understandings* about how to carry out a practice, this does not mean that agreement exists. Instead, practices are inherently open to multiple interpretations. What is considered a correct or an incorrect way of practising is continuously being negotiated via power relations (Gordon *et al.* 2009; Mørk *et al.* 2010; Benn *et al.* 2013).

The mesh of these three concepts of power, knowledge and practice is depicted as a triangular relationship in figure 4.1. It is much like the metaphor of a three-legged stool whose legs help form an interdependent structure, in which removing one leg causes the entire construction to fall apart.

CONCLUSION AND PRACTICAL IMPLICATIONS

In this chapter, we have advocated the idea that power, knowledge and practice are inseparable, as captured in the metaphor of a three-legged stool. Although we have argued that power is produced by practices, we posit that the concepts of practice and power are in a recursive relationship. Just as power contributes to perpetuating a practice, power contributes to its transformation as well. Practices and accepted ways of practising are understood to be in constant negotiation and therefore shift (Benn *et al.* 2013). We consider power to be as much produced by practices as it contributes to producing practices (Levina & Orlikowski 2009; Mørk *et al.* 2010). At the same time, knowledge is central to our understanding of both power and practice. We cannot have power relations without knowledge and vice versa, just as a practice can only be performed by doing (i.e., knowing), which, in turn, facilitates power (Hardy & Clegg 2006).

This chapter suggests several practical implications that may give readers a starting point for reflecting on their own practices. As demonstrated by our examples, every practice, or a 'bundle' of multiple practices, is unique in exhibiting different understandings, knowledge associated with it, ends, or rules. Power relations, too, differ from practice to practice. Our practice-power approach may be used as a heuristic to appreciate the wider power dynamics within a particular work environment. It may assist practitioners, across a range of fields and professions, to think about how they are positioned in their local practices, and how they exercise and experience power. The practice approach we have taken highlights that power dynamics are more than what happens in the here and now (Seidl & Whittington 2014). Instead, we have illustrated the wider context that may not be directly visible in an instance of power, but that is still at play.

Since practices are in constant negotiation, practitioners may question whether the organisation has the systems in place to recognise these changes, whether they are aware of what makes these changes happen, and what the consequences are for existing power relationships due to these changes. Relatedly, since not only practices shift but power relations do, too, this entails asking how this may affect the existing work practices. Might work practices need to be revamped in order to account for the shifting power dynamics? Also, can power be exercised purposively as a means to achieve changes in a given practice?

Concerning issues of legitimacy, practitioners can reflect on how power dynamics contribute to determining 'the correct' way of practising. Which actors or groups are involved and who is excluded? Related to our previous point, can this be changed by exercising the dispositional power one may have according to one's position in a practice bundle?

In conclusion, we adopt a view that assumes the social world consists of practices (a practice ontology), and integrate the concepts of episodic (i.e., the exercise of power), dispositional (the power a person 'has' given his or her social position, such as tenure, expertise, social capital), and systemic power (power that stems from the social system). In doing so, we highlight how power functions in correspondence with everyday practice. This is what we call practice-power, a concept for illuminating how practice and power stand in mutual relation to each other, and how practices produce (and disrupt) power relations, and vice versa.

Based on the integration of episodic, dispositional and systemic power, the practice-power approach developed in this chapter contributes to existing conversations that aim to further our understanding of the relationship between practice and power, as well as the role of knowledge. Rather than considering these concepts in isolation, they enrich each other. As shown in figure 4.1, the notion of practice affords deeper insight into understanding how power relations are produced in everyday practising. Power, meanwhile, elucidates how boundaries and legitimate ways of practices are set, thereby producing and reproducing these practices. Knowledge, at the same time, brings practices to life.

SUGGESTED FURTHER READINGS

Clegg, S.R. (1989) *Frameworks of power*. London: SAGE.
This has been an influential text in fields including organisation studies and sociology. Clegg discusses different social science frameworks for understanding power and offers his own contribution, which points to the idea of circuits of power.
Lukes, S. (2005) *Power. A radical view*. 2nd Ed. London: Palgrave Macmillan.
Lukes made a landmark contribution by offering his 'radical view' of power and its third face. In this second edition of the 1974 book he provides an additional introduction and two new chapters responding to critics and elaborating further on his ideas.
Mørk, B.E., Hoholm, T., Ellingsen, G., Edwin, B., & Aanestad, M. (2010) Challenging expertise: On power relations within and across communities of practice in medical innovation. *Management Learning*. 41(5): 575–592.
This excellent article draws on empirical research in healthcare and uses a power lens to analyse the relations between different communities of practice.

REFERENCES

Arendt, H. (1970) *On violence*. New York: Harcourt Brace.
Bachrach, P., & Baratz, M.S. (1962) Two faces of power. *The American Political Science Review*. 56(4): 947–952.
Benn, S., Edwards, M., & Angus-Leppan, T. (2013) Organizational learning & the sustainability of community of practice: The role of boundary objects. *Organization Environment*. 26(2): 184–202.
Clegg, S.R. (1989) *Frameworks of power*. London: SAGE.
Clegg, S.R., Courpasson, D., & Phillips, N. (2006) *Power & organizations*. London: SAGE.
Contu, A. (2014) On boundaries & difference: Communities of practice & power relations in creative work. *Management Learning*. 45(3): 289–316.
Dahl, R. (1957) The concept of power. *Behavioral Science*. 2(3): 201–215.
Foucault, M. (1977) *Discipline & punish: The birth of a prison*. London: Allen & Lane.
Foucault, M. (1978) *The history of sexuality, Volume 1*. London: Penguin.
Foucault, M. (1980) *Power/ knowledge: Selected interviews & other writings 1972–1977*. Brighton: Harvester Press.
Gergen, K.J. (1991) *The saturated self: Dilemmas of identity in contemporary life*. New York: Basic Books.

Gherardi, S. (2006) *Organizational knowledge: The texture of workplace learning*. Oxford: Blackwell.

Gherardi, S. (2013) *How to conduct a practice-based study: Problems & methods*. Cheltenham: Edward Elgar.

Giddens, A. (1984) *The constitution of society: Outline of the theory of structuration*. Cambridge: Polity Press.

Gordon, R., Clegg, S., & Kornberger, M. (2009) Embedded ethics: Discourse & power in the New South Wales police service. *Organization Studies*. 30(1): 73–99.

Goss, D., Jones, R., Betta, M., & Latham, J. (2011) Power as practice: A microsociological analysis of the dynamics of emancipatory entrepreneurship. *Organization Studies*. 32(2): 211–229.

Hardy, C., & Clegg, S. (2006) Some dare call it power, in S. Clegg, C. Hardy, T.B. Lawrence, & W.R. Nord (eds.), *The SAGE handbook of organization studies*. Thousand Oaks, CA: SAGE, pp. 754–775.

Hardy, C., & Thomas, R. (2014) Strategy, discourse & practice: The intensification of power. *Journal of Management Studies*. 51(2): 320–348.

Haugaard, M. (2003) Reflections on seven ways of creating power. *European Journal of Social Theory*. 6(1): 87–113.

Haugaard, M. (2010) Power: A 'family resemblance' concept'. *European Journal of Cultural Studies*. 13(4): 419–438.

Haugaard, M. (2012) Power & truth. *European Journal of Social Theory*. 15(1): 73–92.

Haugaard, M., & Clegg, S.R. (2009) Introduction: Why power is the central concept of the social sciences, in S.R. Clegg & M. Haugaard (eds.), *The SAGE handbook of power*. London: SAGE, pp. 1–24.

Heizmann, H. (2011) Knowledge sharing in dispersed a network of HR practice: Zooming in on power/knowledge struggles. *Management Learning*. 42(2): 379–393.

Huzzard, T. (2004) Communities of domination? Reconceptualising organisational learning & power. *The Journal of Workplace Learning*. 16(6): 350–361.

Jacobs, C., & Coghland, D. (2005) Sound from silence: On listening in organizational learning. *Human Relations*. 58(1): 115–138.

Lave, J., & Wenger, E. (1991) *Situated learning: Legitimate peripheral participation*. Cambridge: Cambridge University Press.

Lawrence, T.B. (2008) Power, institutions & organizations, in R. Greenwood, R. Oliver, K. Sahlin, & R. Suddaby (eds.), *The SAGE Handbook of Organizational Institutionalism*. London: SAGE, pp. 170–197.

Levina, N., & Orlikowski, W.J. (2009) Understanding shifting power relations within & across organizations: A critical genre analysis. *Academy of Management Journal*. 52(4): 672–703.

Lukes, S. (1974) *Power: A radical view*. London: Macmillan.

Lukes, S. (2005) *Power: A radical view*. 2nd Ed. London: Macmillan.

Marx, K. (1975) *Early writings*. Harmandsworth: Penguin.

McGabe, D. (2009) Strategy-as-power: Ambiguity, contradiction & the exercise of power in a UK building society. *Organization*. 17(2): 151–175.

Mørk, B.E., Hoholm, T., Ellingsen, G., Edwin, B., & Aanestad, M. (2010) Challenging expertise: On power relations within & across communities of practice in medical innovation. *Management Learning*. 41(5): 575–592.

Nicolini, D. (2009) Zooming in & out: Studying practices by switching theoretical lenses & trailing connections. *Organization Studies*. 30(12): 1391–1418.

Nicolini, D. (2011) Practice as the site of knowing: Insights from the field of telemedicine. *Organization Science*. 22(3): 602–620.

Nicolini, D. (2013) *Practice theory, work, & organization: An introduction*. Oxford: Oxford University Press.

Parsons, T. (1967) *Sociological theory & modern society*. New York: Free Press. As cited in: Lukes, S. (2005) *Power: A radical view*. 2nd Ed. London: Macmillan.

Pfeffer, J. (1981) *Power in organizations*. Marshfield, MA: Pitman.

Rasche, A., & Chia, R. (2009) Researching strategy practices: A genealogical social theory perspective. *Organization Studies*. 30(7): 713–734.

Salancik, G.R. & Pfeffer, J. (1977) Who gets power and how they hold on to it: A strategic contingency model of power. *Organizational Dynamics*. 5: 2–21.

Schatzki, T.R. (2002) *The site of the social: A philosophical account of the constitution of social life & change*. Pennsylvania: Pennsylvania State University Press.

Schatzki, T.R. (2005) Peripheral vision: The sites of organizations. *Organization Studies*. 26(3): 465–484.

Schatzki, T.R. (2006) On organizations as they happen. *Organization Studies*. 27(12): 1863–1873.

Schatzki, T.R. (2012) A primer on practices, in J. Higgs, R. Barnett, S. Billett, M. Hutchings, & F. Trede (eds.), *Practice-based education: Perspectives & strategies*. Rotterdam: Sense Publishers, pp. 13–26.

Seidl, D., & Whittington, R. (2014) Enlarging the strategy-as-practice research agenda: Towards taller & flatter ontologies, *Organization Studies*. 35(10): 1407–1421.

Weber, M. (1954) *Max Weber on law in economy & society*. New York: Simon & Schuster.

Weber, M. (1978) *Economy and society: An outline of interpretive sociology*. Berkeley: University of California Press.

Weber, M. (1981) 'Bureaucracy', in O. Grusky and G.A. Miller (eds.), *The sociology of organizations: Basic studies*. New York: Free Press, pp. 7–36.

Wenger, E. (1998) *Communities of practice: Learning, meaning, & identity*. Cambridge: Cambridge University Press.

Wittgenstein, L. (1967) *Philosophical investigations*. Oxford: Oxford University Press.

5 Perspectives on Knowledge Work

Toma Pustelnikovaite and Shiona Chillas

INTRODUCTION

The terms 'knowledge work' and 'knowledge workers' first emerged as central concepts in the discourse around changing socio-economic conditions in the 1970s and then again in 1990s. In the 1970s, Daniel Bell (1999) forecasted that knowledge workers would be at the forefront of the emerging post-industrial society. He postulated the growth of the service sector, an increased supply of workers with specialist education, which reconfigured the social order from one based on empirical knowledge (such as that of artisans) to one based on theoretical knowledge, acquired through higher education (Blackler *et al.* 1993:853). The accompanying change in the mode of production from manual to mental labour would lead, it was thought, to more professional and technical jobs, and improve working conditions. In the 1990s, Drucker (1993) elaborated on Bell's idea that knowledge workers are the primary resource of a post-capitalist society by adding that a shift from generalised to specialised knowledge also requires a management revolution. He suggested that finding ways to organise knowledge and make it productive is a key societal challenge. The same decade also saw the emergence of literatures on the knowledge-creating company (Nonaka 1991), communities of practice (Lave & Wenger 1991; Brown & Duguid 1998) and organisational knowledge (Tsoukas & Vladimirou 2001), which all share the idea of an organisation as a living organism in which knowledge is both personal and collective, embodied in individuals and embedded in work practices. The emphasis these literatures put on the tacit and social nature of knowledge made a case that every employee can be said to "know more than we can tell" (Polanyi 2013:4). As a result, from the 1990s the idea that knowledge was inherent in all types of work led scholars to claim that all workers are considered knowledge workers.

From these bodies of work, it becomes clear that conceptual understanding of knowledge work remains far from homogeneous, but instead contains a variety of views on knowledge and its relationship with work.

On one hand, there is debate around the definition of knowledge, questioning whether knowledge work is a separate category of work. On the other, scholars argue that knowledge work is distinctive, yet disagree over what makes it so. Categorisations of knowledge work range from the broad to the specific: some argue that knowledge work is synonymous with service work (Stevens 1998); others that it is confined to certain occupational groups such as information technology (IT) (Reed 1996; Scarbrough 1999) or scientists, technicians and managers (Drucker 1993); yet others see it as work where theoretical knowledge is used for product and process improvement (Warhurst & Thompson 2006; Darr & Warhurst 2008).

Our chapter has two aims: to explore how knowledge work is conceptualised in the literature and to evaluate what these conceptualisations reveal about the nature of knowledge work. To address the first, we propose a typology of perspectives on knowledge work and outline the existing debates within each. Specifically, we suggest classifying the literature into 'cognitive', 'content', 'temporal' and 'contextual' streams. The 'cognitive' view considers different types of knowledge, the 'content' approach looks at the use of knowledge within specific labour processes, the 'temporal' perspective emphasises recently formed occupations that are connected with new technology and information handling, and the 'contextual' viewpoint embeds knowledge work in the wider social structure. Table 5.1 outlines the key features of each perspective, and this is discussed in more detail in the next section. The value of our typology lies in its ability to uncover the links between knowledge, work practices, occupations and the political economy, and to expose common misconceptions in the literature on the subject—in particular, the tendency to conflate knowledge with information and to focus only on knowledge work or knowledge workers. As a result, we offer a holistic framework that captures the nature of knowledge work.

Our second aim examines the implications of the typology, leading to the proposition that knowledge work is a stratified phenomenon of social action. We argue that knowledge work contains a number of inextricably linked categories and layers that are determined by existing social arrangements: for instance, by the way work is organised or by power dynamics in society. Here, we interpret power as "the pre-given reality of structural forms that both enable and constrain human conduct" (Isaac 2004, cited in Kogan 2005:11). In simple terms, power is "vested in those who have command of the structures" (Kogan (2005:11) and comprises, for instance, governments or managers. (For further discussion of power in relation to knowledge and practice, see Chapter 3.)

Table 5.1 A typology of knowledge work

Perspective	Cognitive	Content	Temporal	Contextual
Classification by	Type of knowledge	Use of knowledge	Occupations	Purpose of knowledge work
Key debate	Which knowledge is valuable?	How is knowledge used at work?	Which occupations are engaged in knowledge work?	What purpose (and whose) is knowledge work serving?
Manifestation	• All work is knowledge work: all knowledge is valuable vs • All work is knowledge work: language makes up for knowledge vs • Only some work is knowledge work: theoretical knowledge is valuable	• Knowledge work: the creative use of theoretical knowledge is enabled in the workplace vs • Knowledgeable work: relies on the use of practical knowledge and routines in the workplace	• Knowledge work is working with knowledge: it is done by the new occupations that handle information vs • Knowledge work is working from knowledge: it is done both by the newer and the older occupations that require theoretical knowledge in their work	• State priorities: capitalise on knowledge to enhance national competitive advantage; the knowledge worker is empowered vs • Organisational priorities: capitalise on knowledge to maximise value; the knowledge worker is disempowered

UNDERSTANDING KNOWLEDGE WORK

The Cognitive Perspective

The epistemological underpinnings of the knowledge work debate are covered by the 'cognitive' perspective, which focuses on different types of knowledge (see Chapter 2—knowledge). The key debate lies between perspectives that argue that all work requires knowledge, and those who posit that with reference to work, valuable knowledge is primarily theoretical in nature.

Practice-based theorising relies on the idea that knowledge is 'alive', embodied in people and embedded in work practices. Workers' practice articulates and influences knowledge (Gherardi 2000). Scholars have produced various classifications of the types of knowledge emerging from practices. Early perspectives suggested a broad differentiation between explicit and tacit knowledge, where explicit knowledge entails codified knowledge, and tacit knowledge is a combination of practical and theoretical knowledge that cannot be clearly articulated (Polanyi 1962, 2013). Tacit knowledge means that one is aware of the constitutive elements of an action, knows that an action happens because those elements combine in a specific way, is able to attribute a meaning to the action, and understands that only a specific joint combination of constitutive elements will lead to a particular practice (Polanyi 2013). Interpreters, for instance, subconsciously perform this sequence when translating from one language to another—a skill that cannot be learned by reading from a book. Other scholars have added to the types of knowledge. The key example is Blackler's (1995) embrained, embodied, encultured, embedded and encoded knowledge, which refers to cognitive, action-oriented and social knowledge, knowledge of routines, and knowledge that is codified, showing that knowledge resides in different places (such as one's brain or a book) and derives from different sources (such as routines or actions). More recent studies suggest even more detailed differentiations in knowledge types. For instance, Rennstam and Ashcraft (2013:4) refer to communicative knowledge, which is "knowledge about interaction that is also created and used in interaction", whereas Kamoche and Maguire (2010) suggest 'pit sense' as a new form of knowledge required by a specific occupational group (tunnellers) to assess risk at work. With a number of different types of knowledge to draw on, and varying degrees of applicability, analysis of knowledge work lies on the types and character of knowledge, which are then used in a variety of jobs and/or work situations (Hislop 2008:580). Because all work involves some knowledge, there is no hierarchy of knowledge work and 'not' knowledge work, or knowledge worker and 'not' knowledge worker.

Sharing the premise that all work can be considered knowledge work to some extent, post-structuralist scholars suggest that knowledge work is language work (Alvesson 1993, 2011; Alvesson & Spicer 2012). Alvesson's argument is that knowledge work is merely a language game within economies of persuasion. In other words, knowledge work as a separate analytical category is a myth, because knowledge workers manufacture a seductive image of their work using rhetorical devices and persuasive skills to make it *appear* distinctive. At the workplace level a paradox arises because knowledge work also means knowing when to deploy "functional stupidity", which requires the suppression of reflexivity and a disinterestedness in organisational structures, values and decisions (Alvesson & Spicer 2012). Functional stupidity manifests when, for instance, employees decide to comply with agreed-upon business procedures regardless of their own moral beliefs because "[w]hat is right in the corporation is what the guy above you wants from you" (Jackall 2010:4). In short, then, knowledge work within organisations also means knowing when knowledge should be withheld.

Another viewpoint within the 'cognitive' stream prioritises embrained theoretical knowledge compared to other knowledge types, because it is seen as more relevant for the competitive advantage of an organisation (Drucker 1993). As a result, knowledge work is enacted by specific occupational groups with a high degree of theoretical knowledge, such as professionals, executives and managers. This is not to suggest that the tacit and social nature of knowledge has been ignored within this perspective. Literatures on the knowledge-creating company, communities of practice and organisational knowledge that turned every employee into a knowledge worker made the case for tacit and social knowledge to be explored alongside explicit knowledge. However, communities of practice that are expected to facilitate the extraction of tacit and social knowledge are often envisioned as being composed of specialised knowledge workers (Thompson *et al.* 2001). Moreover, it is not necessarily the case that communities of practice will engage in the activities expected of them, nor indeed that their remit is entirely knowledge related. Ritzer (2011), for example, observed a reduction in the knowledge content of academics' and healthcare professionals' work, despite academics and doctors being accepted as knowledge workers. To illustrate this point, he pointed to the use of multiple-choice examinations that could be graded by a computer, or at the so-called "pathways" that comprise a standardised series of steps when dealing with medical problems. This process of de-professionalisation suggests that knowledge as the property of an individual is to be viewed separately from knowledge as property of a job, and hence 'knowing' and 'doing', or knowledge worker and knowledge work, are analytically distinct (Thompson *et al.* 2001).

The Content Perspective

Overall, although the cognitive perspective shows the variety of knowledge types possessed by individuals and possibly required in work, it also suggests that not all types of knowledge are of equal value to the firm, nor is knowledge necessarily applied in work, as in communities of practice.

Looking at the social practices around knowledge application in the workplace reminds us that there is a need to question the relationship between occupation and knowledge, and also to take into account the division of labour within organisations.

Claims that assembly line workers are becoming more educated (Neef 1998:3) do not necessarily mean that packing mushrooms suddenly requires a degree in biology; at times the employer may demand more from an employee than the work content itself (Darr & Warhurst 2008). The 'content' perspective overcomes the assumption that knowledge work is necessarily done by knowledge workers by emphasising the utilisation of knowledge within particular labour processes. In other words, instead of looking at *what* knowledge is used at work, the content perspective emphasises *how* knowledge is used, including how it may be manipulated or extended. Here knowledge is a "capacity for action" (Stehr 1994:120) whose application occurs within a specific institutional context. The context is referred to as "workplace knowledge" and comprises, for example, systems of organisational hierarchy and control, work intensity, effort bargain, and professional or occupational structures and cultures, as well as state, political economy and other institutional conditions of work that enable or constrain the utilisation of knowledge (Warhurst & Thompson 2006).

Within the content perspective, there is a view that the use of theoretical knowledge is what makes knowledge work distinctive. The essential characteristic of knowledge work is the meaningful use of theoretical knowledge within a labour process. For example, referring to Yanow's (1999) renowned study on flute-making, Swart and Kinnie (2003:62) rightly point out that "doing a clever thing over and over does not mean that it is knowledge-intensive". The perspective does not imply that manual work, for instance, does not require knowledge—rather, the 'content' view draws a distinction between knowledge work and knowledgeable work, which primarily relies on contextual, practical or social types of knowledge (Thompson *et al.* 2001).

In summary, then, the 'content' perspective argues for a conceptual shift from "knowledge work" to "knowledge in work" (Thompson *et al.* 2001). Although analytically distinct, knowledge work and knowledge workers are nonetheless deemed to be engaged in a labour process without which it is difficult to think of work and workers. However, this perspective has not yet adequately addressed the relationship between "knowledge in work" and the broader expert division of labour that comprises occupations whose work requires a specialised knowledge base, and who also develop specific power strategies to protect their expertise (Reed 1996). An attempt to link work and occupations has been made within the 'cognitive' perspective; however, providing a restricted list of occupations supposedly engaged in knowledge work does not take into account that new occupations may try to enhance their status by making claims to possess specialised knowledge in order to imitate other high-profile occupations such as law or medicine. For example, project managers or management consultants may aim to create links with local universities, form professional bodies, rely on project-based organising or create new managerial fads (Hodgson 2007; Kipping 2011; Muzio *et al.* 2011). Since occupational groups do not remain stable over time, the inception and trajectory of knowledge work merits some attention.

The Temporal Perspective

Scholars taking a 'temporal' view on knowledge work explore the relationship between knowledge and new technology, debating the extent to which knowledge work is a new phenomenon. This debate results in discussion of the "new economy thesis" (Fleming *et al.* 2004; Thompson & Smith 2009) and a "continuity thesis" (Freidson 2001; Muzio *et al.* 2007).

One of the key proponents of the new economy thesis, Castells (1996), argued that the technological revolution and accompanying changes in management and labour process technologies created a demand for educated and autonomous workers, or knowledge workers, who would be "able and willing to program and decide entire sequences of work" (Castells 1996:241). The work would involve the application of "knowledge and information to knowledge generation and information processing/communication devices" (Castells 1996:32). A view supportive of the new economy thesis, yet less focused on the deterministic role of IT, emerges from Reed's (1996) and Fincham's (2012) works. In this view knowledge work is a subdivision of the expert division of labour. Knowledge work is performed by workers who rely on the application of an intangible, hard-to-standardise knowledge base using analytic problem-solving capabilities, which are apparent in the new service sectors such as consulting, IT or e-business. In short, they portray knowledge workers as a new group of workers that work "*with* knowledge", and not "*from* knowledge" (Scarbrough 1999:7, italics in the original).

This last point exemplifies the confusion inherent in the new economy stance, namely that of conflating knowledge and information (Bell 1999; Dean 2014). Work "with knowledge" entails the separation of knowledge from the individual, meaning that knowledge is codified and objectified. As a result, it remains precisely what information is defined to be, the "communication of knowledge" (Castells 1996:21), or knowledge conveyed by symbols and signs (Blackler 1995). It is therefore questionable to restrict the term 'knowledge worker' to those who work with information using new technology.

This misconception is tackled in the literature on the sociology of professions. The key idea in the 'continuity' argument is that the knowledge work phenomenon itself is hardly new, and at present is merely expanding to encompass the work of new occupational communities. As a result, occupations from the new service sectors are more appropriately conceptualised as the "new knowledge workers" (Ackroyd 1996), whose emergence is tied to practices of knowledge institutionalisation as opposed to signalling the rise of a new type of demanding work. Knowledge institutionalisation involves the creation of an "organized system for the production of producers" (Larson 1977:70), established by forming professional bodies or seeking links with educational institutions, as illustrated by the case of project managers and management consultants mentioned above. The desire for status relates to the rewards, power and prestige that are expected to benefit members of certain privileged occupations once their specialist knowledge claims are legitimised.

The main premise of the temporal stream concerns the 'newness' of knowledge work. While it could be argued that knowledge work arose from the emergence of new economic sectors and new technology, which in some circumstances entailed more complex work carried out by specialist individuals capable of dealing with this technology, this group represents only a small proportion of the division of labour. The "continuity" argument that knowledge work is not new and at present is merely growing to encompass new occupations (that can demonstrate possession of expert knowledge, autonomy in task execution, normative orientation and high status associated with high-profile occupations such as law, medicine or the clergy) is more persuasive (Gorman & Sandefur 2011).

The Contextual Perspective

The preceding three streams expose different aspects of knowledge work; namely, there can be multiple types of knowledge involved ('cognitive'), the focus can be shifted from 'knowledge' to 'work' ('content'), and a debate exists on whether knowledge work involves working "from knowledge" (Scarbrough 1999) or with information ('temporal'). The discussion thus far, however, has not been explicit about the wider social context within which knowledge work is embedded. This is not to suggest that context has been absent in the preceding perspectives. The 'cognitive' perspective, for instance, demonstrates that not all types of knowledge may be seen as being of equal value to the firm, and neither are all types of knowledge beneficial to the firm, as illustrated in the 'functional stupidity' argument. The 'content' perspective made reference to 'workplace knowledge' that determines how knowledge is used in the workplace. The 'temporal' stream noted that some new occupations endeavour to institutionalise their knowledge and also that the technological revolution has created a demand for new types of workers. Nevertheless, this chapter has not yet elaborated on the impact of context on knowledge work.

The 'contextual' perspective embeds knowledge work within the political economy, looking at work from two levels of analysis: namely, the national/international and the organisational. Situating work within these two levels of analysis takes into account that knowledge work is an economic activity, derived from an underlying premise that there are opportunities to capitalise on knowledge. The national/international level perspective represents the 'knowledge economy' argument and posits that capitalising on knowledge helps to fulfil the priorities of a nation state or of a region such as the EU. Literatures examining the workplace level point at the ways in which knowledge work can maximise shareholder profit in the private sector or contribute to efficiency and effectiveness in the public sector.

At the national/international level, knowledge work as an employment category becomes an instrument to create knowledge economies characterised by "the economics of abundance, the annihilation of distance, the de-territorialization of the state, and, investment in human capital" (Olssen & Peters 2005:331). The notion that knowledge work enhances national competitive advantage has been heavily influenced by the accounts of Bell (1999) and Reich (1993) amongst others. These accounts have argued that national competitive advantage depends upon the accumulated knowledge of the nation's workers. This idea is now one of the three main priorities of the Europe 2020 strategy (European Commission 2010; Hervás Soriano & Mulatero 2010) and is also embraced by international bodies such as the OECD, IMF or NAFTA (Warhurst & Thompson 2006; Thompson & Harley 2012). The image of knowledge promoted by such a new economy vision is that of certified and measurable intellectual property that can generate invention and innovation (Bell 1999:xvii). This type of knowledge is believed to empower workers: knowledge workers own, and can sell, their knowledge, becoming more internationally mobile as a result (Drucker 1999:87). For example, an academic coming from a non-EU country would find it easier to immigrate to the UK than an unskilled labourer, because host societies aim to ensure migrants' economic and social contribution to the country, and associate contribution with skill (Menz 2009).

In the shadow of the "high-profile [knowledge economy] discourse" lies the idea of shareholder value maximisation, which has an impact on current understanding of knowledge work at the organisational level (Thompson & Harley 2012:1371). Profit maximisation on the one hand means trying to "legitimise" the knowledge of the workers, and to transform workers' skills and abilities into an organisational resource available to all organisational members (Fleming *et al.* 2004:729). On the other hand, treating knowledge as an economic commodity involves maximising knowledge workers' contribution to the organisation, often without reciprocal employment security.

To transform workers' knowledge into an organisational resource, sociotechnical management techniques aimed at making knowledge saleable and shareable has been developed (Pan & Scarbrough 1999). Making knowledge saleable involves establishing practices designed to separate knowledge from the knower, despite some scholars claiming that this separation is not possible (see Despres & Hiltrop 1995). Such practices involve, for instance, knowledge codification, standardisation and accessibility, which have been facilitated by the increased use of information and communication technologies in the workplace. Making knowledge shareable involves creating new managerial approaches to foster supportive organisational environments where knowledge sharing and creativity is encouraged. In particular, this approach occurs through establishing communities of practice to encourage socialisation of employees within or across organisations, or by designing flexible working practices to tackle dispersed organisational knowledge (Becker 2001; Swart & Harvey 2011). Sociotechnical management practices, however, are based on the assumption that tacit knowledge cannot be hidden and that knowledge workers will voluntarily participate in the knowledge exchange, sharing their knowledge and receiving that of others (McKinlay 2005). However, McKinlay (2002) points out that although the general organisational goal to harness employee knowledge remains present, knowledge management is not always effective, given that workers can actively or passively resist managerial practices.

Contemporarily, employers may choose to intensify work and be reluctant to invest in the training of knowledge workers because the latter can transfer their knowledge elsewhere rather easily (Smith 2006; Keep & Mayhew 2010). In the public sector, for example, new public management practices have increased the accountability of professionals to management, state, funding bodies or clients, leading to the intensification of work (Alvesson & Thompson 2005). Others tell a cautionary tale about project work, which is often presented as offering independence for knowledge workers who, supposedly, can freely trade their knowledge for the best financial offer (Barley & Kunda 2004). For instance, in the case of research scientists, short-term contract employment limits access to opportunities that determine long-term career success (Harney *et al.* 2011). Similarly, tradable knowledge is not a sufficient asset for freelance journalists and performing artists, whose specialist and contextualised knowledge may become obsolescent in the process of job-hopping (D'Amours & Legault 2013).

Summing up, examining knowledge work as embedded in national and organisational contexts reveals a dichotomy. On the national level, the potential to engage in knowledge work empowers the worker to capitalise on knowledge. At the organisational level, the 'empowered worker' is disempowered by practices that may exploit their expertise.

KNOWLEDGE WORK AS A STRATIFIED PHENOMENON

In isolation, none of the four perspectives outlined in table 5.1 can fully explain knowledge work. For example, knowledge work *could* be associated only with the newer occupations that work with the information and communications technology ('temporal' perspective), but attention to the knowledge types within the 'cognitive' perspective provides a basis to argue that knowledge and information are not the same. Similarly, the 'content' perspective rightly points out that how knowledge is used matters, but does not explain why it is the use of theoretical knowledge (and not, for instance, the knowledge of routines) that distinguishes between knowledge work and knowledgeable work. This explanation is instead provided by the 'contextual' perspective that reveals potentially competing interests in evaluating knowledge work. In summary, then, table 5.1 demonstrates that knowledge work is a phenomenon whose explanation has to take into account the types of knowledge associated with the working environment, how the knowledge is used, by whom, and to what ends.

By considering the four perspectives holistically, tensions in the nature of knowledge work are revealed and a separation between a socially just and a politicised view of knowledge is uncovered. Drawing on an analogy from linguistics helps to illustrate this point. Linguistically, all language varieties are deemed equal to an arbitrary language standard because they all have the power to effectively communicate the message. In other words, a message conveyed in a Cockney accent is no different to one conveyed in BBC English, because the content is identical. However, when the same message is situated within social practices such as work, a socially perceived value of how that message is conveyed comes into play, in some cases leading to a linguistic variation (accent) becoming a cause for employment discrimination or bullying (Williams & Connell 2010; Edwards 2014). Accordingly, from a social justice standpoint, all types of knowledge are valuable, as processes of knowing and doing are interconnected through work practices (Orlikowski 2002). Yet, through considering knowledge as embedded within a production process that happens within a political economy (that is at the nexus between economics, law and politics) the utility of knowledge becomes more important than knowledge *per se,* with the result that it becomes politicised. Given that knowledge is susceptible to value judgements, it is a stratified phenomenon of social action.

Stratification occurs among the different types of knowledge described in the 'cognitive' stream: codified and embrained knowledge become privileged over social and tacit knowledge. Arguably, codified and embrained knowledge became more highly valued because they are easier to measure and, at the national/international level, also constitute the types of knowledge deemed necessary to produce economic advantage and national competitive advantage (as the 'contextual' perspective has already established). Indeed a number of proxies have been used to measure knowledge. At the national level, for example, Warhurst and Thompson (2006) cite several proxies used to measure and assess the extent to which a country is a knowledge economy: the numbers of people with higher education (human capital measure); activities (such as released patents, investment in education, information technologies); and employment numbers in specific occupations. At the organisational level, employers make judgements on the value of certain credentials privileging, for example, those who have attended prestigious universities (Brown & Hesketh 2004).

The variety of proxies available to measure knowledge means that an arbitrary political decision over which measurement to choose has to be made. For instance, looking into the data from the EU that shows the increasing percentage of total population having completed at least upper secondary education (EUROSTAT 2013), or that from the European Patent Office which, albeit with some fluctuations, indicates a rise in the number of patents (EPO 2013), would support the attainment of knowledge economies in Europe. By contrast, looking into the knowledge content of jobs shows that in the UK, for instance, the major area of employment growth is in lower-level service jobs (Thompson *et al.* 2001). Others have found evidence of an 'hourglass economy', a term used in reference to patterns of growth only in occupations associated with servicing or new technologies, as well as rising employment in lower occupational levels. For example, in her exploration of the UK's Standard Occupational Classification 2000, Anderson (2009) found support for the argument that both the high-level and the low-level occupations are expanding because occupations at the middle level are being reclassified. On the whole, then, the grounds on which theoretical knowledge is prioritised over other types are questionable, yet knowledge stratification persists and, arguably, expands. Stratification is now visible *within* theoretical knowledge, so that a hierarchy of disciplines emerges from the pressures put on researchers to ensure that their work "yields value for taxpayers' money" (Taylor 2011:202). According to this logic, physics knowledge is more valuable than history knowledge because physics knowledge is more practically applicable (Kogan 2005).

Having established that knowledge is stratified, the typology presented in table 5.1 helps to illustrate how knowledge stratification also permeates the realm of work. Within the 'cognitive' perspective, for instance, the ability to evaluate risk ('pit sense') is valuable knowledge for tunnellers to have (Kamoche & Maguire 2010). However, "[m]anagers tended to discount the existence of pit sense and spoke of it in disparaging terms" (736). Within the 'temporal' perspective, knowledge stratification is visible from the attempts of recently formed occupations to establish links with universities or to create professional bodies in order to codify their body of knowledge and thereby enhance status. Furthermore, in their study of the accounting profession in the UK, Stevenson, Ferguson & Crawford (Chapter 9 Accounting) illustrate how links with universities and professional bodies can lead to the stratification of knowledge within the professional community. The outcome of such stratification—that is, whether research-based or practice-informed knowledge is considered more valuable—determines which knowledge is available in the workplace to be used by knowledge workers. Moreover, workers may possess different types of knowledge, but organisations may deem some forms of knowledge uncomfortable and accordingly develop strategies such as denial, dismissal, divergence or displacement to suppress that knowledge (Rayner 2012). This example is accounted for by the focus on knowledge use within the 'content' perspective. Within the 'contextual' stream, knowledge stratification shows how the knowledge worker may become empowered by knowledge on the national level as a means to fulfil policymaker agendas, yet may also be disempowered in the workplace.

CONCLUSION

In conclusion, this chapter has provided a critical review of theoretical perspectives on knowledge work. In doing so, it has categorised these perspectives by way of their 'cognitive', 'content', 'temporal' and 'contextual' aspects, set out in table 5.1. The discussion has noted key messages from each perspective, which, it is argued, has contributed to the blurred understanding of knowledge work. We suggest that a framework that shows analytical links between knowledge, the political economy, occupational trajectories and work practices is valuable in representing the complexity of knowledge work. We propose that the typology reveals stratification within each stream of literature, and conclude that knowledge and knowledge work are stratified forms of social action.

SUGGESTED FURTHER READINGS

Frenkel, S.J., Korczynski, M., Shire, K., & Tam, M. (1999) *On the front line*. Ithaca, NY: Cornell University Press.
  This book focuses on the dynamics and organisation of the front-line work. It offers an analysis of eight companies in the United States, Japan and Australia, and provides an account on how work differs in service, sales and knowledge-based settings.
Barley, S.R., & Kunda, G. (2004) *Gurus, hired guns, & warm bodies: Itinerant experts in a knowledge economy*. Princeton, NJ: Princeton University Press.
  An ethnography that focuses on knowledge workers engaged in contractual work. This book reveals the contemporary realities of knowledge work and takes into account the perspectives on temporary work of the workers themselves, as well as of their employers, colleagues and staffing agencies.
Gorman, E.H., & Sandefur, R.L. (2011) 'Golden Age', quiescence, & revival: How the sociology of professions became the study of knowledge-based work. *Work & Occupations*. 38(3): 275–302.
  This article brings together the historical and the modern perspectives on knowledge-based occupations. The paper analyses the changes that have occurred in professions, and identifies four key themes that unify professional and knowledge-based work.

REFERENCES

Ackroyd, S. (1996) Organization contra organizations: Professions & organizational change in the United Kingdom. *Organization Studies*. 17(4): 599–621.

Alvesson, M. (1993) organizations as rhetoric: Knowledge-intensive firms & the struggle with ambiguity. *Journal of Management Studies.* 30(6): 997–1015.

Alvesson, M. (2011) De-essentializing the knowledge intensive firm: Reflections on sceptical research going against the mainstream. *Journal of Management Studies.* 48(7): 1640–1661.

Alvesson, M., & Spicer, A. (2012) A stupidity-based theory of organizations. *Journal of Management Studies.* 49(7): 1194–1220.

Alvesson, M., & Thompson, P. (2005) Post-bureaucracy?, in S. Ackroyd, R. Batt, P. Thompson, & P.S. Tolbert (eds.), *The Oxford handbook of work & organization.* Oxford: Oxford University Press, pp. 485–507.

Anderson, P. (2009) Intermediate occupations & the conceptual & empirical limitations of the hourglass economy thesis. *Work, Employment & Society.* 23(1): 169–180.

Barley, S.R., & Kunda, G. (2004) *Gurus, hired guns, & warm bodies. Itinerant experts in a knowledge economy.* Princeton, NJ: Princeton University Press.

Becker, M.C. (2001) Managing dispersed knowledge: Organizational problems, managerial strategies, & their effectiveness. *Journal of Management Studies.* 38(7): 1037–1051.

Bell, D. (1999) *The coming of post-industrial society: A venture in social forecasting.* 3rd Ed. New York: Basic Books.

Blackler, F. (1995) Knowledge, knowledge work & organizations: An overview & interpretation. *Organization Studies.* 16(6): 1021–1046.

Blackler, F., Reed, M., & Whitaker, A. (1993) Editorial introduction: Knowledge workers & contemporary organizations. *Journal of Management Studies.* 30(6): 851–862.

Brown, J.S., & Duguid, P. (1998) Organizing knowledge. *California Management Review.* 40(3): 90–111.

Brown, P., & Hesketh, A. (2004) *The mismanagement of talent: Employability & jobs in the knowledge economy.* New York: Oxford University Press.

Castells, M. (1996) *The rise of the network society: The information age: Economy, society & culture, Volume 1.* Oxford: Blackwell.

D'Amours, M., & Legault, M.-J. (2013) Highly skilled workers & employment risks: Role of institutions. *Labor Studies Journal.* 38(2): 89–109.

Darr, A., & Warhurst, C. (2008) Assumptions, assertions & the need for evidence: Debugging debates about knowledge workers. *Current Sociology.* 56(1): 25–45.

Dean, K. (2014) *Capitalism, citizenship & the arts of thinking: A Marxian-Aristotelian linguistic account.* Oxford: Routledge.

Despres, C., & Hiltrop, J.M. (1995) Human resource management in the knowledge age: Current practice & perspectives on the future. *Employee Relations.* 17(1): 9–23.

Drucker, P. (1999) Knowledge worker productivity: The biggest challenge. *California Management Review.* 41(2): 79–94.

Drucker, P.F. (1993) *Post-capitalist society.* Oxford: Butterworth Heinemann.

Edwards, K. (2014) Shut yer face! I'm fed up being ridiculed for my regional accent in academia. *The Telegraph.* Available: http://www.telegraph.co.uk/women/womens-life/11270980/British-universities-Im-fed-up-of-being-ridiculed-for-my-regional-accent.html?fb. Accessed: January 28, 2015.

EPO (2013) *European patent applications 2004–2013 per country of residence of the first named applicant.* Available: http://documents.epo.org/projects/babylon/eponet.nsf/0/22470C8932722D8CC1257C910042620A/$File/European_granted_patents_by_country_of_origin_2004_2013.xlsx. Accessed: October 8, 2015.

European Commission (2010) Europe 2020. A European strategy for smart, sustainable & inclusive growth. *Resources, Conservation & Recycling*. Brussels. Available: http://linkinghub.elsevier.com/retrieve/pii/S0921344910000856. Accessed: January 15, 2015.

EUROSTAT (2013) *Upper secondary or tertiary educational attainment, age group 25–64 by sex.* Available: http://ec.europa.eu/eurostat/tgm/table.do?tab=table&init=1&plugin=1&language=en&pcode=tps00065. Accessed: December 16, 2014.

Fincham, R. (2012) Expert labour as a differentiated category: Power, knowledge & organisation. *New Technology, Work & Employment*. 27(3): 208–223.

Fleming, P., Harley, B., & Sewell, G. (2004) A little knowledge is a dangerous thing: Getting below the surface of the growth of 'knowledge work' in Australia. *Work, Employment & Society*. 18(4): 725–747.

Freidson, E. (2001) *Professionalism: The third logic*. Cambridge: Polity Press.

Gherardi, S. (2000) Practice-based theorizing on learning & knowing in organizations. *Organization*. 7(2): 211–223.

Gorman, E.H., & Sandefur, R.L. (2011) 'Golden age', quiescence & revival: How the sociology of professions became the study of knowledge-based work. *Work & Occupations*. 38(3): 275–302.

Harney, B., Monks, K., Alexopoulos, A., Buckley, F., & Hogan, T. (2011) University Research scientists as knowledge workers: Contract status & employment opportunities. *The International Journal of Human Resource Management*. 25(16): 2219–2233.

Hervás Soriano, F., & Mulatero, F. (2010) Knowledge policy in the EU: From the Lisbon strategy to Europe 2020. *Journal of the Knowledge Economy*. 1(4): 289–302.

Hislop, D. (2008) Conceptualizing knowledge work utilizing skill & knowledge-based concepts: The case of some consultants & service engineers. *Management Learning*. 39(5): 579–596.

Hodgson, D. (2007) The new professionals: Professionalisation & the struggle for occupational control in the field of project management, in D. Muzio, S. Ackroyd, & J.F. Chanlat (eds.), *Redirections in the study of expert labour: Medicine law & management consultancy*. Basingstoke: Palgrave, pp. 217–234.

Jackall, R. (2010) *Moral mazes: The world of corporate managers*. 20th Anniversary Ed. Oxford: Oxford University Press.

Kamoche, K., & Maguire, K. (2010) Pit sense: Appropriation of practice-based knowledge in a UK coalmine. *Human Relations*. 64(5): 725–744.

Keep, E., & Mayhew, K. (2010) Moving beyond skills as a social & economic panacea. *Work, Employment & Society*. 24(3): 565–577.

Kipping, M. (2011) Hollow from the start? Image professionalism in management consulting. *Current Sociology*. 59(4): 530–550.

Kogan, M. (2005) Modes of knowledge & patterns of power. *Higher Education*. 49: 9–30.

Larson, M.S. (1977) *The rise of professionalism: A sociological analysis*. Berkeley: University of California Press.

Lave, J., & Wenger, E. (1991) *Situated learning: Legitimate peripheral participation*. Cambridge: Cambridge University Press.

McKinlay, A. (2002) The limits of knowledge management. *New Technology, Work & Employment*. 17(2): 76–88.

McKinlay, A. (2005) Knowledge management, in S. Ackroyd, R. Batt, P. Thompson, & P.S. Tolbert (eds.), *The Oxford handbook of work & organization*. Oxford: Oxford University Press, pp. 242–263.

Menz, G. (2009) *The political economy of managed migration: Nonstate actors, Europeanization, & the politics of designing migration policies*. Oxford: Oxford University Press.

Muzio, D., Ackroyd, S., & Chanlat, J. (2007) *Redirections in the study of expert labour*. Basingstoke: Palgrave Macmillan.

Muzio, D., Hodgson, D., Faulconbridge, J., Beaverstock, J., & Hall, S. (2011) Towards corporate professionalization: The case of project management, management consultancy & executive search. *Current Sociology*. 59(4): 443–464.

Neef, D. (1998) *The knowledge economy*. Woburn, MA: Butterworth Heinemann.

Nonaka, I. (1991) The knowledge-creating Company. *Harvard Business Review*. (November–December): 96–104.

Olssen, M., & Peters, M.A. (2005) Neoliberalism, higher education & the knowledge economy: From the free market to knowledge capitalism. *Journal of Education Policy*. 20(3): 313–345.

Orlikowski, W.J. (2002) Knowing in practice: Enacting a collective capability in distributed organizing. *Organization Science*. 13(3): 249–273.

Pan, S.L., & Scarbrough, H. (1999) Knowledge management in practice: An exploratory case study. *Technology Analysis & Strategic Management*. 11(3): 359–374.

Polanyi, M. (1962) Tacit knowing: Its bearing on some problems of philosophy. *Reviews of Modern Physics*. 34(4): 601–616.

Polanyi, M. (2013) *The tacit dimension (with a new foreword by Amartya Sen)*. Chicago: University of Chicago Press.

Rayner, S. (2012) Uncomfortable knowledge: The social construction of ignorance in science & environmental policy discourses. *Economy & Society*. 41(1): 107–125.

Reed, M.I. (1996) Expert power & control in late modernity: An empirical review & theoretical synthesis. *Organization Studies*. 17(4): 573–597.

Reich, R.B. (1993) *The work of nations: Preparing ourselves for 21st century capitalism*. London: Simon & Schuster.

Rennstam, J., & Ashcraft, K.L. (2013) Knowing work: Cultivating a practice-based epistemology of knowledge in organization studies. *Human Relations*. 67(1): 3–25.

Ritzer, G. (2011) *The McDonaldization of society*. 6th Ed. Thousand Oaks, CA: SAGE.

Scarbrough, H. (1999) Knowledge as work: Conflicts in the management of knowledge workers. *Technology Analysis & Strategic Management*. 11(1): 5–16.

Smith, C. (2006) The double indeterminacy of labour power: Labour effort & labour mobility. *Work, Employment & Society*. 20(2): 389–402.

Stehr, N. (1994) *Knowledge societies*. London: SAGE.

Stevens, C. (1998) The knowledge-driven economy, in D. Neef (ed.), *The Knowledge Economy*. Woburn, MA: Butterworth Heinemann, pp. 87–97.

Swart, J., & Harvey, P. (2011) Identifying knowledge boundaries: The case of networked projects. *Journal of Knowledge Management*. 15(5): 703–721.

Swart, J., & Kinnie, N. (2003) Sharing knowledge in knowledge-intensive firms. *Human Resource Management Journal*. 13(2): 60–75.

Taylor, J. (2011) The assessment of research quality in UK universities: Peer review or metrics? *British Journal of Management*. 22(2): 202–217.

Thompson, P., & Harley, B. (2012) Beneath the radar? A critical realist analysis of 'the knowledge economy' & 'shareholder value' as competing discourses. *Organization Studies*. 33(10): 1363–1381.

Thompson, P., & Smith, C. (2009) Labour power & labour process: Contesting the marginality of the sociology of work. *Sociology*. 43(5): 913–930.

Thompson, P., Warhurst, C., & Callaghan, G. (2001) Ignorant theory & knowledgeable workers: Interrogating the connections between knowledge, skills & services. *Journal of Management Studies*. 38(7): 923–942.

Tsoukas, H., & Vladimirou, E. (2001) What is organizational knowledge? *Journal of Management Studies*. 38(7): 973–993.

Warhurst, C., & Thompson, P. (2006) Mapping knowledge in work: Proxies or practices? *Work, Employment & Society.* 20(4): 787–800.

Williams, C.L., & Connell, C. (2010) 'Looking good & sounding right': Aesthetic labor & social inequality in the retail industry, *Work & Occupations.* 37(3): 349–377.

Yanow, D. (1999) The language of "organisational learning": A palimpsest of terms, in Easterby-Smith, M., Araujo, L., Burgoyne, J. (eds.), Organizational Learning. Proceedings of the 3rd International Conference, Lancaster University, June 6–8. 2: 1075–1086.

6 Identity, Knowledge and Practice

Nic Beech, Gail Greig and Louisa Preston

INTRODUCTION

How might we understand and research the links between practice and identity? What are the mutual consequences of how one might answer the related questions of who we are, what we know and what we do? In many cases, work activities form part of a person's identity, their self-perception and the expectations that others have of them. Such activities are not merely the behaviour of work but the knowledge, access to resources, and skill in activity-process which are part of the meaning of work. Simultaneously, identities, or aspects of identity, are needed in order to carry out many work functions. Adherence to codes of professional ethics as a personal commitment is crucial as part of who health workers are if they are to be trusted by patients and service users. Eating a meal cooked by a star chef or listening to a concert by a celebrated musician is simply not the same if they send a deputy instead of performing the work themselves, no matter how good the deputy. Various theories of knowledge, practice and identity are available, but we will argue that a productive combination is of theories which adopt a processual view (Nayak & Chia 2011)—that is, theories which focus on action and interaction over time. In this chapter we focus on identity work theory and activity theory. We do not explain these theories in total, but rather set out areas of potential synergy where there is complementarity. We conclude by drawing inspiration from Bakhtin's (1968) conception of the 'carnivalesque' as a way of highlighting the insights to be gained from focusing on the abnormal.

IDENTITY WORK THEORY

The literature on identity is enormous and occurs in philosophy, sociology, psychology and a range of arts and humanities disciplines. Within the management field a range of approaches, often reflecting more general theories of identity, have been applied and extended. An initial question is whether we are concerned with individual identities (those that define a

person including, for example, personal characteristics) or collective identities (such as a group defined by its position in an organisation, a social class
or an ethnic identity). The approach adopted here is that individual and collective identities are constructed in relation to each other. An individual may
claim as part of their personal identity an identification with a class or ethnic
group. Equally, they may seek to dissociate themselves from such a form of
collective identity that other people 'project' onto them but which they do
not regard as being central to their own being. One classic conception is that
identity is the core of the self, which remains constant in different contexts:
the self that is true, or authentic in different social, psychological or political
contexts. This way of thinking has had an impact on the way that, for example, some psychology has been applied to management, such as the analysis
of the personality characteristics of leaders or entrepreneurs—identifying
particular characteristics as resulting in success in the practice of leadership
or entrepreneurship. However, we will argue that a more dynamic conception of identity may be of significant utility in enhancing our understanding
of knowledge and practice (or knowing and practising). A dynamic, process-
oriented perspective on identity is known as 'identity work'.

Recent research under the heading of identity work has conceptualised
identity as being 'in process', something that is 'worked' upon as people
live their lives at work. Identity work is a set of processes in which people are "forming, repairing, maintaining, strengthening or revising the
constructions" of their selves, which produces a sense of "coherence and
distinctiveness" (Alvesson & Willmott 2002:626). From this viewpoint,
people are seen as continuously working towards a sense of self that is clear
and which fits with a narrative of self (Watson 2009). Few theorists would
regard the outcome of identity work as a static or fully stable identity. However, one stream of research has concluded that the processes can lead to a
quasi-stable equilibrium. For example, Kreiner *et al.* (2006) analyse how
Episcopal priests' identities adjust and evolve to find a self-concept that fits
with their role and work. An alternative perspective agrees that identity is
in process but argues that the process never stops and that the 'outcome' is
ongoing change. For example, Thomas & Davies (2005) show the nature
of police work and identity to be in a continuous crafting process. In some
circumstances, the level of disruption can be so great that a person's identity is perpetually liminal, a state of being betwixt and between, especially
when their sense of self is disrupted by the assumptions and projections of
others (Beech 2011). This can be observed, for example, amongst management consultants who live a nomadic existence, spending more time in other
organisations than their own and more time with clients than with team
members (Sturdy *et al.* 2006).

Identity work processes are those through which people's identities
are reproduced and altered by their participation in work. This can entail
'claims' and 'grants' (Brown 2015) through which people assert a form of
identification and others agree or project an alternative onto the individual.

For example, a manager may hold a self-identity perspective of himself or herself as being honest and helpful, whilst others may project different perspectives onto that person, based on their expectations of such a role as, perhaps, being deceitful or manipulative. Hence at root there is a relational or dialogical process in which identity work is a social composite (Beech 2008). Identity work is conducted not only by the individual, but by others who have role expectations, stereotypes associated with characteristics and knowledge of the person.

Expectations, language, behaviour and the expression and embodiment of knowledge can all be resources used in the practice of identity work. The management consultants studied by Sturdy *et al.* (2006) adopt certain dress codes, operate with a particular 'tool kit' and are adept at certain forms of analysis and presentation. Their adopting of the customs, way of being or 'habitus' (Bourdieu 1990) of the consultant constitutes a use of resources to make a claim to the identity of 'consultant'. Their claim is effective to the extent that they and others believe and accept the claim. This interactive process reaches its zenith when no one thinks to question it—when the consultant just *is*. At this stage, much of the knowledge and behavioural content of being a consultant has become intuitive, natural and tacit.

The identity work perspective does not presume that a person has only one identity. Rather, it assumes that people have multiple 'strands' of identity (Ybema *et al.* 2009) and that the way that identity is exercised in different contexts may result in quite different meanings being associated with knowledge, skills and practices. Bendrups (2006) produces a reflexive account of his dual identity as musician and researcher. Having been a professional musician, he embarked on a PhD studying the music and culture on the Polynesian island of Rapanui. One might have expected his experience to enable him to connect with the Rapanui musicians and to develop a shared understanding. However, as he says:

> My initial interactions with the Rapanui musicians gave me the impression that I was expected to behave like an anthropologist or sociologist rather than as an artist or performer . . . as a non-guitarist I found it difficult to convince some of the Rapanui musicians that I was a competent musician myself. Years of experience as a freelance trombonist in various contexts meant nothing on Rapanui, where this instrument has only ever been seen as occupying a perfunctory role in military band performances.
>
> (2006:23)

What counts as a convincing embodiment of an identity in one context may not translate into other contexts, and hence it is not simply the case that competent performance is a route to effectively claiming an identity. In this short extract we can also see that there is a significance to tools and their associated meanings—in this case the status of a trombone as a legitimate musical instrument. As discussed in Chapter 3 (practice), the issues of tools, technology and materiality are also highly significant in practice-based theories, and we discuss this below when considering activity theory.

In addition to 'getting it right', getting it wrong but in the right way can be part of establishing an accepted identity. Alvesson and Robertson (2006) studied aeroplane pilots whose identity was closely related to their occupation—incorporating as it does (self-) images of technologically proficient, adventurous high achievers. However, in something of a subversion of this image, pilots were also found to discuss near misses and other mistakes with close colleagues in their crew rooms at airports. The mistakes were not so dangerous as to be reported automatically or formally, but they could be fairly alarming for the travelling public. However, being competent in the identity of a pilot included being able to tell mistake-stories in the back room, away from management or passengers. These confidential confessions to each other, done in the right way, were part of how experienced pilots identified with each other. Less established pilots would be less likely to tell such stories or make such confessions. Hence, part of the inhabiting of the identity was the knowledge of when and how to display a *lack* of skill to select others.

Therefore, from an identity work perspective, what people do at work, how they do it and the styles and tastes that are revealed through their enactment of an identity to audiences who understand the nuances are central to their achieved identity. In the next section we will consider a version of practice-based theory, activity theory, and the (potential) role of identity in its analysis.

ACTIVITY THEORY

Blackler and colleagues (2000), influenced in particular by Engeström (1990), develop the application of activity theory in a way that emphasises the connection between individuals, communities and objects of activity. "Activities imply the motives and goals of participants . . . activities provide the link between the individual and society . . . societies can be conceptualized as an interlacing pattern of different activities" (Blackler *et al.* 2000: 96). The object of activity emerges as individuals operate as part of communities through the use of tools and technologies, following and adapting rules and procedures and developing a division of labour. Chapter 7, on being a maker, provides an illustration of experience of the object (pot, vase, jug) that has been produced being inseparable from its producer, and her identity as a 'bona fide' maker. In this case, the intention, skill and knowledge is embedded in the physical object, which carries symbolic meaning. Meaningful activities are never absolutely individual as even a person acting apparently alone is doing so in a social, cultural and historical context that provides the language and symbolism with which to accomplish meaning.

The social context is that which provides the tools to use and the learning that has led to the person being able to act with intention.

Activities interact in a conceptual system, not necessarily in agreement and in a complementary fashion with each other, but often incorporating tension between differing purposes and objects (Orlikowski 2002). The role of the community is particularly important in negotiating priorities and symbolic meaning, allocating resources and enabling learning—sometimes explicit or codified, but often based on socialisation and informal cultural learning. Although activity theory places less emphasis on the explicit notion of identity than, for example, social learning theory (e.g., Wenger 1998), the issues of personal and social identities arise in the use of the concepts of community and division of labour. For example, Nicolini (2013) uses this theoretical basis to explore activities in telemedicine. Clinicians and nurses, in a community encompassing other healthcare practitioners, operate with a division of labour in which key decisions are allocated to (and expected from) particular professional roles and operate with professional codes of practice to deliver specific activities in the provision of care to their patients. Nicolini reveals how changes in technology can result in significant alterations to practice; for example, by enabling patient monitoring to occur while the patient is at home rather than in hospital. This type of change is not only technological but can entail a re-identification of the participants. The patients may have to take on greater responsibility and accountability for the use of monitoring equipment and the transmission of results to clinicians, things that were previously part of the day-to-day activities of technicians and nurses in hospitals. The role of clinicians shifts from being *in charge* of the patients, their environment and the measures that are taken, towards an engagement with a more *active or participating* patient. Such changes are manifested not only in the division of labour but also in a change in how people in a system of activities relate to each other, how power and influence are distributed, and in what it means to be a good patient, clinician, nurse, etc. These issues are crucial in understanding how people produce identities in relation to each other, what they do, and how they and their activities are valued.

In a somewhat different context, Bechky and Okhuysen (2011) adopt a practice-based approach to explore how film crews adapt their practices to unexpected surprises. This focus is particularly helpful, as having to cope with the *unusual* highlights both what is usual and how crews can enact speedy learning. Bechky and Okhuysen identify organisational bricolage as the route to adaption to new circumstances. Bricolage involves putting resources together in ways in which they may not have been combined previously. This is likely to include material resources, but crucially also entails social and cognitive resources. The bricolage they observed included role shifting, reorganising routines and reordering work. For example, when a lead actor was suddenly unwell during filming, the crew discussed what to do. Their answer was to shoot the Steadicam shots of the location. This made use of the expensive equipment and operator whilst not needing the actors. Subsequently, these shots could be edited together with action shots including the actors. This would mean a change to the editing process and a change in the schedule, but provided a highly efficient way of continuing. The decision-making required crew members to act as a community—sharing ideas to produce an outcome that may not have been achieved individually, a preparedness to break with established routine and to change how the work was being done. It also meant that crew members had to act outside their traditional role identities to enable a different way of thinking and acting. Key aspects of knowledge, such as the potential for a different approach to editing or the financial cost and value of the Steadicam, had to be accessed by different members of the community.

These ways of understanding and analysing practice, or the activities that constitute systemic practices, call forth an account of identity. That is, although the focus within the action and interaction is on the activity, those interactions also relate to who the participants are being while engaged in the practice. For example, it might be expected that only senior staff would be involved in deciding to vary from established routine, but in this case more junior people take on part of the occupational identity of the senior staff. Practices are only regarded as such when they are meaningful (not mere behaviour or reaction), and meaning is established in and through culture, which incorporates self and group identity. In the next section we will suggest one way of relating these ideas to enquiry into practice.

STUDYING THE ABNORMAL—INSIGHTS FROM THE CARNIVALESQUE?

Bakhtin's (1968) conceptualisation of the carnivalesque has influenced organization studies (e.g., Linstead 2010), and we argue that it could provide some direction for the future studies of knowledge and practice and the aspect of identity in particular. Medieval carnivals were forms of festival that enabled, and relied upon, certain reversals. Traditional religious festivals contained ritual, ceremony and symbolism, which represented and reinforced hierarchies of status, knowledge and practice. Religious ceremonies highlighted the separation between the ordained members of the church and the common folk in word, deed, dress and place.

Processions separated the audience from the officially appointed processors who typically had special access to symbols such as relics or ceremonial artefacts, which were used only on special days. Hence the sacred and the profane were separated in knowledge and practice, and the identities of those in the sacred realm were publically re-established in a hierarchical division from the everyday. In contrast, in carnivals, such boundaries of practice and identity were blurred and often reversed. For example, in the Feast of Fools the lower orders of cathedrals were elevated to leading roles in rituals for the duration of the festivities. The body, rather than spirituality, was emphasised with fun being made of bodily functions and sex, and the corporeal similarities between people, regardless of their status, were stressed. The higher learning and wisdom of those in authority was openly questioned and practices of separation between central participants and the audience were challenged by, for example, common folk joining in processions, adapting dress styles and indulging in normally prohibited behaviours.

Many of these reversals would be performed with humour, which allowed for a certain mocking of normal practice. However, although the normal rules of knowledge and practice were suspended for the duration of the carnival, these were specific and time-limited events, often followed by times of strong and clear reimposition of the traditional order, as happens in Lent. Bakhtin points out that modern-day carnivals are not the equivalent of medieval carnivals as they typically incorporate the norms of separation: division of performers from the audience, maintenance of the rule of law, and increasingly commercialisation, including, as we now see, the justification of carnivals on the basis of increasing tourism and economic impact (Page & Connell 2012)—the established norms of reasoning in the mainstream.

Notwithstanding the modern version of carnival, the Bakhtinian interpretation may offer some insights of value. In commercial and not-for-profit enterprises there has been a rise in networked and 'de-coupled' organisations. Rather than one company or organisation exercising ownership along the value chain, supply agreements and outsourcing have increased over a considerable period. At the same time, traditional connections between organisations and their customers and service users have been shifting. Marketing and brand building used to be within the purview of organisations but increasingly the nature of mediation between product/service providers and consumers has become less controlled and managed. For example, in the creative industries, whilst publishers, film-makers, theatre producers and music companies continue to initiate, brand and sell projects or products, purchasing decisions have become subject to multiple influences (Bilton & Cummings 2014). Advertising, industry standards and awards which were formerly used to 'position' products and hence gain publicity have not been supplanted, but are now to some degree rivalled by non-industry, 'non-expert' mediation. Hence, critics who previously held sway over theatre and film audiences through newspaper and magazine reviews now sit alongside customer/user reviewers who can post commentaries and recommendations instantaneously. Traditional book reviews and prizes decided upon over a twelve-month period by a panel of experts sit alongside customer reviews on book-purchasing websites, and those websites also offer purchasing recommendations based on previous consumer behaviour. This form of 'non-expert' influence could be regarded as a form of carnivalesque influencing, itself being influenced by changes in practice and identity. The very non-expert status of the customer reviews may be a factor in people paying attention to them rather than to difficult-to-read professional reviews.

Informality and speed may replace academically informed, considered professional criticism. Beyond this, self-publishing and crowdsourced funding for publishing literature, drama, film and music is further disrupting traditional forms of investment decision-making that was previously professionalised and removed from the direct influence of the customer. This is not to say that the organisationally framed, professional approach is better or worse than the decentred, more open forms of mediation. However, in order to understand these practices, a genuine questioning of what it means to do the practice of producing, customering, customer-reviewing, patienting and so on should not be removed from an understanding of who people are being when they undertake these, and any, practices.

The metaphor of the carnival encourages us to question the taken-for-granted assumptions of knowledge, practices and identities in the communities we research with. Like pilots who discuss near misses in a confidential, trusted setting or film-makers who devise ways of filming without the need for actors, sometimes it is possible to learn about the meaningful nature of practices when things are not normal. The abnormal can throw light onto the normal in that it reveals the boundaries of who people can be and what is legitimate for them to do at work. The idea of inverting the conventional hierarchy plays through subsequent chapters on environmental policy (Chapter 10), knowledge co-production (Chapter 14), and the Collaborations for Leadership in Applied Health Research and Care (CLAHRCs—Chapter 11), in which traditional notions of whose voice is privileged or who drives the process of knowledge creation are overturned.

CONCLUSION

Identity work theory is concerned with what people do as they seek to construct a narrative of self for themselves and for others. Practice-based theories, and activity theory in particular, are concerned not with mere behaviour but with meaningful activity in which tools and resources are used in a knowing way, through a division of labour and with workers having legitimacy to carry out activities in part because of their professional or occupational identities. Both theories are concerned with process over time: the interweaving of action and interaction, in a cultural and technological context, which enables an embodied sense-making of people and their practices. Such embodied sense-making is occurring both for practitioners and for researchers engaging with the practitioners and so it is common for practice-based research to adopt longitudinal methodologies such as ethnography, action research or engaged research. The crucial skill in such research is the ability to belong to, or at least be close enough to, two different communities to understand their local theories of how and why things are as they are—the practice community and the community of research practitioners. This should not be impossible as, from an identity work perspective, we are normally part of, on the way into, and on the way out of several meaning-making communities at any one time.

SUGGESTED FURTHER READINGS

Blackler, F., Crump, N., & McDonald, S. (2000) Organizing processes in complex activity networks. *Organization*. 7: 277–300.
This paper provides not only an interesting research application of activity theory but has appendices that introduce activity theory in a succinct and accessible way. There are alternative ways of thinking about activity theory that are not discussed by Blackler, but which are covered by Nicolini.

Nicolini, D. (2013) *Practice theory, work, & organization*. Oxford: Oxford University Press.
This book offers a rounded view of the field. Nicolini explains the theoretical underpinnings of activity theory and practice-based research and shows how insights from philosophy, psychology and sociology can be applied to management research. He introduces detailed examples that show how analysis can be conducted.

Kenny, K., Whittle, A., & Willmott, H. (2011) *Understanding identity & organizations*. London: SAGE.
This book provides a thoughtful and thorough introduction to a range of identity theories. It covers core issues of the relationship between identity, power and resistance, diversity, and the impact and possibilities that new technologies and new organisational forms bring for identity work.

REFERENCES

Alvesson, M., & Robertson, M. (2006) The best and the brightest: The construction, significance and effects of elite identities in consulting firms. *Organization*. 13(2): 195–224.

Alvesson, M., & Willmott, H. (2002) Identity regulation as organizational control: Producing the appropriate individual. *Journal of Management Studies*. 39: 619–644.

Bakhtin, M. (1968) *Rabelais & his world*. Cambridge MA: MIT Press.

Bechky, B.A., & Okhuysen, G.A. (2011) Expecting the unexpected? How SWAT officers & film crews handle surprises. *Academy of Management Journal*. 54: 239–261.

Beech, N. (2008) On the nature of dialogic identity work. *Organization*. 15: 51–74.

Beech, N. (2011) Liminality & the practices of identity reconstruction. *Human Relations*. 64: 285–302.

Bendrups, D. (2006) Researchers, musicians or record producers? Negotiating roles & responsibilities in music ethnography. *Context: Journal of Music Research*. 31: 21–35.

Bilton, C., & Cummings, S. (2014) *Handbook of management & creativity*. Cheltenham: Edward Elgar.

Blackler, F., Crump, N., & McDonald, S. (2000) Organizing processes in complex activity networks. *Organization*. 7(2): 277–300.

Bourdieu, P. (1990) *The logic of practice*. Stanford: Stanford University Press.

Brown, A.D. (2015) Identities & identity work in organizations. *International Journal of Management Reviews*. 17(1): 20–40.

Engeström, Y. (1990) *Learning, working & imagining: Twelve studies in activity theory*. Helsinki: Orientat Konsultit.

Kreiner, G.E., Hollensbe, E.C., & Sheep, M.L. (2006) Where is the 'me' amongst the 'we'? Identity work & the search for optimal balance. *Academy of Management Journal*. 49: 1031–1057.

Linstead, S. (2010) Popular culture as carnival: The clash, play & transgression in the aesthetic economy, in B. Townley & N. Beech (eds.), *Managing creativity: Exploring the paradox*. Cambridge: Cambridge University Press, pp. 60–80.

Nayak, A., & Chia, R. (2011) Thinking, becoming & emergence: Process philosophy & organization studies, in H. Tsoukas & R. Chia (eds.), *Philosophy & organization theory*. Bingley: Emerald, pp. 281–309.

Nicolini, D. (2013) *Practice theory, work, & organization: An introduction*. Oxford: Oxford University Press.

Orlikowski, W.J. (2002) Knowing in practice: Enacting a collective capability in distributed organizing. *Organization Science*. 13(3): 249–273.

Page, S.J., & Connell, J. (2012) *The Routledge handbook of events*. Abingdon: Routledge.

Sturdy, A., Schwarz, M., & Spicer, A. (2006) Guess who's coming to dinner? Structures & uses of liminality in strategic management consultancy. *Human Relations*. 59: 929–960.

Thomas, R., & Davies, A. (2005) Theorizing the micro-politics of resistance: New public management & managerial identities in the UK public services. *Organization Studies*. 26: 683–706.

Watson, T.J. (2009) Narrative, life story & manager identity: A case study in autobiographical identity work. *Human Relations*. 62: 425–452.

Wenger, E. (1998) *Communities of practice: Learning, meaning, & identity*. Cambridge: Cambridge University Press.

Ybema, S., Keenoy, T., Oswick, C., Beverungen, A., Ellis, N., & Sabelis, I. (2009) Articulating identities. *Human Relations*. 62: 299–322.

Part B

Context-Specific Discussions of the Relationship between Knowledge and Practice

7 Sensing Bodies

The Aesthetics of Knowing and Practising

Anna Brown, Gail Greig and Emilia Ferraro

INTRODUCTION

The abstractions of people, places, minds and bodies in rational, cognitive models of knowledge and learning go against the very notion of being alive. The world is not, after all, made up of pieces that slot into place to form a comprehensible whole. It is far more fluid, unpredictable and interchangeable. This chapter is firmly rooted in the theoretical concepts of practice, wherein knowing is inherently entangled with doing and understood as an ongoing, emergent, social process (Nicolini *et al.* 2003, see Chapter 3 Practice). Using craft as a specific example, this chapter explores the material aspects of practice by focusing on what professional craftspeople or 'makers' do. Through the process of making we discuss the embodied nature of practice and present a case for a bodily understanding of knowing, sensed through one's immersion in the world.

We begin the chapter with a brief discussion of sociomateriality and the usefulness of this conceptual approach in practice-based studies. From here, we explore 'knowing from the inside' (Gherardi 2006; Ingold 2013) and present an empirical account of one author's journey to becoming a professional craft maker. This ethnography specifically addresses the sensible nature of our relationship with tools and materials, showing how the five senses are used beyond their prescribed function when engaging in making. This developing relationship between maker, environment and practice brings about ways of knowing that are also ways of being.

THE SOCIOMATERIALITY OF PRACTICE

The material dimension of practice is just that, the stuff that things are made of: the environment in which we live, from man-made and natural structures to the weather. It encompasses both raw and 'cooked' materials, from the objects that surround us to the minerals in the ground (Marchand 2010; Ingold 2011). The social is that of people and the relations between them: what we do and say, and how we act. In theories of sociomateriality these two aspects of practice—the social and material—are inherently entwined: there is no social that is not also material, and no material that is not also social (Orlikowski 2007:1437).

The social nature of practice, however, has often led, in organisation studies and social science more generally, to the material dimension of organisational life being overshadowed by a concentration on individuals. This has provided more or less nuanced accounts of what people say, and sometimes of what they do, but has largely either disregarded or implied the sociomateriality of practices and practising (Orlikowski 2010). More recent developments in practice theory have begun to specifically consider the sociomateriality of practice, bringing to the fore the entanglement of people and environment, where participants are never separated, but always entwined with others and things in the world (Ingold 2000, 2011, 2013; Barad 2007; Sandberg & Tsoukas 2011; Dall'Alba & Sandberg 2014).

Sociomateriality is inherent both to theories of practice and practising. From this perspective there can be no separation between people and environments, minds and bodies, or individual action and organisation: tools, materials, environments, people and things are woven together in the fabric of our lives through an ongoing process of becoming (Sandberg & Tsoukas 2011; Ingold 2013). This approach is helpful as it presents opportunities to explore how practitioners, as socially constituted beings (Bakhurst & Sypnowich 1995), are ordinarily involved in a relational whole rather than made separate, set against—or acting 'outside'—the world they inhabit (Ingold 2000, 2011, 2013; Shotter 2006; see suggested reading). It is in such circumstances that we find ourselves being part of and *within* a world that is indivisible and continually unfolding (Shotter 2013) as opposed to one that is rational, systematic and predictable. Hence we can understand the world in a way that is closer to how it might be experienced, bringing to the fore the immersive nature of being alive, where people engage in practice with their entire being, not just learning *about* but learning to *be* (Sandberg & Tsoukas 2011).

KNOWING FROM THE INSIDE: AESTHETICS OF PRACTICE

If knowing emerges from practice, through participation in the activities at hand, then the whole body must be engaged: from tongue to toe, and gut to heart. Such an immersion in practice exposes practitioners to direct encounters with the sights, sounds, smells, feelings and emotions involved in carrying out the activities that constitute any given practice. These experiences provide participants with alternative ways of knowing to those abstracted and curiously disembodied forms of knowledge frequently prescribed by conventional cognitive models. 'Knowing from the inside' (Gherardi 2006; Ingold 2013) highlights the aesthetic dimension of practice (Strati 2007) where a practical understanding (Schatzki 2014) of the activities at hand, the relationship between practitioners, and the tools and materials of a practice is fundamental to knowing and becoming knowledgeable.

Knowing from the inside is an essential part of our understanding of the world. Wherein an immersion in practice and our entanglement in the world leads to the development of morals and world views, creating affiliations that "knit together objects, people and ways of doing things" to form practitioners' professional—and personal—identities (Brown & DuGuid 1991; Lave & Wenger 1991; Amin & Roberts 2008:359; Marchand 2010). Thus to know from the inside is to feel, to sense, and to be party to the joys and frustrations of an activity (Ingold 2013), where ways of doing are distributed throughout the entire body—not just the mind—and contextualised in relation to the world of practice. To this end, practice both shapes and is shaped by our actions (Gherardi 2006), making it impossible to separate what we do from who we are (Sandberg & Tsoukas 2011; Ingold 2013). Hence what is learned through the body is "not something one has, like knowledge that can be brandished, rather, it is something that one *is*" (Bourdieu 1990:73).

The field of organisational aesthetics (*see* Taylor and Hansen 2005 *for a review*) has emphasised the sensible and corporeal nature of learning and organising (Strati 2000, 2007; Gartner 2013; Viteritti 2013), or how quality and value judgements are made based on taste, for example (Cook & Yannow 1993, Gherardi *et al.* 2007; Gherardi 2009; Merilainen *et al.* 2015). Whilst these studies have shown how sensible knowing and aspects of the body are used in understanding and constructing organisational life, they leave room to explore the multisensory nature (Pink 2011) of how we experience the world with our whole being, where aesthetic engagement in practice blurs the boundaries of the individual senses and allows us, for example, to use our hands to both feel and 'see'.

A METHODOLOGY TO BECOMING A MAKER

Craft provides an excellent example of sensible knowing. It is an unequivocally physical form of labour where novice makers learn about and *through* the processes that bring objects into being. The physical nature of work brings to the fore the role of the body and senses in knowing, highlighting the ways in which people don't just learn about, but learn to be. Therefore, we follow the ebb and flow of materials in the world of craft practice, and in particular their relationship with the maker's body. In doing so, we explore the relationship between bodies and materials—and tools—in ceramics practice, and ask, what do these relations tell us about how ways of knowing emerge through the body?

We base our discussion on an ethnographic study—and apprenticeship—undertaken in a working pottery. Author one (Anna) carried out the fieldwork following prior experience in ceramics, whilst authors two and three (Gail and Emilia) prompted reflections on practice through ongoing discussions throughout that time, to enable reflection on the auto-ethnographic aspect of the apprenticeship. We tied this to other ethnographic aspects of the study, which involved Anna in participant observation during her apprenticeship, and the conduct of a range of interviews with practitioners at varying stages of their careers, including an extended life history interview with a pivotal senior practitioner in the field. Together with archival documentary data, these combined data allowed us to see how the practice of ceramics has developed over time more broadly, whilst capturing the sense of *being* together with data *about* becoming a craft practitioner (Shotter 2006; Ingold 2013).

The pottery concerned was established in 1981, and has space for six ceramicists. These 'makers' are at varying career stages, with the pottery owner having been involved in ceramics for over forty years, and each of the other makers for between two and twenty years. The pottery has a city centre location, in the basement of a traditional tenement. Maintaining a domestic feel, the space is faced by a small gallery, which is open to the public, and has three rooms towards the back of the building that house its six residents.

We locate ourselves in the pottery studio with Anna as she begins her journey and shares her changing experience of becoming a maker 'from the inside'.

Figure 7.1   Inside the studio

What the Eyes Cannot See and the Ears Cannot Hear

On arriving in the pottery I was immediately drawn to the sensory nature of the studio (figure 7.1). There was so much to look at, to see, to touch, to hear. Things around me were catching my eye and piquing my interest. In this new environment a raft of questions emerged: how would I work? How did others work? How would I set up my space? What should I do? What tools did I have? What did I need? I was yet to discover that I already had most of what I needed, standing in the studio that day, excited, scared, apprehensive: taking it all in.

I had been given access to an old Shimpo wheel in the pottery (figure 7.2). Its heavy metal body vibrated on the stone floor of the studio and created a din that was at once monotonous and all-encompassing. I can still feel the hum from the wheel transferring from my feet and my hands, through my arms and legs, to overtake my senses. On throwing a pot, the wheel should

Figure 7.2   Shimpo wheel

turn away from your dominant hand, so for right-handed people—like me—it would turn anticlockwise. I sat up at the wheel, rested my foot on the drive pedal and flicked the 'on' switch. The wheel was spinning, but in a clockwise direction. Sarah had told me that if this were to happen, to correct the direction of travel I should wait for the wheel to come to a complete stop and flick the 'on' switch in the opposite direction. That sounded like a simple instruction, but as I waited for the wheel to stop turning and flicked the switch off, and back on again, confusion crept in:

> I had a problem with the wheel. My confusion reigned, as I could not get it to turn anti clockwise. I asked Catherine and she came through. I had to wait for the wheel to stop whirring before I could change the direction. There was a bit of a knack to it. Catherine said 'try now' and it worked. I wasn't sure what she'd heard or been listening for, but there was obviously something (and that was why Sarah had insisted it came to a complete stop before the switch was flicked). Next time I switched off the wheel I listened carefully: sure enough, you could hear the mechanisms come to a complete stop. I flicked the switch and the direction changed again.
>
> (Field notes B: 52)

I was expecting the sound of the wheel stopping to be obvious, but the whirr and the click that I heard as the mechanisms came to a halt were a few seconds after the wheel itself had stopped spinning. It was a quiet sound, subtle, and could be easily missed. I had to tune my ear to a sound that came after the din, to continue listening even though all visible motion and audible sound had stopped. This, it turned out, became a common theme in my developing knowing.

Listening to Materials

Listening with my ears was an important part of studio life. I could hear the clicks of the kiln elements as they intermittently turned on, telling me the kiln was heating up rather than cooling down. I could hear the chatter of my tools as they bounced off the clay and I knew it was too dry to turn. I could hear the squelch of the wet clay on my plaster bat as I tried to knead it to the right consistency; and the tap, tap, tap of the fired objects as I tried to chip them off kiln shelves after a glaze run, or when a lid had stuck to its pot.

> One of the pot lids was jammed on but was moving, [Sarah] took the pot in the water and tapped along the seal—sure enough after a couple of taps the lid came free. I tried with the other pots. I tapped for ages. Sarah kept saying that I'll hear a change in tone when they come undone.
>
> (Field notes, B: 247)

The audible sounds of making represented waymarkers, and a change in tone or frequency was a means of my communicating between with these 'inanimate' objects and raw materials. As I progressed through my apprenticeship these sounds of the studio would enable me to navigate the process of making and see what was not observable. In the beginning I used my five senses as prescribed: ears for listening, eyes for seeing, tongue for tasting, nose for smelling, skin for touching. It became apparent, however, that the senses were more fluid than I had once thought as, gradually, I found there were other ways to listen, to hear, and to see.

Hands As Ears

The risk of failure was high; it was inherent in everything I did and it was through each failed attempt that my body grew in knowing. I quickly came to realise that it was not possible to work with the material if it was too wet or too dry, so I had to find a way of knowing when the clay or glaze was in the optimum state for the next part of the process. Over time and with practice this became instinctive as I continually listened and responded to my materials: I could get a sense from the clay passing between my hands, as to how thin the walls were, what the shape of the pot might become, how I could manipulate it and whether it was going to collapse. I soon came to realise that being able to respond to the materials and wider environment was an integral part of being a maker.

> The clay is full of these rather smug little lessons. You know, you can't do it now, you've got to wait 'til it's right. And it does tell you what, you've got to learn to listen to what the clay wants . . .
> (Life History Interview: 105)

Certainly, the relationship I developed with my materials involved listening to something that was innate, that didn't make a sound without my intervention. I began to understand the natural limits of my materials: too much water will weaken the clay, too much pressure will throw it off-centre, and too thin a wall would cause the pot to collapse. The process of making, no matter how routinised it became, was never identical twice, and that was where the ability to 'hear' what the materials were telling me became an essential part of making. I noticed this especially when talking to others about my developing practice:

> I found myself saying quite often that 'the clay will tell you when it's had enough and if you push it too far it will flop'.
> (Field notes, B: 858)

My whole body became a measure and a means of making, but it had been a gradual process of getting to know what both I and the materials could do. I was responding to the environment aesthetically, through my sense of touch: my hands became my eyes, but perhaps less obviously they sometimes became my ears. My developing awareness of the subtleties of the feedback I received from the clay as it spun on the wheel—the texture, dampness, firmness and weight of the material—fed into my understanding of the practice of making. These ways of knowing were not just limited to the raw materials (like the clay), but enabled me to interact with many tools and stages of production.

The Body As a Tool

Just like with throwing, losing pots in a firing is an inherent part of making. You have little control of what goes on inside a kiln and the heat distribution and results can vary depending on how tightly the kiln is packed, and the relative size of the pots. As a maker I had to learn to let go of the outcomes and give in to the natural flow of the materials I was working with. The uncertainty in making was all part of following and responding to the rhythms of the practice. There were, however, ways to prevent faults occurring in the work and to manage the process to my advantage by using my body as a tool to read and respond to the environment.

In the beginning I had always relied on the pyrometer (a sophisticated temperature gauge inside the kiln, with a controller on the outside) (figure 7.3) to tell me what the temperature inside the kiln was. Or on firing the kiln I used pyrometric cones that responded to 'heatwork' over time, watching them bend as the kiln reached temperature (figure 7.4). But as I progressed in the studio, I developed new ways of knowing. Just like these heat-sensitive tools, I was able to tell whether the kiln had cooled sufficiently and was safe to open by holding my hand against the kiln door, held slightly ajar—or 'cracked'—thereby using my hands to 'feel' the temperature *inside* the kiln: a place that, until the kiln was cool enough, remained unseen.

> I suggested [we crack the kiln] maybe at 150/140 degrees. Jennifer said what she does is open the kiln slightly and if she can't hold her hand next to the crack—if it's too hot—then it's still too hot to open it. But we agreed that 140 would probably be OK.
>
> (Field notes, B: 575)

My hands became a tool for seeing and listening to the internal, unseen workings of the kiln and the pots that were snugly settled inside. It was as if my body had become attuned to those of the pots: if I could withstand the temperature difference without discomfort, so too could they. I used other parts of my body too, to understand and aesthetically read my environment. When it came to understanding the fired work and knowing whether the kiln

Figure 7.3 Pyrometer

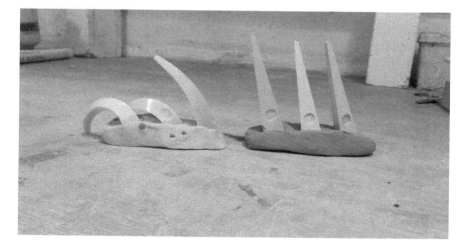

Figure 7.4 Fired and unfired pyrometric cones

had fired to the right temperature, I was able to use my mouth to understand what perhaps my eyes and hands could not tell me:

> Sarah took me through to her studio and asked, "do you know how to tell if the bisque is over fired?" When I responded no, she told me to pick up a piece of fired ware and touch it with my tongue. As I did this, she said, "do you feel that, clawing on your tongue? That means it's still porous." The fired clay had drawn the saliva from my tongue and as a result had gripped onto my taste buds.
>
> (Field Notes, C: 1)

By using my tongue and feeling the fired clay grip to my taste buds I was at once able to know that the material was still porous: I could tell that the 'cooking' was complete, but that the pots were not 'over-fired'. In that moment I was offered another way of knowing my materials, using my body and muscles but perhaps not as they were intended or had been prescribed: in ways I hadn't imagined. The way the fired clay gripped to my tongue that day imparted more knowledge than I could have gained from any one of my other senses: what my eyes could not see, my ears could not hear, and my fingertips could not feel.

KNOWING AND BEING

The empirical example shows how knowing is not limited to rational thought processes, but instead is also sensed or felt. Knowing emerges through an engagement in practice that encompasses the whole body, not just the mind or the senses in isolation (Strati 2007). Anna's experiences using her hands to both see and hear show how the division of bodily capabilities is a means of ordering and rationalising our experiences of the world (Pink 2011), when in fact the way we actually engage in everyday life is much more subtle and immersive (Sandberg & Tsoukas 2011). Anna's time in the studio demonstrates the ways in which practitioners negotiate with all that surrounds them: feeling the consistency of the clay, sensing feedback from tools or paying attention to the humidity in the room.

It is possible to see how Anna began to use her body in ways we perhaps would not consciously consider in order to follow the flows of her materials and processes; for example, she used her tongue to taste how porous the clay was. This experience of being in and part of the world (Shotter 2006; Ingold 2011) led to a deep and meaningful connection between Anna and her practice. Here she developed a deep understanding of the objects she was producing as she began to tune into her materials and the process of making (Ingold 2000). This was shown most clearly as she began to sense the temperature of the kiln with her hands rather than the prescribed tools.

Anna's tools become an extension of her body and the body an extension of the tools, each allowing the other to fulfil its purpose.

Although the empirical example focuses on the process of making, and specifically life inside the studio, it is possible to see how these experiences might be reflected in other aspects of everyday life. The immersive nature of knowing and being in the world suggests that knowing can be derived by means other than the application of cognitive or canonical knowledge in a given situation. For example, the way in which Anna's knowing became instinctive over time pertains to the ways in which we make everyday decisions on our actions. As we become socialised we are able to perform and participate in new and different ways. And just as the process of making is routinised, so too are our everyday lives. Each journey we take to work may follow the same patterns and processes, and begin to feel monotonous and banal, but each experience will be slightly nuanced, from the weather determining what we wear, to the people we encounter along the way. As we sense and feel, we trust our gut and begin to 'just know'.

In following the processes of making, participation is shown to be as transformative of the materials as it is of the makers as the body adapts to find new ways of knowing. Over time practitioners become attuned to their practice (Ingold 2013), developing a deep and meaningful bond that enables them make instinctive, or intuitive, decisions. In 'just knowing', practitioners are able to trust their sensibilities of tools and materials, as well as of their own selves. Knowing through the senses becomes deeply ingrained in the fibres of the body as much as it is in the fabric of everyday life. Each failed attempt is not lost, but settles in the body, leaving in its trail a more nuanced understanding of both the practice and practitioner. Knowing therefore is a continuous process where mastery is never truly accomplished, other than perhaps in the eyes of one's peers. The practitioner senses that as their practice continues so too will the process of discovery, both in practical ability and in self. Thus who we are and what we do are irrevocably bound in the world we inhabit, making it impossible to separate what one knows, or where one practices, from whom one is (Bourdieu 1990; Sandberg & Tsoukas 2011; Ingold 2013).

CONCLUSION

A practice approach allows us to explore the world as we experience it. By approaching making from inside the practice we have shown the ways in which knowing is both embodied and enacted in practice (Ingold 2000, 2011; Sandberg & Tsoukas 2011). Making highlights the ways in which we know *from* the world, rather than *about* the world (Shotter 2006; Ingold 2011) through a process that is transformational for both maker and made.

To this end, this chapter has illustrated how practitioners not only engage in their environment, but are immersed in it: hearing, seeing, feeling, sensing and *being* with their entire bodies.

Practitioners use their bodies in many different ways, outside of those prescribed by rational thought processes: where the senses blur to produce a deep and complex understanding of the processes at play in the contexts in which they are played out. This chapter specifically looks at issues of craft and making, as physical processes that rely heavily on the material world. There is however room to explore other practices and areas of work in which the materiality of process plays out in much more subtle ways. Here we can explore further how ways of knowing emerge from the practice itself, binding the actions of the individual and their environs.

ACKNOWLEDGEMENTS

Dr Ferraro's contribution is part of her association with the "Knowing from the Inside" research project, financed by the ERC and led by Prof. Tim Ingold.

SUGGESTED FURTHER READINGS

Ingold, T. (2000) Earth, sky, wind, & weather, in T. Ingold (ed.), *Being alive: Essays on movement, knowledge and description.* London: Routledge, pp. 115–125.
   This chapter explores Ingold's theory of 'dwelling' and expands on the ideas presented here about the entanglements of life: where we are part of the world, rather than set against it.
Lave, J. (2012) Changing practice. *Mind, Culture & Activity.* 19: 156–171.
   Based on a keynote address to the 2011 International Society for Culture, Activity and Research, this article focuses on relational theories of learning and reflects on critical ethnographic practice, apprenticeship learning, and the relations between knowledge and identity.
Strati, A. (2007) Sensible knowledge & practice based learning. *Management Learning.* 38(1): 61–77.
   This article focuses on the relevance of sensible knowledge in practice-based studies and provides an overview of aesthetics in organisation studies.

REFERENCES

Amin, A., & Roberts, J. (2008) Knowing in action: Beyond communities of practice. *Research Policy.* 37: 353–369.
Bakhurst, D., & Sypnowich, C. (1995) *The social self.* London: SAGE.
Barad, K. (2007) *Meeting the universe halfway: Quantum physics & the entanglement of matter & meaning.* Maine: Duke University Press.
Bourdieu, P. (1990) *The logic of practice.* Stanford: Stanford University Press.

Brown, J.S., & Duguid, P. (1991) Organisational learning & communities of practice: Toward a unified view of working, learning, & innovating. *Organization Science.* 2(1): 40–57.

Cook, S.D.N., & Yannow, D. (1993) Culture & organizational learning. *Journal of Management Inquiry* 2(4): 373–390.

Dall'Alba, G., & Sandberg, J. (2014) A phenomological perspective on researching work & learning, in S. Billet, C. Harteis, & H. Gruber (eds.), *International handbook of research in professional & practice-based learning.* Dordrecht: Springer, pp. 279–304.

Gartner, C. (2013) Cognition, knowing & learning in the flesh: Six views on knowing organization studies. *Scandinavian Journal of Management.* 29: 338–352.

Gherardi, S. (2006) *Organizational knowledge: The texture of workplace learning.* Oxford: Blackwell.

Gherardi, S. (2009) Practice? It's a matter of taste! *Management Learning.* 40(5): 535–550.

Gherardi, S., Nicolini, D., & Strati, A. (2007) The passion for knowing. *Organization.* 14(3): 315–329.

Ingold, T. (2000) *The perception of the environment: Essays on livelihood, dwelling & skill.* London: Routledge.

Ingold, T. (2011) *Being alive: Essays on movement, knowledge & description.* London: Routledge.

Ingold, T. (2013) *Making: Anthropology, archaeology, art & architecture.* London: Routledge.

Lave, J., & Wenger, E. (1991) *Situated learning: Legitimate peripheral participation.* Cambridge: Cambridge University Press.

Marchand, T.H.J. (2010) Making knowledge: Explorations of the indissoluble relation between minds, bodies & environment. *Journal of the Royal Anthropological Institute.* 16: 1–21.

Merilainen, S., Tienari, J., & Valtonen, A. (2015) Headhunters & the 'ideal' executive body. *Organization.* 22(1): 3–22.

Nicolini, D., Gherardi, S., & Yanow, D. (2003) *Knowing in organizations: A practice-based approach.* New York: M.E. Sharpe.

Orlikowski, W.J. (2007) Sociomaterial practices: Exploring technology at work. *Organization Studies.* 28(9): 1435–1448.

Orlikowski, W.J. (2010) The sociomateriality of organisational life: Considering technology in management research. *Cambridge Journal of Economics.* 34: 125–141.

Pink, S. (2011) Multimodality, multisensorality and ethnographic knowing: Social semiotics and the phenomenology of perception. *Qualitative Research.* 11: 261–276.

Sandberg, J., & Tsoukas, H. (2011) Grasping the logic of practical rationality. *Academy of Management Review.* 36(2): 338–360.

Schatzki, T.R. (2014) Art bundles, in T. Zembylas (ed.), *Artistic practices: Social interactions & cultural dynamics.* London: Routledge, pp. 17–31.

Shotter, J. (2006) Understanding process from within: An argument for 'Withness'-Thinking. *Organization Studies.* 27(4): 585–604.

Shotter, J. (2013) Reflections on sociomateriality: From inter to intra-thinking in performing practices, in P. Carlile, D. Nicolini, A. Langley, & H. Tsoukas (eds.), *How matter matters: Objects, artefacts & materiality in organization studies.* Oxford: Oxford University Press, pp. 32–57.

Strati, A. (2000) *The aesthetics of organization.* London: SAGE.

Strati, A. (2007) Sensible knowledge & practice-based learning. *Management Learning.* 38(1): 61–77.

Taylor, S.S., & Hansen, H. (2005) Finding form: Looking at the field of organizational aesthetics. *Journal of Management Studies.* 42(6): 1211–1231.

Viteritti, A. (2013) It's the body (that does it)! The production of knowledge through body in scientific learning practice. *Scandinavian Journal of Management.* 29: 367–376.

8   Everyday Creative Development Practices in Advertising

Christian Grahle and Paul Hibbert

INTRODUCTION

The everyday creative development processes in advertising agencies provide a good setting for studying the relationship between process knowledge (c.f. Hibbert & Huxham 2005) and the collaborative enactment of practice. Advertising agencies employ staff with different perspectives and roles in the development and delivery of advertisements, including strategists, creatives, producers, project management and others. Considering how these individuals work together and resolve tensions between divergent goals and understandings provides insight into how different practitioners put their distinct understandings into practice, and how process knowledge is constituted through participation in practices.

Research describing the practices that comprise 'everyday' creative development processes at advertising agencies is rather limited. This is because the literature has instead tended to focus on broad phase/stage models of the advertising development process. The rather generic step-by-step advertising development model offered by Pratt (2006) is typical of this genre. While this kind of research gives a useful overview of the scale and scope of the advertising development process, there has long been an opportunity for a different kind of research study, one which describes how advertising practitioners collectively organise their creative processes, and use and generate knowledge through their practices.

There are, however, a limited number of cases that provide a more detailed view of particular aspects of the creative advertising development process, or provide a new way of looking at the process as a whole. For example, the collective creative processes in the industry have been described as being organised through ritual processes (De Waal Malefyt & Morais 2010) in which tensions inherent in working with brands are resolved. Similarly, others suggest the organization of creative advertising processes to be a contested performance of authenticity in which the tastes of different groups, especially clients and product consumers, are in tension (Moeran 2005). Resolution from this perspective is commercial; in order to sell ideas, the tastes of clients are favoured over tastes of consumers and the rationalisation of ideas, divergent goals and creative influences takes place, rather uncomfortably, in a post-hoc phase of the creative process (Moeran 2005, Morais 2007).

It seems that creative tensions and rationalisations suggest that how the creative process (and creativity) is understood has an important bearing on how the creative advertising process proceeds (Nyilasy *et al.* 2013). Research suggests that advertising practitioners share specific understandings "about how to produce the creative product, including how the product should look" (Stuhlfaut 2011:284). As McLeod *et al.* (2011:118) explain, "service-led agencies are associated with 'low risk' creative work, since they prioritize processes that deliver effective, efficient client service. In contrast, creatively-led agencies seek to produce strong creative work with award-winning potential. 'Creatives' in these agencies tend to have more room to experiment and produce 'riskier' work than their service-led counterparts".

Despite these emergent insights on the creative tensions that help to shape the advertising development process, there is still a need to understand how this plays out in the practices that advertising professionals engage in during the creative process. The aim of the research reported in this chapter was to investigate the practices advertising practitioners are immersed in when developing advertisements as well as the potential tensions and rationalisations they might arise. Five key practices were identified and these are discussed below, but first an overview of the methods used to investigate these practices is explained.

METHODS

A practice-based approach to studying everyday creative development processes at advertising agencies was chosen. As discussed in Chapter 3, practice theory is still quite new to organisational research and different approaches to the concept of practice exist (Whittington 2011). According to Geiger (2009:129), "the common starting point of [. . .] practice-based approaches in organization studies is the desire to shed new light on organizational phenomena by getting closer to the 'real' work in organisations".

The essential idea of practice theory is that "the social" resides in "a mesh of practices and material arrangements" and that social life emerges out of such "practice-arrangement bundles" (Schatzki 2005:472–473). More broadly, Nicolini (2011:602) defined practices as "meaning-making, identity-forming, and order-producing activities". Applied to organisational studies, practice theory suggests that practice arrangement bundles constitute the site of an organisation, and that organisational phenomena transpire through and are effects of these bundles (Nicolini 2011). Thus, the recurrent reproduction of practices contributes to the production of social order in an organisation as well as to other organisational phenomena such as knowledge and purposiveness (Gherardi 2009; Nicolini 2011). This led

Gherardi (2009:536) to conclude that "practices are not only recurrent patterns of action [. . .] but also recurrent patterns of *socially* sustained action".

To explore and account for the practices through which creative advertising processes are effected, ethnographic research was carried out at a London-based advertising agency over a period of five months. Taking into account the multiple ways in which the advertising field can be mapped out, the advertising firm can be best described as a large, independent, full-service agency with a particular focus on creativity. Research in this agency involved participant observation throughout the period, along with the collection of semi-structured interview data. In particular, 40 interviews with members of the agency's main disciplines (strategy, creative, production, project management and others—each supposedly hierarchically equivalent), were conducted, leading to roughly 650 pages of transcribed conversation. Interviewees spanned a diverse range of seniority, experience, gender and age characteristics. They are identified by codes in order to maintain their anonymity: C refers to a creative; CD to a creative director; S to a strategist; P to a producer; and HCR to the head of creative resources. Finally, documentary sources such as emails, briefings and scripts for TV advertisements were also collected.

Although this study was conducted at a single agency, this chapter discusses the general practices that participants in the study indicated, both implicitly and explicitly, in various responses. These practices were not unique to the fieldwork agency as they also tallied with individuals' experiences in other advertising agencies. Through iterative rounds of coding and analysis, five key practices constituting the development of advertisements were identified and characterised: kicking off the creative process, developing strategies, generating ideas, realising concepts and evaluating the effects of ideas. In the following section these practices are described. The chapter concludes with a discussion of the insights on knowledge and practice gained from this research.

THE FIVE PRACTICES OF EVERYDAY DEVELOPMENT IN ADVERTISING

Kicking Off the Creative Process

'Kicking off the creative process' describes the gathering and analysis of a wide range of information to localise the clients' problems. The agency's advertising development started shortly after the organisation received clients' briefs, which included outlines of the communication problem they were facing. Client briefs served to define the problems clients were facing at that time—that is, their particular sales and marketing goals and challenges as they saw them—and thus the reasons why clients were approaching the advertising agency for help. Unsurprisingly, advertising practitioners therefore described their day-to-day job as 'problem solving'. As S9 noted, for example, "It's just about problem solving at its simplest. And yeah, helping clients to solve their problems to be able to exploit it for competitive advantage, really".

However, often clients were unsure about the exact outline of the issues they were facing, or they thought they had to tackle certain problems even though the real troubles lay somewhere else. Therefore, in addition to the information provided in clients' briefs, strategists normally gathered more information, both quantitative and qualitative in nature. Through processing and analysing this information they sought to enrich their understanding, and thereby get closer to the clients' situations. As S2 noted, "You'd take the brief from the client and kind of try and flesh [it] out as much as you can with the client, you know, the brief in terms of if you think there are any holes in it, if you think there are any sort of discrepancies or anything, or you think you're missing any information—[just] trying to get it sort of as shaped as you can". Sometimes this meant that clients provided access to business-relevant information only, to allow the strategist to develop a client brief for them. On these occasions it was thus not about shaping clients' briefs but engaging in their development. Through the shaping of the information provided by the clients, the advertising practitioners not only made sense of the problem at hand but also began developing initial ideas on how to tackle it. As noted by S4, "Very much what we do is we pose the advertising problem and then we solve the advertising problem".

Besides demographic information, such as age, gender or residency, strategists were particularly keen to identify 'consumer insights', which were characterised as rather hidden and hitherto unknown consumer characteristics they could build their solutions upon. For them, finding those hidden consumer characteristics was important in order to increase the solution's relevance as well as its unexpectedness (that is, its captivating originality). Sometimes the advertising practitioners tried to combine multiple consumer insights in order to connect with a broader range of people. To remain original, the particular consumer insight advertising practitioners would build upon would be "different in every situation," as S3 noted, but generally "there should be something human and interesting about it—not just a regurgitation of all the stuff that client's brought you".

The identification of consumer insights could take multiple forms. Strategists made use of specific cultural research services (e.g., trend reports), commissioned their own research (e.g., focus groups) and even used academic literature to get closer to the peculiarities of the target audiences (e.g., research studies). In addition, several advertising practitioners reported that they would interview family members and friends that matched the profiles of their clients' target consumers. S9 even reported that she read books with titles such as *The Mommy Myth, Confessions of a Scary Mommy* or *Mommy Wars* to sharpen her understanding of mothers, which were the target audience for a project she was developing a strategy for. Often, however, gathering information about the client as well as consumers appeared to be deductive rather than inductive in nature. In some ways it was driven by intuition; participants suggested that the goal was to "verify your own instinct", as S9 noted, and thus to confirm the advertising practitioners' initial gut feelings.

Developing Strategies

'Developing strategies' was rooted in the identification and organisation of interesting insights within information gathered and analysed by the agency staff, and their synthesis into creative briefs. In tandem, after all of the information that had been gathered throughout the 'kicking off the creative process' practices (alluded to above) had been processed and analysed, it was synthesised by individual strategists and transformed into a specific strategy that defined the particular steps required to solve the clients' problems and thus to achieve their marketing objectives. Thus the practice 'developing strategies' usually went hand in hand with the development of a creative brief, which functioned as a short record of the strategy on paper; in effect, description and prescription were melded together to a degree. As S1 noted, "So my role is to help identify what the business problems are, if there are any, and what the market context is, who we should be talking to, why we should be talking to them, what we should say, and then write that in theory, write that into a brief, which then I give to the creatives and they write an ad". The advertising practitioners, however, emphasised that strategies can involve a range of different solutions, of which only one would be the production of 'ads'. Despite the common generation and use of typical or classic advertisements (e.g., TV, radio or print advertisements), the advertising agency also developed business solutions (e.g., setting up a call centre to increase customer satisfaction) and experiential solutions (e.g., setting up events to activate a new product), as well as complex digital installations (e.g., creating a solution involving augmented reality to increase brand engagement).

In the process of arriving at the diverse possibilities for advertising solutions, creative briefs were important working documents in the creative teams' efforts to develop ideas. Creative briefs contained the essential information required to develop ideas that support the clients' marketing objectives (e.g., the advertising objectives; motivation, thoughts and feelings of the target audience; or the brand positioning and personality, primary outcome or 'take away', as explained in Shimp & Andrews 2013), and thus provided the framework in which 'generating ideas' had to take place. Most importantly, however, these creative briefs gave a sense of initial direction—and thus functioned as inspirational input and 'jumping-off points' on which creative teams could then build. Creatives had a degree of freedom, within limits; to ensure that the creative direction was addressing the perceived marketing problem, creative briefs were signed off by clients before being passed on to creative teams. Thus, since the creative brief combined input from the client, the agency, and also the consumers (e.g., through consumer research), it somehow captured the expectations of the gatekeepers and stakeholders with an interest in the creative work to follow.

Generating Ideas

'Generating ideas' describes the practice of the development of potentially realisable concepts for advertisements that built upon the creative briefs. After creative briefs were signed off, they were communicated to creative teams. In contrast to strategists, who were responsible for laying out the underlying strategy of the clients' solutions, creative teams were responsible for delivering the specific 'means': that is, they needed to generate specific ideas for TV, radio, print, business, or experiential or digital solutions that would support the clients' marketing objectives. Thus, as soon as the strategists shared creative briefs with the creative department, creative teams went away to develop creative executions.

However, before they actually started they engaged in the preceding practice alluded to above—'kicking off the creative process'—themselves; that is, they conducted their own research on clients and target audiences as well, to sharpen their own understanding of the clients and consumers for whom they were creating ideas. In addition, creative teams looked for inspiration in a variety of ways. Besides the use of various websites and internet media, many creative teams reported working outside the office to be closer to the people they are supposed to reach in order to gain inspiration. As CD1, for example, noted, "My inspiration is mainly from life and living and chatting to people". In this study creatives worked in a similar way to those in most other advertising agencies—as a team of two (a copywriter and an art director), enabling them to bounce ideas off each other before they were presented to the wider team. 'Generating ideas' was commonly referred to as 'delivering against the brief' (e.g., HCR1), thus emphasising the limitations the creative brief puts onto the creative team's practice. The circumscription of creativity this entailed was considered to be important; besides being 'original', creative executions had to be relevant and thus take the information stated in the creative brief into consideration.

Creative executions were regularly presented in reviews. Whereas 'creative reviews' were meetings in which ideas were presented internally to creative directors (and strategists), 'client reviews' were occasions in which clients judged ideas and decided which should be developed further. During these meetings 'routes' (i.e., advertising messages that could be executed in various different ways) that initially appeared to be promising were suddenly found to be inappropriate and were dropped while others were opened up for exploration. The practice of 'generating ideas' was therefore highly iterative in nature. In this way, advertising practitioners were "trying to discover ['right' ideas] through writing stuff" (C2). As CD1 noted, "Certainly on [brand name] we're reinventing the brand so we're learning and setting up principles as we write".

As soon as clients favoured specific ideas, creative teams developed variations of those ideas. This included suggestions about how these ideas might translate into other communication channels and thus what an entire campaign might look like. If the initial idea was, for example, an idea for a TV advertisement, suggestions were made about how this idea might come out in a digital, print or radio environment. As CD7 noted, ". . . you [. . .] come up with, kind of, the overview and then detail it out, like TV scripts and press and posters and other bigger ideas". Moreover, favoured ideas were taken into 'advertisement testing' in which consumers were asked to evaluate them. The resultant feedback from consumers could impact heavily on the clients' final decision—particularly if it was in line with the particular personal judgements of clients. Eventually, the clients signed an idea off that was then passed on into production.

If it was an idea for TV, directors were approached and asked to suggest their interpretation of the idea. Directors were expected to add their take on an idea (e.g., by shooting an idea in a 'Wes Anderson style'). The directors' 'treatments' (an in-depth, visual as well as discursive translation of the creative team's script) were preselected by the creative team and those most outstanding were suggested to the client. Finally, as soon as the client decided on a director's treatment, the idea was realised in the chosen media.

Realising Concepts

Realising concepts describes the production and thus transformation of ideas into final advertisements, after ideas were signed off by clients. That is, in 'realising concepts', advertising practitioners turned the creative execution that the creative teams came up with "into something more tangible, more practical" (P5). At this stage, producers seemed to take over the advertising development process. However, although producers became highly involved at this stage of the advertising development process, they worked in close contact with the creative team, who created the ideas and wanted to make sure that ideas were realised as envisioned.

The process of production began with the pre-production of the idea that had been signed off, which meant the detailed planning of its realisation. As with 'generating ideas', the production took place within strict frameworks, which were mainly defined by the timing and budget allocated to the project at hand. In pre-production all factors constituting an idea, such as the location and people involved, as well as a timetable, were discussed and decided upon with the advertising agency's staff, clients and external production companies. Due to the number of people involved in the realisation of an advertising idea, production days were heavily expensive and thus had to be kept to an absolute minimum. Through pre-planning, unforeseen troubles, which might risk the production of advertisements in time and on budget, were avoided to the greatest possible extent.

In pre-planning the signed-off 'treatment' of the director, which, as revealed above, included illustrations of the scenes and interpretations of ideas, formed the basis on which producers planned the production. As noted by P2, pre-planning takes place "in quite a logical way. So if I've got a script I'll break it down and work out how many people are in it. And therefore how many artists I need to cost for, kind of generally chat to the creatives to trying get an idea of the scale of it, to work out how many days you think you might need quite roughly. But often things like that are dictated by how much money you have". Consequently, as a producer, knowing the right external resources and being able to manage them as the production progressed was fundamentally important.

In actual production, the material (e.g., photos, audio, or video footage) required to construct the story, as illustrated in the director's 'treatment', was produced. In this step all of the people involved (e.g., creative teams, creative directors, the producer, clients and appropriate people from external production companies) came together at the production site and followed the detailed production plan that was worked out in pre-production. Creative teams as well as creative directors made sure that the director executed the idea as envisioned and agreed upon. Moreover, they made sure that the clients were happy with the production. As C6 noted, "the main thing you do [at a production site] is try and make sure that what you've imagined in your head or on paper, or however you imagined it, fully comes to life on the shoot". The producer, on the other hand, was responsible for ensuring that the production took place on time (and on budget). As P7 noted, "On the actual shoot day you get a shooting schedule from the production company, [. . .] [and] my main job is making sure that [this actually] happens".

After the raw material required to bring an idea to life was captured, it was passed on into 'post-production'. The raw material was then reviewed to identify those visuals that were most suitable for the purpose of telling the creative team's story. The material, which was thus filtered out, was then strung together to compile the first draft of the later TV, radio, print, business, experiential or digital solution. Finally, the draft was refined further. For a TV commercial that meant that the draft was processed in edit or sound suites, where it was graded and where sound, sound effects, and computer-animated elements were also added.

Evaluating the Effects of Ideas

Soon after ideas had been produced, they were launched in the market. Thus, evaluating the effects of ideas effectively describes the analysis of the effect of ideas on consumers, once they were launched in markets. That is, the advertising practitioners evaluated the performance of the advertising agency's ideas based on a range of different data—at least to a certain extent.

The process upon which the evaluation was based depended on the specific client the advertising practitioners was working with. Clients normally had their own specific methods of evaluation, as S8, for example, explained: "Different clients have different ways of doing it and we tend to fall in line with the way that the client wants to evaluate the research, rather than have our own set way of doing". Surprisingly, however, some advertising practitioners reported that not all clients would be interested in the evaluation of their campaigns or that data to evaluate campaigns would exist, but would not be shared with the advertising practitioners. Therefore, as S2 pointed out, "Understanding how it's working can sometimes be quite complex enough in itself".

However, for some advertising practitioners, measuring the success and failure of a campaign and thus knowing how well campaigns had worked out was considered "a sort of pride thing" (P5). Different levels and kinds of interest in the evaluation of the performance of ideas existed on the advertising agency side. Whereas strategists (as well as digital and experiential producers) seemed to care about the performance of ideas, creative teams were less interested. As P2 explained, "Generally once it's on air I kind of stop thinking about it and I move on to the next thing". In a similar vein C8 noted, "It's good to know if it's helped business and stuff, but I think that's kind of out of our bounds a little bit, you know?"

If creative teams monitored the success or failure of their idea, they were rather more interested in its very immediate effects and thus preferred qualitative instead of quantitative data. Thus Facebook, Twitter and YouTube were the favourite channels for creative teams to see how their ideas performed. CD2 explained the advantages of Facebook, Twitter and YouTube as follows: "It's incredible 'cause like it's so immediate and it's so raw and visceral, unmoderated. [. . .] You get what it is—what it says on the tin". Clients and other advertising practitioners also used these communication channels to monitor the performance of particular ideas, in addition to the evaluation of advertisements through conventional measures. As S6 noted, "As soon as an ad goes on air, the client will look straight [. . .] to YouTube views and they're looking on Twitter about what somebody said about their new commercial [. . .]. So unless you got your arms around that and see if you can respond accordingly and manage the client, what this all means accordingly then, yeah, you kind of need to do it basically".

Summary: A Process Constituted through Five Practices

The five practices that have been articulated above collectively provide a feel for the creative advertising development process, in its commercial context. These practices are summarised in table 8.1 below. The summary provided in the first five rows of the table—and the preceding sections of this chapter, which have provided a more detailed articulation of each of the practices—suggests a rather linear process. It should be noted, however, that

Table 8.1 Everyday development process practices

Practice	Description
Kicking off the creative process	The gathering and analysis of a wide range of information to localise the clients' problems.
Developing strategies	The identification of interesting insights within information gathered and analysed and their synthesis into creative briefs.
Generating ideas	The development of ideas for advertisements, which built upon the creative briefs.
Realising concepts	The production and thus transformation of ideas into final advertisements, after ideas were signed off by clients.
Evaluating the effects of ideas	The analysis of the effect of ideas on consumers, once they were launched in markets.
Working in discontinuity	The advertising practitioners' constant 'shifting' between one of the above practices and another.

most advertising practitioners were constantly 'shifting' between a range of the practices that have been described. This is because many advertising practitioners were working across different brands, across different projects of a brand, and across projects involving different forms of media, which impacted on the specific design of the advertising development processes in which they were involved. This is normal for the industry. Moreover, the projects were normally at different stages of the advertising development process and thus demanded different types of action. Thus, the practices of 'kicking off the creative process', 'developing strategies', 'generating ideas' and 'realising concepts' often overlapped. Consequently, there was not simply one advertising development process at any one time within the advertising agency, but multiple advertising development processes at the same time. The broad blending of practices thus applied to almost all advertising practitioners, with the temporary exception of those who were working on larger productions and thus allocated to a limited range of projects only. Thus a 'meta-practice', of working in discontinuity, is also included within the summary table.

DISCUSSION AND CONCLUSION

Overall, this research identified practices of five kinds, which can be regarded as representative of the industry as a whole, as repeatedly confirmed by participants. These practices provide useful insights into ways in which everyday development processes at advertising agencies are organised and thus provide new insights into the ways the advertising practitioners' day-to-day doings and process knowledge (c.f. Hibbert & Huxham 2005) are enacted. The account reveals how advertising practitioners work with each other and their clients in the process of developing and delivering advertisements.

The account falls short in explaining how advertising practitioners put their distinct creativity *understandings,* through some type of shared or contested *aesthetic* knowledge, into practice. That is, although they explain 'standard' practices common at many advertising agencies, they fail to expose the distinctive understanding of advertising practitioners regarding ways in which advertisements should be produced and how they should look and thus what distinguishes the particular 'creative code' (as Stuhlfaut 2011 refers to it) of an individual advertising agency from the creative code of another. The practices do, however, provide a useful generic understanding of creative process knowledge in the advertising industry that offers more detail than the insights offered by earlier studies—and begins to reveal interesting tensions.

In particular, this chapter has shown some divergent views (for example, in relation to evaluation) at work within the enactment of everyday development practices; in common with the creative processes at most advertising agencies these seem to be related to tensions emerging from conflicts between art and commerce, as reported in previous literature (Hirschman 1989; Hackley & Kover 2007; De Gregorio *et al.* 2012). The different creative understandings of advertising practitioners in different roles seem potentially to have some bearing on the ways in which such tensions play out; implicitly, there is a relationship between differences in role-related knowledge and the tensions evident when the practices that support creative processes are enacted. And while the agency studied in this research sought to be creatively led, the advertising practitioners reported many similarities to everyday practices at other agencies. Thus one can speculate that diverging from practices common at many advertising agencies might also be a source of tensions and confusion, even if such disruption was argued to foster creativity. Alternatively it may be argued that the practice of 'generating ideas' (as described above) contains the potential disruption of novelty within activities that are regarded as reserved for just a few creative specialists—leaving the commercial process that circumscribes generative creative practices largely unchanged.

SUGGESTED FURTHER READINGS

Amabile, T.M. (1996) *Creativity in context.* Boulder, CO: Westview Press.
    This offers a good overview of creative processes *per se,* with a focus on what *individuals* do in such processes. It is widely cited in research that spans a range of industries beyond advertising, and will be helpful for those reflecting on how the insights in this chapter might relate to other contexts and individuals in a range of professions.

Hibbert, P., & Huxham, C. (2005) A little about the mystery: Process learning as collaboration evolves. *European Management Review*. 2(1): 59–69.

This paper considers the complex relationship between the process of learning how to work collaboratively and the generation of 'new knowledge'. It is therefore helpful as a starting point for reflection on how different forms of learning and 'knowledge creation' processes can be understood and engaged with, extending the insights of this chapter beyond 'pure' creative settings.

Davey, N. (2013) *Unfinished worlds: Hermeneutics, aesthetics and Gadamer*. Edinburgh: Edinburgh University Press.

This provides a Gademerian 'take' on aesthetics in relation to the possibility of participation in shared meaning. It will appeal to those who want to explore the problems of aesthetic understanding raised in this chapter through philosophical reflection.

REFERENCES

De Gregorio, F., Cheong, Y., & Kim, K. (2012) Intraorganizational conflict within advertising agencies: Antecedents & outcomes. *Journal of Advertising*. 41(3): 19–34.

De Waal Malefyt, T., & Morais, R.J. (2010) Creativity, brands, & the ritual process: Confrontation & resolution in advertising agencies. *Culture & Organization*. 16(4): 333–347.

Geiger, D. (2009) Revisiting the concept of practice: Toward an argumentative understanding of practicing. *Management Learning*. 40(2): 129–144.

Gherardi, S. (2009) Practice? It's a matter of taste! *Management Learning*. 40(5): 535–550.

Hackley, C., & Kover, A.J. (2007) The trouble with creatives: Negotiating creative identity in advertising agencies. *International Journal of Advertising*. 26(1): 63–78.

Hibbert, P., & Huxham, C. (2005) A little about the mystery: Process learning as collaboration evolves. *European Management Review*. 2(1): 59–69.

Hirschman, E.C. (1989) Role-based models of advertising creation & production. *Journal of Advertising*. 18(4): 42–53.

McLeod, C., O'Donohoe, S., & Townley, B. (2011) Pot Noodles, placements & peer regard: Creative career trajectories & communities of practice in the British advertising industry. *British Journal of Management*. 22(1): 114–131.

Moeran, B. (2005) Tricks of the trade: The performance & interpretation of authenticity. *Journal of Management Studies*. 42(5): 901–922.

Morais, R.J. (2007) Conflict & confluence in advertising meetings. *Human Organization*. 66(2): 150–159.

Nicolini, D. (2011) Practice as the site of knowing: Insights from the field of telemedicine. *Organization Science*. 22(3): 602–620.

Nyilasy, G., Canniford, R., & Kreshel, P.J. (2013) Ad agency professionals' mental models of advertising creativity. *European Journal of Marketing*. 47(10): 1691–1710.

Pratt, A.C. (2006) Advertising & creativity, a governance approach: A case study of creative agencies in London. *Environment & Planning A*. 38(10): 1883–1899.

Schatzki, T.R. (2005) Peripheral vision: The sites of organizations. *Organization Studies*. 26(3): 465–484.

Shimp, T.A., & Andrews, J.C. (2013) *Advertising promotion & other aspects of integrated marketing communications*. Mason, OH: Cengage Learning.

Stuhlfaut, M.W. (2011) The creative code: An organisational influence on the creative process in advertising. *International Journal of Advertising*. 30(2): 283–304.

Whittington, R. (2011) The practice turn in organization research: Towards a disciplined transdisciplinarity. *Accounting, Organizations & Society*. 36(3): 183–186.

9 Mind the Gap! Exploring Academics' and Professional Practitioners' Views of Accounting Knowledge

Lorna Stevenson, Louise Crawford and John Ferguson

INTRODUCTION

As with many other professions, there are disputes about what counts as appropriate knowledge within the accounting profession. Who creates and defines knowledge for the accounting profession is intertwined in a "jurisdictional battle" between professional accountancy firms, professional accountancy bodies, and accounting academics. This chapter examines differing perspectives on knowledge within the profession, particularly during the process by which aspiring accountants become professionally qualified. Drawing on insights from those with a stake in knowledge production in accountancy practice, we explore perceptions of credentialed knowledge in accounting, sources of new knowledge, the role of research, and how students might be exposed to research findings. In this sense, our chapter explicitly considers the knowledge-practice interface, and whether (or the extent to which) research knowledge is brought into the accountancy education process.

This chapter draws on the perceptions of key constituencies in the accountancy knowledge production process: (i) representatives from the education departments of professional accountancy bodies, (ii) representatives from the research departments of professional accountancy bodies, and (iii) accounting academics. From our research, we see different epistemologies in accounting practice and research, and contested perceptions of what is considered valuable in the context of knowledge production and use. We suggest that this results in what could be termed a "jurisdictional battle" between accountancy practitioners and accounting academics, with the professional bodies, although far from independent of practitioners, mediating from the middle.

The next section provides an overview of professional accountancy bodies in the UK, their programmes of professional education, and the influence of the "Big 4" accountancy firms. This is followed by a discussion of knowledge as it pertains to the accountancy profession. The findings from 20 semi-structured interviews with professional body representatives and accounting educators are then presented. Finally we offer some concluding comments on knowledge and knowing in accountancy.

ACCOUNTANCY BODIES, PROFESSIONAL EDUCATION AND THE "BIG 4" ACCOUNTANCY FIRMS

The initial establishment and history of the UK's accountancy profession might be seen to reflect the needs of the industrial revolution; for example, the world's first professional accountancy body, the Institute of Chartered Accountants of Scotland (ICAS), was established in 1854. Contemporary professional accountancy trainees have to complete a 3-year period of relevant practical experience and pass formal professional examinations prior to being admitted to professional body membership. While much accounting work may be done by unqualified practitioners, a professional qualification is required to undertake certain state-sanctioned tasks, such as the audit of companies' statutory financial statements.

The UK government is responsible for maintaining a legal framework for audit regulation, mostly derived from EU directives. However, it delegates the detail of oversight, supervision and qualification of statutory auditors to the UK Financial Reporting Council (FRC)—which is responsible for overseeing the activity of six professional accountancy bodies in the UK. The oversight and training of professional accountants is largely controlled by the professional bodies themselves, each of whom is responsible for developing and delivering a programme of professional education; assessing putative members; validating professional experience; and admitting, supervising and disciplining members.

Professional Accountancy Bodies

There are six chartered accountancy bodies in the UK. The number of professional accountancy bodies is partly due to the different specialist roles practised by professional accountants, and different jurisdictions in the UK (although the accountancy bodies are now positioning themselves as global bodies and not jurisdiction restricted). The six accountancy bodies are the Association of Chartered Certified Accountants (ACCA); the Chartered Institute of Management Accountants (CIMA); the Chartered Institute of Public Finance and Accountancy (CIPFA); the Institute of Chartered Accountants in England and Wales (ICAEW); Chartered Accountants Ireland (CAI); and the Institute of Chartered Accountants of Scotland (ICAS). All, apart from CIMA, have responsibility for offering a statutory auditor qualification and for supervision of the work of statutory auditors. Different accountancy bodies have emerged to focus on different niches—and in many cases their current students continue to reflect that history. For example, over 80% of ICAS, CAI and ICAEW students are located in public practice, largely undertaking audit and consultancy; CIMA's niche is industry and commerce, where 76% of its students are employed and directly engaged in organisational management and decision-making; and the ACCA's students are more evenly distributed across all employment sectors, although 78% of its students are located outside the UK and Ireland (FRC 2015a). In total, the professional bodies governed by the FRC have over 335,000 (166,000) members (students) in the UK and Ireland, and over 485,000 (545,000) worldwide (FRC 2015a).

In addition to being under FRC oversight, the six UK chartered accountancy bodies are members of the International Federation of Accountants (IFAC). IFAC has four boards that set international standards for professional accountants in Audit, Ethics, Education, and Public Sector Accounting. As IFAC members, the UK professional bodies obligate themselves to comply with these IFAC standards (IFAC 2015). In addition, IFAC member bodies are obligated to comply with the International Financial Reporting Standards (IFRS) issued by the International Accounting Standard Board (IASB). Indeed, since 2005, listed companies operating in the European Union are required under statute to prepare IFRS-compliant financial statements.

Influenced by this framework of regulation and standards, programmes of professional education tend to focus on the technical aspects of accounting and audit practice, and how to interpret and comply with standards and legislation. Nevertheless, each of the UK professional bodies develops and regulates its own particular programme of professional education and training, controlling their own syllabi and employing experienced examiners to assess their students. Each professional body also offers different routes to attain a professional qualification in terms of entry and practical experience requirements. For example, over 90% of ICAS and CAI training contracts required degree entry in 2014; 79% of CAI students were recruited with a degree recognised by CAI as "relevant" to their professional accounting qualification (discussed further below), whereas around 50% of students training with ICAS held a non-relevant degree (FRC 2015a). In terms of practical experience requirements, trainees with CAI, ICAS and ICAEW obtain training contracts with accredited employers and acquire their practical experience at the same time as taking their professional exams. ACCA takes a different approach, whereby practical experience and professional examinations can be acquired at different times. Notwithstanding these differences, the changing needs of society, developments in business and strong forces of homogenisation mean that the professional bodies, especially ICAS, ACCA, ICAEW and CAI, increasingly mimic one another's syllabi and routes to qualification in their competition for students and members. table 9.1 sets out key characteristics of five of the six professional accountancy bodies in the UK—the ones examined in our study.

The education syllabi of the professional accountancy bodies represent standardised accounting knowledge and have a strong influence on many

Table 9.1 Key characteristics of five UK professional accountancy bodies

Name of body	Year established	Qualification route* (membership nomenclature)	Number of members (students) in 2014 (FRC 2015a)	Percentage of students holding a (relevant) degree in 2015 (FRC 2015a)	About us/continuing professional development (CPD) required?
Association of Chartered Certified Accountants (ACCA)	1904	• 14 exams (nine exemptions available) • 36 months' experience in a relevant role • (ACCA)	174,000 (374,000)	51 (26)	"We are the world's leading body for professional accountants, with over 110 years of experience, innovation and excellence. We champion opportunity within accountancy, demonstrate excellence through our qualifications, and act as a driving force within the accounting profession to constantly improve working practices". CPD required. (ACCA)
Institute of Chartered Accountants of Scotland (ICAS)	1854	• 11 exams (5 exemptions available) • 450 days' relevant practical experience • (CA)	20,000 (3,000)	98 (42)	"ICAS is a professional body for more than 20,000 world class business men and women who work in the UK and in more than 100 countries around the world. Our members have all achieved the internationally recognised and respected CA qualification (Chartered Accountant). We are an educator, examiner, regulator, and thought leader". CPD required. (ICAS)
Institute of Chartered Accountants in England and Wales (ICAEW)	1880	• 15 exams (maximum 5 exemptions) • 450 days' practical work experience • (ACA)	144,000 (22,000)	78 (20)	"We provide our members with knowledge and guidance based on the highest ethical and technical standards. We shape opinion, understanding and delivery to ensure the highest standards in business and in the public interest". CPD required. (ICAEW)

(Continued)

Table 9.1 (Continued)

Name of body	Year established	Qualification route* (membership nomenclature)	Number of members (students) in 2014 (FRC 2015a)	Percentage of students holding a (relevant) degree in 2015 (FRC 2015a)	About us/continuing professional development (CPD) required?
Chartered Accountants Ireland (CAI)	1888	• 10 exams (exemptions vary) • 3 years' practical work experience • (CA)	24,000 (7,000)	94 (79)	"Chartered Accountants Ireland (The Institute) is a membership body representing 23,000 influential members throughout the globe. Our role is to educate, represent and support our members. Our members work in senior positions in practice and industry. We are committed to restoring confidence at every level of the economy. We work with governments and businesses to raise awareness of the importance of sound financial advice". CPD required. (ICAI)
Chartered Institute of Management Accountants (CIMA)	1919	• 12 exams (exemptions vary) • 3 years' verified relevant work experience • (ACMA)	100,000 (128,000)	54 (45)	"CIMA is the world's largest and leading professional body of management accountants. Our mission is to help people and businesses to succeed in the public and private sectors. We have more than 227,000 members and students in 179 countries. They work at the heart of business in industry, commerce and not for profit organisations. We have strong relationships with employers, and sponsor leading research". CPD required. (CIMA)

* Different routes to qualification are available depending on whether the student is a school-leaver, a graduate, a holder of a relevant degree or post-graduate qualification, a person changing careers, or already a member of a different accounting body. The indicative routes highlighted here are the most prominent on each body's website.

Note: Professional accountancy bodies regularly review and amend their approaches to programme delivery and assessment prior to admission to membership. In this respect, the details elaborated in Column 3 of table 9.1 reflect the approach taken by these bodies at the time of writing.

undergraduate accounting degree curricula. This means that a) holders of such degrees are exempt from some of the professional bodies' examinations, and b) many undergraduate students of accredited education programmes experience little choice in what they study on their accounting degree programme. Due to the four-year rather than three-year honours degree programmes in Scotland, students may have the option to study non-accredited material, often critically informed by social science, in the final year of their honours degree (Bunniss 2006; Duff & Marriott 2012).

With the exception of CAI, individuals who wish to qualify as accountants need not possess an accounting degree in order to undergo professional training or to be eligible to study for the professional qualifying examinations; thus professionally qualified accountants have graduated from a wide range of degree programmes. Nonetheless accounting is a popular degree choice in UK universities—made by 33,000 students in 2008/9 (see Target Jobs 2015)—even though many accounting graduates do not go on to work in the accountancy profession (HESA 2010 in Duff & Marriott 2012:17). Where a university wishes to offer a professionally accredited accounting degree, it must undergo regular inspections and accreditation exercises with each of the professional institutes whose marque it seeks. Each accountancy body has different criteria for accreditation, and so universities offering accounting undergraduate education must decide which, if any, of the bodies they wish to be accredited by. Universities are at liberty to seek as many or as few accreditations as they wish, and often deploy professional body recognition as a marketing tool in their own student recruitment efforts.

Employers Including the "Big 4" Accountancy and Professional Service Firms

Some indication of the power of the "Big 4" accountancy firms—Deloitte & Touche, Ernst & Young, PriceWaterhouseCoopers and KPMG—over accounting practice and related educational development may be illustrated in two ways. Firstly, by their domination of the audit market for the UK's largest companies listed on the London Stock Exchange: for financial statements ending in 2014, 94 of the top 100 (and 234 of the top 250) companies had Big 4 auditors. Secondly, the professional accountancy curricula, as well as accredited undergraduate equivalents, are heavily influenced by the needs of these Big 4 employers (Duff & Marriott 2012:4). Not only is the content of accounting education shaped by their needs, but these firms indirectly shape codified accounting knowledge in another important respect. In particular, course content (in both professional and university contexts) reflects the developments and content of accounting standards (i.e., the guidelines for financial reporting that specify how transactions are to be recognised, measured, presented and disclosed in financial statements). In this respect, it seems apposite to note that the Big 4 accountancy firms "are centrally involved in regulation" (Cooper and Robson 2006:433). In particular, they directly affect the accounting standard-setting process by virtue of having representation on regulatory bodies and standard setting boards; directly funding standard-setting boards; and lobbying extensively during the standard-setting process (Cooper and Robson 2006; Larson and Kenny 2011).

KNOWLEDGE SYSTEMS IN ACCOUNTANCY

Knowledge in accountancy is often seen in terms of three arenas: (i) the practice dimension; (ii) that which is taught via formally educating students; and (iii) research knowledge contained in academic journals. Echoing discussions in Chapter 2 (knowledge), we might see "empirical knowing" as *either* knowledge of the content and application of accounting standards *or* research-informed understanding of the societal impact of accountancy; "theoretical knowing" as *either* an ability to prepare financial statements *or* conceptual understanding of the logical cohesion of the various accounting standards; and "experiential knowing" as *either* the professional practitioner's "craft and mastery" *or* the academic's craft. Making sense of debates about knowledge in accounting demands that we understand which "knowledge" or system of knowledge is being discussed—especially as Freidson (1988:xiii) notes:

> Practitioners, administrators and teacher-researchers . . . [e]ach has a different perspective on the relevance and use of the profession's formal knowledge in the different tasks one performs. This creates differences in what knowledge is actually employed [and, we show below, what knowledge is valued]. The outcome is sufficiently variable and indeterminate to require us to adopt an interactive view of the relations between knowledge and power.

Sources of knowledge in accountancy and the processes by which these permeate the discipline have long been discussed in the accounting literature, though settled views have not yet emerged. For example, Rodgers & Williams (1996:52) noted, "There seems to be an acknowledged problem with the process of knowledge creation in the accounting academy, but there has yet been little systematic analysis of that knowledge process". Similarly, Hopwood (1988:573) called "for a much more substantial investigation of the functioning and control of knowledge in professionalised accountancy".

Accounting academics undertake research—sometimes funded by professional accountancy bodies—and professional firms also publish research of a more "applied" nature. However, findings in academic journals are rarely accessed by professional students or accountants. Indeed it is often noted that, in both the university and professional body context, "the accounting curriculum has included a significant amount of rules-based and technique-driven content, arguably at the expense of more conceptual, principles-based and contemporary material" (e.g., Duff & Marriott 2012:3). At its core there has been a long-standing tension around the role of research in the university teaching of accounting. This is somewhat exemplified by Sterling's (1973:49) observation that

> [accounting] education and practice seem to be complementary in that educators teach accepted practice and practitioners accept and practice what they are taught. This complementary relationship excludes research from the chain of events that determine what is taught and what is practiced. Research is an isolated activity in accounting.

Although accounting academic research is often viewed as disconnected from what is happening in the profession, we see benefits in exposing practising accountants to research-informed knowledge because this is more likely to result in reflective practitioners, who are more cognizant of their public interest obligations (which may differ from the narrower expediency of their organisational or employer goals). In order to understand some of the challenges of moving in this direction, we next provide an outline of participants' views of the accountancy profession's knowledge system(s).

INTERVIEWS WITH RESEARCH AND EDUCATION DEPARTMENT REPRESENTATIVES OF THE PROFESSIONAL ACCOUNTANCY BODIES

We sought to examine the extent to which academic research in accountancy was seen by representatives of professional accountancy bodies and accounting academics as contributing to accounting knowledge (and practice). We undertook semi-structured interviews with both the education and research arms of the five professional bodies listed in table 9.1. These two arms represent syllabus matters and knowledge advancement respectively. Four interviews were conducted with the education representatives of these bodies and five interviews with the research representatives. A further eleven interviews were undertaken with accounting academics, who were delivering professionally accredited accounting programmes in eleven different Scottish universities. All the interviews were conducted in 2009–2010 and they were either face-to-face or via telephone, lasting between thirty minutes and two hours. Table 9.2 describes each of the interviewees and their affiliations.

The interviews explored perceptions of credentialed knowledge and sources of new knowledge in accountancy, the role of research, and how students might be exposed to research findings. The findings from the interviews are discussed below in relation to two themes: sources of knowledge in accountancy and whose knowledge is taught in accounting education.

Table 9.2   Overview of interviewee affiliations

Interviewee*	Affiliation	Connection to professional body (PB)
Vivien—PB1-R	PB1**	Research (R) representative
Jan—PB2-R	PB2	Research representative
Lesley—PB3-R	PB3	Research representative
Kim—PB4-R	PB4	Research representative
Nikita—PB5-R	PB5	Research representative
Stevie—PB2-E	PB2	Education (E) representative
Robin—PB3-E	PB3	Education representative
Charlie—PB4-E	PB4	Education representative
Frankie—PB5-E	PB5	Education representative
Alex—AA1	University—accounting academic (AA)	Member (M) of PB3
Chris—AA2	University—accounting academic	Member of PB1
Ronnie—AA3	University—accounting academic	Member of PB1
Sam—AA4	University—accounting academic	Member of PB1
Jamie—AA5	University—accounting academic	
Jerry—AA6	University—accounting academic	Member of PB4
Bobby—AA7	University—accounting academic	Member of PB2
Andy—AA8	University—accounting academic	
Freddie—AA9	University—accounting academic	Member of PB1
Laurie—AA10	University—accounting academic	Member of PB2
Jesse—AA11	University—accounting academic	

* Names were randomly chosen to anonymise interviewees and do not reflect real names, nationalities or gender.
** The Education representative of Professional Body 1 declined to be interviewed without providing a reason
PB = Professional Body; AA = Accounting Academic; R = Research; E= Education

Sources of Knowledge in Accountancy

Professional Body Research Arm Interviewees

Accountancy firms, industry, consultancies, think tanks, professional bodies, standards and regulatory organisations, university academics, competitor institutes, and political and economic developments were all cited as sources of new knowledge in accounting by the PB research arm interviewees. For example, Jan (PB2-R) noted the importance of the academy, practice, consultancies, technology, political and economic climate—for example, compliance and Fred Goodwin [the infamous head of Royal Bank of Scotland (RBS) at the time of the 2007 global financial crisis], and external shocks

as sources of new accountancy knowledge; nonetheless this interviewee suspected that "professional body research impact is less than we would want it to be".

New standards from regulatory bodies such as the International Accounting Standards Board (IASB) were identified by Nikita (PB5-R) as new accounting knowledge, echoing Abbott (1988:177): "Some professions . . . receive new knowledge willy-nilly from external sources, as does accounting from regulatory bodies".

Jan (PB2-R) further noted that one of their magazines was purely for student members and that findings from research work funded by the PB were regularly reported in that publication; in addition signposts to research findings and their implications were also regularly displayed for an online community of student members. Reflecting the distinction made in Chapter 2 between "knowing *that* and knowing *how*", Kim (PB4-R) disseminated research findings exploring "how" topics are taught to education colleagues, but saw research on "what" topics are taught as of less interest to those colleagues. Stevie (PB2-E) expressed concern that, given the speed of change and of new knowledge development, university education needed to focus on teaching students *how* to think, rather than emphasising *what* to learn.

Vivien (PB1-R) distinguished between practice-oriented research and what was termed "blue-sky" research; this interviewee stated that accounting degree holders will "come across lots of different research during their studies" but that graduates with "non-relevant" (non-accounting) degrees "probably won't even be aware that there is any research in accounting". It was further stated, "I cannot imagine at any [Institute] Committee meeting discussing how any research is, or can be, used in our teaching—it's *never* on the agenda" (*emphasis* in original).

Highlighting the indeterminacy of accountancy knowledge, and the consistent view of it as a "thing", external to individuals' lived experience, Lesley (PB3-R) noted that students were exposed to new accounting knowledge via "[academic] journals, newsletters, professional body materials, tuition and workshops, and on the job training"; we are struck by the absence of practical experience in this list.

Professional Body Education Arm Interviewees

Interviewees from the educational arm of professional bodies saw their roles as focused on delivering employer-relevant education and ensuring that the education content and process were fit for that purpose. Thus new knowledge in the form of research—unless it related to how students learn—was deemed of little relevance. Robin (PB3-E) stated that "the curriculum needs to be fit for purpose and for customers' [seen as employers'] needs". Such an observation highlights the existence of "different knowledge processes in accounting" (Rodgers & Williams 1996:52). Indeed, this may help explain why "the academy and profession have perennially 'failed' to settle upon an agreed core of accounting knowledge" (Poullaos 2010:66).

In this sense Frankie (PB5-E) also noted, "We are mindful that the public expects accountants to know certain things" and that in any syllabus "these [techniques and standards] are sacrosanct". Implications of such an approach may be evident in Robin's comment that when reviewing the syllabus, "80% [of the curriculum] is fixed, with [only] 20% available for changes". However, Stevie (PB2-E) also noted that the "professional body curricula lags behind [academic] research; for example CSR [corporate social responsibility] has been on research agendas since [the] 1980s, became more mainstream in accounting research in the 1990s, but professional body curricula only adopted it in the 21st century". Concern that the gap between academics and practice was growing was highlighted by Charlie (PB4-E), who commented that "the academic community should be the engine room of ideas of why we do what we do and how we do it".

University-Based Interviewees

Asked about the source(s) of new knowledge in the accountancy discipline, academic Alex (AA1) noted that "a lot is driven by professional developments and that is reflected in the textbooks and syllabus". Jesse (AA11) too explained, "The lecturer does not create new knowledge, but it comes from the text[book]". This theme of accountancy knowledge as external to lecturers and consumed by them for subsequent relaying to their students was also highlighted by Sam (AA4), who observed "individuals keeping up to date in our reading [professional magazines, professional body bulletins, textbooks, journals] and on what's going on in the profession [and from conferences]". Bobby (AA7) and Chris (AA2) also cited a similar list of influences and external sources of accountancy knowledge.

A rather particular, and perhaps confused, view of knowledge was offered by Ronnie (AA3). He commented that accounting scandals and changes in the regulatory framework were identified as sources of new teaching material, but said, "I do not know if I would go so far as to say [that] anyone here [in this university] creates knowledge". He was "not convinced that the latest IFRS [International Financial Reporting Standard—effectively one of the main sets of rules for accounting] is a new piece of knowledge. It is just a way of dealing with an accounting issue . . . a practical technique . . . [I teach] my understanding of how you might apply a particular technique . . . the knowledge content would be driven by the standard setter". In this perspective, regulation is a source of new knowledge in accountancy. Standard-setters produce knowledge products, which academics then need to translate into know-how (to apply) for students.

Jerry (AA6) saw new knowledge in accountancy coming from "business organisations and clients" in terms of practical developments. He observed that the professional body has "to sit in the middle [between professional firms and academics] listening to what is happening in different areas and bringing that in"; as a consequence the codified knowledge in any emergent syllabus would be a compromise between these competing influences. This comment suggests a mediating role for professional bodies, as opposed to what much of the literature presents as a more controlling role. It also suggests that in accountancy, universities and practice are pursuing different objectives, and thus there is a need for some reconciliatory mediation.

A different, more overarching, view of both relevant and useful knowledges was offered by Freddie (AA9), who noted that although some academic colleagues may see new knowledge coming from the accountancy profession and from commercial practice, he is "trying to encourage students to challenge knowledge structures rather than just absorb [them]". Reflecting debate around accounting standard-setting, Jamie (AA5) too emphasised the need for wider awareness of "whose knowledge gets taught" and "whose rules run things" (see also Flower 1997; Fuller 2004; Botzem and Quack 2009).

Whose Knowledge Is Taught in Accountancy?

Training as a professional accountant is about both passing technical examinations and socialisation and immersion in a practical context. Reflecting this combination, in Chapter 2 (on knowledge) the intertwining of three aspects of knowledge is discussed: episteme ("research informed knowledge"); techne (skill resulting from "hands-on experience"); and phronesis ("judgement, including culturally relevant morals"). Each of these aspects of knowledge could be identified in what interviewees saw as necessary knowledge in accounting. For example, Laurie (AA10) and Andy (AA8) identified research findings (episteme) and accrediting professional bodies' syllabi (techne) as important forms of knowledge. Similarly, Lesley (PB3-R) distinguished between knowledge in terms of "evidence" which comes from research, and other forms of knowing, which "can come from all sorts of places" including work, study and society. However, interviewees were not entirely convinced that these strands were intertwined in professional accountancy education. Many of their comments tended to echo the "perception of a 'schism' between academic and practising accountants" (Rodgers & Williams 1996:52).

We would argue that accounting knowledge is both discovered by researchers and constructed by professional firms and standard-setters, but the latter appear to have the upper hand, especially in professional education. Interviewees presented a view of the accounting education process that is firmly tied to practice in that it seeks to ensure that credentialed practitioners know *that* and know *how* (and two of the authors' own experiences support this). The accounting education process seeks to convey and assess students' grasp of data and information, and their combination of information, experience and judgement.

The emphasis on knowing by doing was not only discussed by professional body interviews. It was also highlighted by academic interviewees, who additionally noted that lack of professional accountancy experience was an impediment for some of their academic colleagues. Such observations accord with findings from studies concerned with the socialisation of professional accountants and the importance of large firms in shaping professional identity and perceptions of what constitutes knowledge—especially knowledge deemed essential for professional success (Anderson *et al.* 2001:101; see also, Power 1991; Covaleski *et al.* 1998; Anderson *et al.* 2005). Research has shown that professional accountancy curricula are heavily influenced by professional accountancy firms, and these syllabi in turn have considerable influence on undergraduate curricula and undergraduate accounting textbooks (Ferguson *et al.* 2008; Duff & Marriott 2012). This was also highlighted by both the professional body and academic interviewees. In the context of a professional body syllabus review process, Charlie (PB4-E) commented on an instance where the "Big 4 employers won on a particular matter" and stated, "The balance of power lies with the big firms, and the employers".

While often acknowledging the heavy influence of the accountancy firms, our professional body interviewees were also keen to point to a wider range of influences on professional accountancy syllabi, including debates among professional bodies, members' views, advice from technical experts, and comments and advice from universities and other educators, as well as the needs of accountancy firms and industry. Indeed, Robin (PB3-E) said that "the world and his wife contribute to syllabus development". Kim (PB4-R) also commented that whether one was a relevant or non-relevant degree holder and the location of one's professional training could also influence what accountancy knowledge was learned. These wider influences, however, do not detract from the overall picture of an accountancy profession where hands-on technical skills and judgement routed in experience trump research-informed knowledge both in training processes and in professional practice.

CONCLUDING COMMENTS

We have explored the views of key actors in the domain of professional accountancy education on where new knowledge in accountancy comes from. Interviewees' responses suggest a limited role for research knowledge in influencing the accredited syllabi of universities, and the professional bodies' own syllabi. Knowing by doing is privileged in professional accountancy in the sense that the professional qualification process focuses on technical skills, experiential learning and the content of technical standards over what might be seen as research-based or theoretical learning (Inanga & Scheider 2005).

Our findings highlight what is perhaps at times a limited and underdeveloped view of knowledge and knowledge diffusion within accountancy education, when compared with the more sophisticated and nuanced discussion of knowledge and practice evident elsewhere in this book. The majority of our interviewees agreed that the main (and sometimes the only) source of change in accounting comes from practice and not from education or research (Sterling 1973). We contend that the apparently limited influence of research-informed knowledge does not accord with either accountancy's role in the academy and society, or the public interest obligations arising from professional bodies' royal charters (Sikka *et al.* 1989). The findings reveal lack of agreement (and some contestation) over what counts as appropriate knowledge in the accountancy profession. Some argue that the professionalisation project is never complete (Macdonald 1999)—accountancy it appears is no different in this regard, and the indeterminacy of accounting knowledge may partly explain why this is so.

ACKNOWLEDGEMENTS

The authors wish to thank the research participants, reviewers and participants in KPEC workshops. We are grateful for the financial support provided by the Carnegie Trust.

SUGGESTED FURTHER READINGS

Duff, A., & Marriott, N. (2012) *Teaching and research: Partners or competitors?* ICAS: Edinburgh.
  This ICAS-sponsored publication provides an overview of the relationship between research and teaching in UK professional accounting education through interviews and a questionnaire survey.
Power, M.K. (1991) Educating accountants: Towards a critical ethnography. *Accounting, Organizations and Society.* 16(4): 333–353.
  This powerful reflection on the author's experience of professional accounting training brings much of the discussion in this arena to life.
BBC Radio 4 (2014) File on 4. *The Accountant Kings.* Available: http://www.bbc.co.uk/programmes/b03wpjjq. Accessed: March 9.
  This investigative radio programme reveals some of the power and influence of the "Big 4" professional accountancy firms in many areas of our lives.

REFERENCES

Abbott, A. (1988) *The system of Professions: An essay on the division of expert labor.* The University of Chicago Press: London.

ACCA. Available: http://www.accaglobal.com/uk/en.html. Accessed: August 10, 2015.

Anderson-Gough, F., Grey, C., & Robson, K. (2001) Tests of time: Organizational time-reckoning and the making of accountants in two multi-national accounting firms. *Accounting, Organizations and Society*. 26: 99–122.

Anderson-Gough, F., Grey, C., & Robson, K. (2005) "Helping them to forget . . . " the organizational embedding of gender relations in public audit firms. *Accounting, Organizations and Society*. 30: 469–490.

BBC (2014) Radio 4, File on 4. *The Accountant Kings*. Available: http://www.bbc.co.uk/programmes/b03wpjjq 9 March. Accessed: August 14, 2015.

Botzem, S., & Quack, S. (2009) (No) Limits to Anglo-American accounting? Reconstructing the history of the international accounting standards committee—A review article. *Accounting, Organizations and Society*. 34: 988–998.

Bunniss, S. (2006) *Purpose and gift; Resisting vocational capture in accounting education: The story from one Scottish University*. PhD thesis, Glasgow: University of Strathclyde.

CAI. Available: https://www.charteredaccountants.ie/. Accessed: August 10, 2015.

CIMA. Available: http://www.cimaglobal.com/. Accessed: August 10, 2015.

Cooper, D.J., & Robson, K. (2006) Accounting, professions and regulation: Locating the sites of professionalization. *Accounting, Organizations and Society*. 31: 415–444.

Covaleski, M.A., Dirsmith, M.W., Heian, J.B., & Samuel, S. (1998) The calculated and the avowed: Techniques of discipline and struggles over identity in Big 6 public accounting firms. *Administrative Science Quarterly*. 43(2): 293–327.

Duff, A., & Marriott, N. (2012) *Teaching and research: Partners or competitors?* ICAS: Edinburgh.

Ferguson, J., Collison, D., Power, D., & Stevenson, L. (2008) *An analysis of the role of the textbook in the construction of accounting knowledge*. ICAS: J. Edinburgh.

Flower, J. (1997) The future shape of harmonization: The EU versus the IASC versus the SEC. *The European Accounting Review*. 6: 281–303.

FRC (Financial Reporting Council Ltd) (2015a) *Key facts and trends in the accountancy profession*, June. London: FRC.

FRC (2015b). *Oversight of the accountancy profession*. Available: https://www.frc.org.uk/Our-Work/Conduct/Professional-oversight/Oversight-of-the-accountancy-profession.aspx. Accessed: August 2015.

Freidson, E. (1988) *Professional powers: A study of the institutionalisation of formal knowledge*. London: University of Chicago Press.

Fuller, S. (2004) Universities and the future of knowledge governance from the standpoint of social epistemology. *Final plenary address at the UNESCO forum Colloquium on Research and Higher Education Policy*, Paris, December 3. Available: https://www2.le.ac.uk/departments/management/research/documents/research/research-units/cppe/seminar-pdfs/2004/fuller.pdf. Accessed: August 14, 2015.

Higher Education Statistics Agency (HESA) (2010) *All HE students by level of study, mode of study, subject of study, domicile and gender 2008/9*. Table 2e. Available: www.hesa.ac.uk/ in Duff, A., & Marriott, N. (2012) *Teaching and research: Partners or competitors?* Edinburgh: ICAS.

Hopwood, A.G. (1988) Accounting research and accounting practice: The ambiguous relationship between the two, in A.G. Hopwood (ed.), *Accounting from the outside*. New York: Garland publishing, pp. 549–578.

ICAEW. Available: http://www.icaew.com/. Accessed: August 14, 2015.

ICAS. Available: https://www.icas.com/. Accessed: August 14, 2015.

IFAC (2015) *Frequently asked questions.* Available: https://www.ifac.org/about-ifac/organization-overview/faq

Inanga, E.L., & Scheider, W.B. (2005) The failure of accounting research to improve accounting practice: A problem of theory and lack of communication. *Critical Perspectives on Accounting.* 16: 227–248.

Larson, R., & Kenny, S. (2011) The financing of the IASB: An analysis of donor diversity. *Journal of International Accounting, Auditing and Taxation.* 20: 1–19.

Macdonald, K.M. (1999) *The sociology of the professions.* London: SAGE.

Poullaos, C. (2010) The profession/academy relationship an entry to professional programs, in E. Evans, R. Burritt, & J. Guthrie (eds.), *Accounting education at a crossroad in 2010.* The Institute of Chartered Accountants in Australia & Centre for Accounting, Governance and Sustainability, University of South Australia, Adelaide, pp. 63–71.

Power, M.K. (1991) Educating accountants: Towards a critical ethnography. *Accounting, Organizations and Society.* 16(4): 333–353.

Rodgers, J.L., & Williams, P.F. (1996) Patterns of research productivity and knowledge creation at the accounting review: 1967–1993. *The Accounting Historians Journal.* 23(1): 51–88.

Sikka, P., Willmott, H., & Lowe, T. (1989) Guardians of knowledge and public interest: evidence and issues of accountability in the UK accountancy profession. *Accounting, Auditing & Accountability Journal.* 2(2): 47–71.

Sterling, R.R. (1973) Accounting research, education and practice. *The Journal of Accountancy.* 36(September): pp. 44–52.

Target Jobs (2015) *An introduction to professional accountancy bodies.* Available: https://targetjobs.co.uk/career-sectors/accountancy-and-financial-management/283313-an-introduction-to-professional-accountancy-bodies. Accessed: August 8, 2015.

10 Negotiating Knowledge through Boundary Organisations in Environmental Policy

Clare Moran, Shona Russell and Lucy Wishart

INTRODUCTION

Often charged with 'saving the planet', environmental policymaking is an arena in which the relationship between knowledge and practice is inherently complex (Hertin *et al.* 2009). While environmental issues may be understood with the help of scientific knowledge, policymakers are faced with issues of spatial and temporal scales and must consider impacts on a global and local level, across current and future generations in pursuit of environmental outcomes. Under the pressure of these 'superhero' aspirations, policymakers engaged in environmental management must make sense of an uncertain, complex and contested knowledge landscape, while also engaging with knowledge producers, including those from science and industry.

In response to challenges of producing policy-relevant knowledge, structures and practices have been created, including boundary organisations and knowledge exchange activities, to facilitate the sharing of useful evidence (Guston 2001, Nutley *et al.* 2007). However, despite the best efforts to provide expert guidance to support environmental policymaking, the process remains inherently messy when learning and knowing often develops in spite of, rather than as a consequence of, system design (Hertin *et al.* 2009).

In this chapter, we examine the structures and practices between science, policy and industry to support the development and implementation of Scotland's waste and water policy, specifically the establishment and development of two national-level organisations—Zero Waste Scotland (ZWS) and the Centre of Expertise on Water (CREW). The two case studies reported here are taken from larger research projects carried out separately by the researchers during 2013 and 2014 in Scotland. Both utilised a range of qualitative data collection methods based upon reflexive methodologies. In each study we spoke to current or former policymakers, specialists, scientists, senior academics, and members of industry; reviewed documents; and observed meetings and conferences.

The chapter is structured as follows: first, we introduce the concept of 'boundary organisations' that will frame the presentation of two cases where we consider how knowledge is produced and mobilised in relation to waste and water policy in the second section. Third, we discuss the cases with reference to the themes of *knowledge, practice and power* that flow through the book. Finally, we comment on the insights gleaned concerning the negotiation of knowledge for environmental outcomes.

ORGANISING KNOWLEDGE FOR ENVIRONMENTAL POLICY

Operating in complex, contested and uncertain knowledge landscapes can be problematic, in terms of determining what constitutes policy-relevant knowledge and how to organise the creation and mobilisation of knowledge amongst producers and users. Credibility, legitimacy and saliency are three tightly joined criteria that need to be met to ensure knowledge is appropriate for policy (Cash *et al.* 2003). In other words policy-relevant knowledge draws on technical evidence that is scientifically adequate *(credible)* and relevant to decision makers' needs *(salient)*, and that reflects and accounts for a spectrum of stakeholder values *(legitimate)* (Cash *et al.* 2003:8086). Efforts to enhance one attribute may be detrimental to others, and tensions in achieving such attributes may be heightened by the number of actors involved in creating, using and mobilising knowledge and the degree to which science-based knowledge is questioned.

Boundary organisations are often presented as solutions to inform decision-making and address contested scientific claims or policy decisions (Guston 2001; Cash *et al.* 2003; Pielke 2007). In engaging with scientific and policy communities, boundary organisations combine scientific and political elements and coordinate activities across various domains, adopting roles of policy broker, issue advocate, science arbiter or pure scientist (see Pielke 2007; Huitema & Turnhout 2009; Pesch *et al.* 2012). These roles are not static, just as the process of producing and mobilising knowledge for decision-making is far from linear (see Chapter 2). Similarly boundaries are ambiguous, contingent and subject to continual negotiation particularly in relation to specific issues, uncertain policy processes, involvement of multiple stakeholders, the stage in the policy cycle, and the sociopolitical context in which policies are being made and implemented (Pesch *et al.* 2012; Hoppe *et al.* 2013; Turnhout *et al.* 2013). Notably, activities of these organisations demarcate the limits of science and policy in relation to social and environmental concerns, and have specific lines of accountability to their respective communities, creating further complexity (Guston 2001; Miller 2001; Jasanoff 2004).

In contrast to work examining boundary organisations in relation to international climate governance (Hoppe *et al.* 2013) or knowledge exchange activities amongst implementing bodies at a project level (Bracken & Oughton 2013), this chapter uses the concept of boundary organisations to examine how two organisations have adapted to changing knowledge needs in the policy domains of waste and water in Scotland.

ORGANISING KNOWLEDGE FOR ENVIRONMENTAL POLICY: THE CASES OF WASTE AND WATER

Since devolution in 1999, the Scottish Government has been responsible for environmental policy and has taken some pioneering actions with regards to environmental concerns. For example, the Scottish Parliament unanimously passed the Climate Change (Scotland) Act 2009, a global frontrunner in laying out an ambitious programme to reduce greenhouse gas emissions and transition to a low-carbon economy involving all sectors of society. These actions are part of the government's five strategic objectives for a Scotland that is wealthier and fairer, safer and stronger, healthier, greener and smarter. These objectives are associated with 16 National Outcomes that articulate the Scottish Government's purpose over a ten-year programme (Scottish Government 2014a), supported by 50 National Performance Indicators that are regularly monitored to assess progress towards the outcomes (Scottish Government 2015).

Amongst a variety of public, private and civil society organisations, Zero Waste Scotland and the Centre of Expertise on Water produce and mobilise knowledge to support waste and water (respectively) policy in Scotland. Specifically, the organisations contribute to the pursuit of those National Outcomes related to the environment: to live in well-designed, sustainable places where we are able to access the amenities and services we need; to value and enjoy our built and natural environment and protect it and enhance it for future generations; and to reduce the local and global environmental impact of our consumption and production. In the rest of this section, we illustrate how these two boundary organisations have engaged with science, policy and industry communities over time in pursuit of these ambitious policy goals.

Zero Waste Scotland

Created in 2010 as the delivery body for the Scottish Government's Zero Waste (ZW) Plan (the Plan), Zero Waste Scotland (ZWS) has developed and changed significantly within its first few years of existence. Originally a subsidiary of the UK-wide resource efficiency organisation, WRAP, in 2014 ZWS became a company in its own right. The organisation provides technical advice, policy updates and project management support to a variety of groups. It also both undertakes and provides limited funds for trials and exploratory research.

ZWS was initially tasked with specific delivery roles within the Plan (Scottish Government 2010), including measuring and monitoring waste movement in Scotland and management of the plastic reprocessing fund. By 2011, the remit of ZWS had expanded to include targets associated with the Scottish Government's low-carbon economy goals (WRAP 2011) with focus placed upon water, energy and waste efficiency within businesses. Cementing its position as the primary advice body for environmental efficiency, in 2013 it created the subsidiary organisation 'Resource Efficient Scotland', which provides tools and support for Scottish businesses. In 2014, ZWS declared itself part of 'Team Scotland': a group of public bodies including the Scottish Government, Scottish Environmental Protection Agency (SEPA) and the Scottish Enterprise Agencies. This group works alongside partners to encourage the advancement of a circular economy in Scotland (Zero Waste Scotland 2014), a development that suggests the organisation now also undertakes a policy role.

There is a high importance placed upon enhancing knowledge of waste in Scotland in the ZW policy; of the 22 action points cited in the ZW Plan, more than half relate directly to educational programmes, enhancing data collection, co-production of knowledge and developing and learning skills. A focus on knowledge flows can show how ZWS acts as an educator, funder and agenda-setter for ZW knowledge in Scotland. In performing these roles ZWS works with a range of stakeholders, acting as a boundary organisation to deliver, shape and facilitate knowledge within the ZW policy.

There is a clear identification within ZWS of its role as an educator. This is, in part, a response to the historical neglect of waste management both in policy circles and as a more general societal concern (Davoudi 2006; Hird *et al.* 2014). Scotland has traditionally operated in a disposal paradigm where management was centralised and for the majority the responsibility for waste was devolved elsewhere. In contrast, as part of the ZW Plan, all stakeholders (seen as the public, business, local authorities and community groups) are being encouraged to view waste as a resource. Part of this journey involves educating groups who have no knowledge of waste management practices. Through programmes such as 'Resource Efficient Scotland' and the 'Zero Waste Volunteers', ZWS is responsible for providing support, advice and basic education on waste measuring, reduction and management to households and businesses. In this sense knowledge can be seen as a product that ZWS delivers.

In the same vein, ZWS is involved in funding and contributing to continued research of best practice within sustainable waste management. In addition ZWS aims to supplement the scant understanding of material flows and resource-use behaviour within Scotland in recognition of the lack of attention there has been to waste in the past. Some of this research is requested from the Scottish Government directly but, on the whole, decisions on what research to undertake is shaped by ZWS's perceptions of policy needs. Most of this research is outsourced, with a continually updated list of tenders advertised on the ZWS website. Although in this sense, knowledge is still conceived as a product, the contributions of ZWS to what that product looks like are far more pronounced.

ZWS does not engage in this agenda-setting activity alone: collaboration with the Scottish Environment Protection Agency (SEPA), the Enterprise Agencies, professional waste bodies and large businesses in developing new research is common. There is a clear commitment to working in partnership both in practice and rhetoric within the ZW policy, as evidenced by the continued and consistent use of consultations, as well as statements of commitment to stakeholder contributions in all key policy documents. This collaborative approach is used to shape future policy but also functions on a smaller scale, with ZWS acting as a conduit between organisations (particularly businesses) by organising workshops, round tables and roadshows to encourage sharing of perspectives on potential problems and solutions for waste management in Scotland.

Centre of Expertise on Water

The Scottish Government launched the Centre of Expertise on Water (CREW) in April 2011, alongside two other Centres of Expertise (CoEs) focused on climate change (CxC) and animal health (EPIC). The CoEs work with universities, research institutes and policy to improve the supply of research to policy: improving collaboration, broadening the supply base, and enhancing knowledge flows within and between policy domains and amongst science, policy and industry communities. CREW aims to deliver 'objective and robust research and professional opinion to support the development and implementation of water policy in Scotland' in conjunction with its users, including Scottish Government policy teams, SEPA and Scottish Water (CREW, 2014). In addition, the organisation aims to increase networks between those working in the field of water management and build skills and capacity to share knowledge appropriately in response to demand by policy and practitioners. The knowledge generated by CREW's activities are intended to generate impact leading to improved environmental, social and economic outcomes (Blackstock *et al.* 2014).

Members of CREW are based in research institutes and universities across Scotland and draw upon engineering, biophysical and social sciences expertise relating to water resource management in rural and urban contexts. The organisation itself is administered by seven individuals, is hosted by the James Hutton Institute—one of the Scottish Government's Main Research Providers (MRPs)—and is overseen by a steering group comprising representatives from the Scottish Government, associated policy agencies, higher education institutions and research providers.

Since its establishment CREW's goal to link research and policy has been realised via a call-down service for policy-commissioned work requiring quick responses, carrying out capacity-building projects, disseminating research and assessing future research needs. CREW's members have informed development of legislation and provided evidence for policy development within the UK and Scottish Governments. In addition, members of CREW are often invited to join advisory groups for policy programmes, such as the Scottish Government's Hydro Nation Agenda. This agenda aims to develop Scotland's water resources and associated economy and contribute to the management of global water challenges. CREW's role includes responsibility for the management of the Hydro Nation Scholarship Programme and representation on the Hydro Nation Forum, which steers the agenda across sectors and supports knowledge sharing amongst policy and science communities.

Over the course of CREW's existence, the organisation has undertaken periodic evaluations of its structures and processes for commissioning and stakeholder engagement (Blackstock *et al.* 2014). Key lessons include the importance of identifying, understanding and translating needs amongst policy and science communities; valuing science and understanding politics; simplifying complexity; and recognition that water is a large subject area. These evaluation processes have supported the capacity building of CREW's staff to facilitate further interaction and develop common understanding and language amongst the organisation's stakeholders. One way in which this has been developed is through the creation of subject-specific networks involving representatives from agencies to ensure that CREW's activities align with the needs of funders and users. These relationships aim to build trust between members, to support efforts to generate policy-relevant outputs, and to inform ways that policymakers or implementers think about a policy issue (CREW interviewee, June 2014). These developments suggest that CREW has shifted from acting as a coordinating body facilitating the transfer of knowledge to a commissioning body negotiating the terms and scope of research required to meet policy needs, and in doing so demarcating the limits of science and policy.

As a boundary organisation, CREW endeavours to facilitate the production and mobilisation of useful knowledge for policy and create relationships between various agencies in line with efforts to undertake collaborative and integrated approaches to water resource management. CREW's activities are subject to other social and political influences, including the complex nature of environmental issues, the respective responsibilities of science and policy, and the development of individual careers, particularly those of scientists. Operating between science and policy communities and priorities, CREW has to negotiate what is seen as 'worthwhile' knowledge work. From the perspective of a CREW interviewee, scientists engaging with policy through CREW recognised the value and "tangible output from scientific endeavour" as compared with academic rubrics of publications and impact factors. However, policy-engaged activity sat alongside scientists' efforts to continue to publish peer-reviewed publications as a marker of the quality of Scottish science (Scottish Government 2014b). As such, the extent to which CREW may be deemed successful in the future may depend on its ability to operate within this negotiated and contingent space between scientific endeavour and policymaking, as well as its continuing to support the pursuit of the stipulated environmental outcomes of the Scottish Government.

REFLECTING ON KNOWLEDGE, PRACTICE AND POWER

Although both cases are situated within the Scottish Government's environmental portfolio, there are distinct differences in the relative engagement and contribution of science, policy and industry. For example, although waste remains of little interest to social science communities in Scotland, through ZWS industry and policy communities have collaborated to reconceptualise waste as a resource issue, and therefore important to economic development. In contrast CREW is part of a broad community of actors engaged in supporting the Scottish Government's efforts to realise and protect the value of Scotland's water. For the remainder of this section we consider the interrelationship between knowledge, practice and power in both subdomains of environmental policy.

Our analysis of dynamic processes—the evolution of arrangements (structures, practices and relationships)—revealed how a delivery body became a diversified educator and service provider (ZWS); and how long-term research programmes became responsive ad hoc advisory mechanisms (CREW). Both case studies accessed the world of practitioners and practice through standard ethnographic methods: elite interviews and document analysis, without explicitly using practice theory (see Chapter 3—practice and Chapter 7—sensing bodies). The 'practice turn' across the social sciences and social theory from the mid-twentieth century onwards (e.g., Giddens 1979) has given social scientists a greater appreciation of the importance of practices and, for organisation studies, the *practitioner*. As part of this broader practice turn in social sciences, researchers have sought to understand and explore what happens in practice; rather than reifying structure (or any other reductive category—see Schatzki *et al.* 2001). Such studies add nuance and fine-grained detail. It would be too simplistic to assume that the existence of structures—for example, knowledge exchange mechanisms—is a signifier of knowledge exchange happening or the achievement of impactful outcomes. Attention to practices and processes uncovers the interactions and outcomes within structures (Meagher & Lyall 2013)—and the varied use of knowledge produced this way (Nutley *et al.* 2007; Ward *et al.* 2009). Practice examples illustrate observed differences between some structures' espoused purposes and their use—even by those who created them (Ettelt *et al.* 2013). This may seem obvious, but attending only to structures, without a critical eye to process, would have obscured the change in purpose and activities that have occurred as a result of the relationships in both of the case studies presented above.

Interfaces between science, policy and industry are challenging spaces for individuals to operate within, whether as a member of a boundary organisation or as an individual with particular expertise. Individuals working at these interfaces are recognised as an emergent community of practice and may be referred to as 'knowledge broker', 'intermediary', 'boundary spanner' or 'research translator' (Ward *et al.* 2009:268). The relative novelty of boundary work has implications for academic researchers: an ambiguous and occasionally precarious career path, imbued with risk as well as difficulty (Lyall *et al.* 2011): not only do individuals stray from traditional, safer career paths, they stray into unknown and unformed territory (see Ward *et al.* 2009). For example, those in research institutions may have to balance commitments to engaged scholarship and impact with requirements to produce high-quality peer-reviewed publications. Similarly managers and decision makers may have to take account of the benefits of engaging in such boundary work in light of uncertainty and expensive investment in time. Cash *et al.* (2003) suggest that the tensions that boundary work creates for individuals can be partially resolved by the existence of boundary organisations, as the "most effective" solutions to tensions arising at science-policy interfaces.

The cases show that boundary organisations are not a panacea, although they relieve some of the pressures on individuals at these interfaces by collectivising and legitimising their activities. For example, ZWS, as a boundary organisation, convenes and commissions research and brings together knowledge from other sources and other sectors. ZWS provides an interface rather than directly engaging in knowledge production—which it nevertheless shapes by setting the agenda of *what* knowledge is produced and what knowledge counts in policy decisions (Davies *et al.* 2000). Conversely in the CREW example, individuals are not only brokers but also the creators of original research knowledge, shaping *how* knowledge is produced. CREW's members may undertake the intermediary function directly with policy, or indirectly through other colleagues within CREW who act as boundary spanners—not necessarily translating the research, but translating the needs of research users to research producers. In CREW this brokering of commissioning occurred through the specialist networks and particular individuals (project managers) that maintained ongoing working relationships with research users. The effectiveness of individual project managers as an organising model can be seen from its use by all three of Scotland's CoEs, but the terminology does not capture the role's breadth:

> . . . you know we're not project managers. We have expertise in a range of fields in the team, and if we don't we go to the likes of [CoE scientists]. So that's really important as well, that we're not just a project management service. The next level down is getting involved in the management groups [in government] and spreading out a little bit further, and I think that's quite important as well. And we can then link into the strategic programme [in government] and the expertise that's there, and advise . . . we only fund research that comes from the customer, but we also have a role in advising them in terms of the science and the evidence and direction of travel perhaps.
>
> (CREW project manager, June 2014)

These designated intermediary roles had also been strengthened in response to the evidence that emerged from CoEs of the challenges for individuals working at the interface. These included the production of insufficiently rigorous evidence by inexperienced researchers; or the need to 'push back' onto policy commissioners of research to better define the product they were requesting, in effect by co-producing a brief for the researchers. The need for an intermediary was not necessarily a response to a skills deficit amongst researchers, many of whom had built their own capacity to work at the interface through secondments into policy areas or through previous jobs in public bodies, or by undertaking training through participation in the CoEs. Rather, the need for intermediaries could be seen as an indication of the inherent challenges of boundary work, which include not only novelty and heterogeneity, but also increased fragmentation and diffusion of activities related to knowledge production and knowledge use. These challenges extend beyond individual researchers' skills, and casting them as solvable by training alone neglects the context within which individuals work; hence the value of sharing evaluation and learning about experiences of individuals and organisations at the boundary. Using the example of CREW's continuous self-evaluation, we can speculate that effective boundary workers can build capacity in their own organisations for future intermediary work, and by building trusting and productive relationships between organisations, increase the chance that this capacity will be recognised, retained, or expanded. The CREW case reveals active participation in the creation of community at both individual and organisational scales, rather than only passive mediation and translation at an interface.

Environmental policy relies on multiple methodologies and forms of knowledge, with relevant contributions coming from science and the humanities (Pahl-Wostl *et al.* 2013), alongside knowledge from lay or practitioner communities (Bäckstrand 2003). Knowledge is far from a "neutral package of 'facts'" (Jordan & Russel 2014). Instead, the package may creatively draw together expert, professional, tacit and experiential knowledge (Bracken & Oughton 2013). In turn boundary organisations may use such packages in their engagement with different communities. For example, ZWS works with individual businesses, applying frameworks to evaluate current practices and identify opportunities for waste reduction. These practical projects are then developed as broader case studies to encourage engagement in waste reduction in the wider sector. Despite such crafting of knowledge for environmental policy, it is possible that packages of facts and evidence may be contested or actively ignored through strategies of denial, dismissal, diversion or displacement (Rayner 2012). In response to such risks, directors and project managers of CREW sought to maintain good relationships and notify ministers and policy-makers of potentially controversial findings prior to final publication of research reports.

However, boundary organisations may also reify certain ways of knowing that exclude others in order to legitimate their own roles and positions, and delegitimise those of others (Gieryn 1983; Latour 1993; Jasanoff 2004; Lidskog 2014). This legitimation may even occur within the research community: for example, where social science may be deemed an addendum and of lesser value to environmental policy compared to biophysical or economic science. In response, one of the main research providers in Scotland has invested in social science capacity to address this imbalance with support from the Scottish Government. In creating boundary organisations meant to broker and produce 'policy-relevant' knowledge, there is a risk of perpetuating or creating approaches to knowledge production that do not reflect normative assertions of the need for interdisciplinary, participative, inclusive or democratising knowledge production in response to complex and uncertain environmental issues (Lane *et al.* 2011).

The production of knowledge is political (Jordan & Russel 2014). The direction of power flows within the case studies were able to illuminate how structure interacted with relational, dynamic aspects of power, present in intertwined themes of expertise, ownership and outsourcing of knowledge or decision-making. Interview data from both cases suggested that these structurally bilateral arrangements of knowledge production contained—in practice—multilateral power relationships arising from institutional and professional power dynamics. Examples of these power dynamics from narrative accounts include perceived power asymmetries between 'experts' (researcher, dominant) and practitioners (in this case civil servants); or the opposite, between the 'capable' policymakers (civil servants, dominant) and researchers 'less capable' in their understanding of particular research or policy contexts. The overemphasis on expert knowledge to the exclusion of lay perspectives has been noted as a particular problem within environmental policy (Petts & Brooks 2006). This exclusion was identified in the one of the case studies, where data highlighted the emphasis on the importance of ZWS working *with* waste experts and Team Scotland, in contrast to the general public, who were portrayed as requiring education on better waste management practices *by* ZWS, rather than as presenting alternative or critical perspectives on the feasibility of the experts' views. These contradictory accounts arise from historic relationships between professional cultures and engagement with the wider public.

There were also nuanced accounts of power arising from or affecting material resource flows. One example concerned sensitivities around institutional funding for HEIs, and perceived competitive 'land grabs' by already dominant organisations into the niche knowledge production spaces of others. Another example was researchers' need for policy champions within government to ensure research use. This need for research use and impact might be felt by individual scientists, particular disciplines, or specific arrangements (e.g., centres) for research production and use. In such examples, the policy actors were dominant and the frequent staff changes within government were destabilising for the organisations that depended upon these relationships. As predicted within the literature, there were also negative views about policy 'ownership', from scientists who felt that the requirement to produce policy-relevant science was an exercise of managerialist power by government as funders (Cash *et al.* 2003).

CONCLUDING COMMENTS

Our examination of the negotiation of knowledge in environmental policy demonstrated that boundary organisations are not static facilitators of knowledge production for policy audiences. Instead, both cases illustrate the active engagement and shaping of knowledge and the science-policy interface in two subdomains of environmental policy. Our findings suggest that the structures and practices of ZWS and CREW have evolved in light of shifting priorities of policy. As a result, individuals operating within boundary organisations have adapted their roles to the ever-changing nature of policies and understanding of environmental issues in scientific, policy and industry communities. The dynamism evident in these empirical cases illustrated how boundary organisations reflect, or indeed amplify, the complexity rather than necessarily providing a perfect solution to uncertain environmental issues.

The cases above illustrate the growing recognition of the value of industry-based and science-based knowledge for environmental policymaking. Knowledge is a process as well as a product, and it involves more than the activities of individual experts. The interplay between individual, organisational and institutional production and use of knowledge for environmental policy requires communities of experts—whether researchers, policymakers or practitioners—to be critical of their own constructions of knowledge and to be reflexive about assumptions and reasons for promoting certain forms of knowledge and certain policy options (Moses & Knutsen 2012; Spash 2012; Hoppe & Wesselink 2014). Furthermore, there is a need to examine the politics, alongside structures and practices, of knowledge production if we are to realise the normative aspirations for participative, inclusive and democratised knowledge production that are deemed integral to attempts to address potentially catastrophic, but still uncertain, environmental risks (Lane *et al.* 2011).

ACKNOWLEDGEMENTS

The authors wish to thank the research participants, reviewers and participants in KPEC workshops. We are grateful for the financial support provided by the Carnegie Trust and the School of Management, University of St Andrews.

SUGGESTED FURTHER READINGS

Cash, D., Clark, W., Alcock, F., Dickson, N.M., Eckley, N., Guston, D.H., Jäger, J., & Mitchell, R.B. (2003) Knowledge systems for sustainable development. *Proceedings of the National Academy of Sciences*. 100(14): 8086–8091.
This article provides a helpful introduction to debates concerning the relationship between knowledge and action to support sustainable development. The authors present a framework to assess the effectiveness of knowledge systems and how they may be developed for long-term transformation to support the pursuit of sustainable development.

Davoudi, S. (2006) The evidence-policy interface in strategic waste planning for urban environments: The technical & the social dimensions. *Environment & Planning C: Government & Policy*. 24(5): 681–700.
In this case study, Davoudi investigates the use of evidence in waste policymaking, identifying the limits of technical expertise and highlighting the need for both social and technical knowledge in developing policy for complex socioecological issues.

Pielke Jr., R.A. (2007) *The honest broker: Making sense of science in policy & politics*. Cambridge: Cambridge University Press.
This insightful book discusses the relationships between scientific advice and the policy process. Pielke Jr. identifies a range of roles scientists may play and how science can contribute to policymaking and democracy.

Ward, V. House, A., & Hamer, S. (2009) Knowledge brokering: The missing link in the evidence to action chain? *Evidence & Policy*. 5(3): 267–279.
This article provides an accessible introduction to the theory and practice of knowledge brokering, and provides some useful analytical frameworks for making sense of it.

REFERENCES

Bäckstrand, K. (2003) Civic science for sustainability: Reframing the role of experts, policy-makers & citizens in environmental governance. *Global Environmental Politics*. 4(4): 24–41.

Blackstock, K., Morris, S., & Hastings, E. (2014) *Evaluating CREW: Summary of findings 2012–13*, CREW. Available: www.crew.ac.uk/publications. Accessed: October 8, 2015.

Bracken, L.J., & Oughton, E.A. (2013) Making sense of policy implementation: The construction & uses of expertise & evidence in managing freshwater environments. *Environmental Science & Policy*. 30: 10–18.

Cash, D., Clark, W., Alcock, F., Dickson, N.M., Eckley, N., Guston, D.H., Jäger, J., & Mitchell, R.B. (2003) Knowledge systems for sustainable development. *Proceedings of the National Academy of Sciences*. 100(14): 8086–8091.

CREW (2014) 'About Us', Centre of Expertise on Water (CREW). Available: http://www.crew.ac.uk/aboutus. Accessed: January 20, 2015.

Davies, H.T.O., Nutley, S.M., & Smith, P.C. (2000) *What works? Evidence-based policy & practice in public services*. Bristol: Policy Press.

Davoudi, S. (2006) The evidence-policy interface in strategic waste planning for urban environments: The technical & the social dimensions. *Environment & Planning C: Government & Policy*. 24(5): 681–700.

Ettelt, S., Mays, N., & Nolte, E. (2013) Policy–research linkage: What we have learned from providing a rapid response facility for international healthcare comparisons to the department of health in England. *Evidence & Policy*. 9(2): 245–254.

144   *Clare Moran et al.*

Giddens, A. (1979) *Central problems in social theory: Action, structure & contradiction in social analysis.* London: Macmillan.

Gieryn, T.F. (1983) Boundary-work & the demarcation of science from non-science: Strains & interests in professional ideologies of scientists. *American Sociological Review* 48(6): 781–795.

Guston, D.H. (2001) Boundary organizations in environmental policy & science: An introduction. *Science, Technology & Human Values.* 26(4): 399–408.

Hertin, J., Turnpenny, J., Jordan, A., Nilsson, M., Russel, D., & Nykvist, B. (2009) Rationalising the policy mess? Ex ante policy assessment & the utilisation of knowledge in the policy process. *Environment & Planning A.* 41(5): 1185–1200.

Hird, M., Lougheed, S., Rowe., R.K., & Kuyvenhoven, C. (2014) Making waste management public (or falling back to sleep). *Social Studies of Science.* 44: 2–25.

Hoppe, R., & Wesselink, A. (2014) Comparing the role of boundary organizations in the governance of climate change in three EU member states. *Environmental Science & Policy.* 44: 73–85.

Hoppe, R., Wesselink, A., & Cairns, R. (2013) Lost in the problem: The role of boundary organisations in the governance of climate change. *WCC Wiley Interdisciplinary Reviews: Climate Change.* 4(4): 283–300.

Huitema, D., & Turnhout, E. (2009) Working at the science–policy interface: A discursive analysis of boundary work at the Netherlands Environmental Assessment Agency. *Environmental Politics.* 18(4): 576–594.

Jasanoff, S. (2004) *States of knowledge: The co-production of science & the social order.* London: Routledge.

Jordan, A., & Russel, D. (2014) Embedding the concept of ecosystem services? The utilisation of ecological knowledge in different policy venues. *Environment & Planning C: Government & Policy.* 32(2): 192–207.

Lane, S.N., Odoni, N., Landström, C., Whatmore, S.J., Ward, N., & Bradley, S. (2011) Doing flood risk science differently: An experiment in radical scientific method. *Transactions of the Institute of British Geographers.* 36(1): 15–36.

Latour, B. (1993) *We have never been modern.* Cambridge, MA: Harvard University Press.

Lidskog, R. (2014) Representing & regulating nature: Boundary organisations, portable representations, & the science–policy interface. *Environmental Politics.* 23(4): 670–687.

Lyall, C., Bruce, A., Tait, J., & Meagher, L. (2011) *Interdisciplinary research journeys practical strategies for capturing creativity.* London: Bloomsbury Press.

Meagher, L., & Lyall, C. (2013) The invisible made visible: Using impact evaluations to illuminate & inform the role of knowledge intermediaries. *Evidence & Policy.* 9(3): 409–418.

Miller, C.A. (2001) Hybrid management: Boundary organizations, science policy, & environmental governance in the climate regime. *Science, Technology & Human Values.* 26(4): 478–500.

Moses, J.W., & Knutsen, T. (2012) *Ways of knowing: Competing methodologies in social & political research.* New York: Palgrave MacMillan.

Nutley, S., Walter, I., & Davies, H.T.O. (2007) *Using evidence: How research can inform public services.* Bristol: Policy Press.

Pahl-Wostl, C., Giupponi, C., Richards, K., Binder, C., de Sherbinin, A., Sprinz, D., Toonen, T., & van Bers, C. (2013) Transition towards a new global change science: Requirements for methodologies, methods, data & knowledge. *Environmental Science & Policy.* 28: 36–47.

Pesch, U., Huitema, D., & Hisschemöller, M. (2012) A boundary organization & its changing environment: The Netherlands Environmental Assessment Agency, The MNP. *Environment & Planning C: Government & Policy.* 30(3): 487–503.

Petts, J., & Brooks, C. (2006) Expert conceptualisations of the role of lay knowledge in environmental decisionmaking: Challenges for deliberative democracy. *Environment & Planning A.* 38(6): 1045–1059.

Pielke Jr., R.A. (2007) *The honest broker: Making sense of science in policy & politics.* Cambridge: Cambridge University Press.

Rayner, S. (2012) Uncomfortable knowledge: The social construction of ignorance in science & environmental policy discourses. *Economy & Society.* 41(1): 107–125.

Schatzki, T.R., Knorr Cetina, K., & von Savigny, E. (2001) *The practice turn in contemporary theory.* London: Routledge.

Scottish Government (2010) *Zero waste plan.* Available: www.scotland.gov.uk/Publications/2010/06/08092645/0. Accessed: January 10, 2015.

Scottish Government (2014a) *National outcomes.* Available: www.gov.scot/About/Performance/scotPerforms/outcome. Accessed: May 24, 2015.

Scottish Government (2014b) *Scottish Government rural affairs & environment. Strategic research strategy 2011–16.* Available: www.gov.scot/Resource/0044/00443642.pdf. Accessed: May 24, 2015.

Scottish Government (2015) *National indicators.* Available: www.gov.scot/About/Performance/scotPerforms/indicator. Accessed: May 24, 2015.

Spash, C.L. (2012) New foundations for ecological economics. *Ecological Economics.* 77: 36–47.

Turnhout, E., Stuiver, M., Klostermann, J., Harms, B., & Leeuwis, C. (2013) New roles of science in society: Different repertoires of knowledge brokering. *Science & Public Policy.* 40(3): 354–365.

Ward, V. House, A., & Hamer, S. (2009) Knowledge brokering: The missing link in the evidence to action chain? *Evidence & Policy.* 5(3): 267–279.

Waste & Resources Programme (WRAP) (2011) WRAP business plan 2011 WRAP. Available: www.wrap.org.uk/sites/files/wrap/Bus_Plan_2011_Final_WEB_2.pdf. Accessed: January 17, 2015.

Zero Waste Scotland (2014) *Inspiring change for Scotland's resource economy: Programme Delivery Plan 2014–15.* Stirling: Zero Waste Scotland. Available: www.zerowastescotland.org.uk/sites/files/zws/Our%20delivery%20plan.pdf. Accessed: March 10, 2015.

11 Organising to Connect Academic Knowledge and Practice in Healthcare

Joyce Wilkinson and Jo Rycroft-Malone

INTRODUCTION

Overall health spending across OECD countries accounted for 9.3% of GDP on average in 2012 (OECD Health Statistics 2014). Policymakers are keen to ensure that this money is spent wisely and that healthcare organisations are efficient, effective and equitable in delivering healthcare services and interventions. They are spurred on by the fact that citizens are also concerned about the cost, quality and accessibility of healthcare. Opinion polls in the UK consistently show that healthcare is one of the three most important issues in deciding which political party the public will vote for (Ipsos MORI 2014). But how can policymakers, health service managers and healthcare practitioners ensure that healthcare funds are spent wisely? One response is that they should pay more attention to what we know as a result of healthcare research. There is widespread recognition that research has the potential to inform and guide the improvement of healthcare services, but there is frustration that this potential is often not fulfilled (Cooksey 2006; CERAG 2008). A gulf continues to exist between what researchers know (the state of the science) and what practitioners do (the state of the art) (Rycroft-Malone *et al.* 2013). As a result, the quality, cost and patient experience of healthcare continue to be compromised (Davis 2006).

These circumstances indicate that healthcare is an important context in which to explore the relationship between knowledge and practice. This chapter does this by discussing an initiative—Collaborations for Leadership in Applied Health Research and Care or CLAHRCs—aimed at improving the connection between academic research and healthcare practice in England. The chapter focuses on an empirical study of three CLAHRCs, highlighting their structure and operation, types of knowledge in use, boundaries, boundary spanning and boundary objects.

CLOSING THE GAP BETWEEN RESEARCH AND PRACTICE

The gap between research and practice was recognised by the Chief Medical Officer's High Level Group on Clinical Effectiveness (CERAG 2008) and led to a recommendation of increased investment in, and the development of an infrastructure to maximise the impact of, health research (Eccles *et al.* 2009). Traditional thinking on increasing research use in healthcare has tended to frame this as a problem that could be addressed by some fairly simple steps, underpinned by a rational decision-making process. This traditional view has been subject to increasing challenge from a growing body of evidence that suggests that research use is not a simple linear process but is instead a social and relational process (Nutley *et al.* 2007) that is also multifaceted, iterative and often unpredictable (Greenhalgh *et al.* 2004; Dopson & Fitzgerald 2005).

In line with a move away from linear models of research use, there has been a growing emphasis on the potential of collaborative and co-productive approaches to knowledge creation and use. Terms such as knowledge transfer, which reflect a more linear conceptualisation of the issue, are being replaced by terms such as knowledge translation and knowledge mobilisation, reflecting perhaps a more dynamic perspective. This shift is in line with Best and Holmes' (2010) conceptualisation of the first transition (from linear to relationship models) in their framework of three generations of thinking about knowledge to action, which was introduced and described in Chapter 2 (knowledge). Consistent with this shift, there has been substantial investment in collaborative approaches to knowledge production and use in healthcare. The CLAHRCs were tasked with both generating applied health research *and* implementing it in practice. The underlying concept of the CLAHRCs was that they would bring the users and producers of evidence closer together and this would catalyse more co-productive ways of working, which would in turn lead to greater amounts of applied health research and greater likelihood that this research would be used in practice (Rycroft-Malone *et al.* 2011; 2013).

AN IN-DEPTH STUDY OF THE IMPLEMENTATION OF THE CLAHRCS INITIATIVE

Joining the book's conversation about co-productive approaches to knowledge creation and knowledge use, this chapter draws on findings from an in-depth implementation study (2010–2014) of three CLAHRCs (Hazeldean, Ashgrove, and Oakdown). The study used a realist evaluation approach (Pawson & Tilley 1997) and multiple qualitative methods to assess what works, for whom, how, why and in what circumstances in the CLAHRCs. Qualitative interviews, observations, documentary analysis and formative feedback sessions included over two hundred participants and four rounds of data collection across the three CLAHRCs (see Rycroft-Malone *et al.* 2011; 2013 for more details about the approach used). We found that there were a number of antecedents, which set the path for subsequent activity within the CLAHRCs. These included the nature of existing relationships between the higher education institutions and health services involved, and existing perspectives about whether research application should be a more or less collaborative act. Existing relationships and connections triggered collaborative action around the implementation of research findings in a shorter period of time. There was potential for flexible interpretation of the funding call in terms of the emphasis placed on knowledge production as opposed to knowledge use, and whether knowledge use was viewed as something that was separate to, or part of, the knowledge production cycle. Across all three CLAHRCs the balance tended towards knowledge production, and to knowledge transfer rather than co-production.

We focus here on findings that shed light on the structures for collaboration in each CLAHRC, how the research use issue was problematised, the types of knowledge that were privileged, the existence of boundaries, and how knowledge and practice were aligned through boundary spanning and boundary objects. These issues are discussed in the remainder of the chapter.

THE STRUCTURE AND OPERATION OF THE CLAHRCS

The CLAHRCs were established and funded by the National Institute for Health Research (NIHR). The funding was conditional on obtaining matched funding from the local NHS and social care organisations involved in each of the collaborations. The number of partners involved in each of the three CLAHRCs is shown in table 11.1. Each CLAHRC adopted a similar structure in that they were all organised on the basis of research programmes or themes, with projects embedded within these. The number of programmes and projects varied across the three CLAHRCs and these are summarised in table 11.1. A key feature of the programmes is the extent to which the production of evidence was prioritised over its implementation. The balance between research production and research implementation set the context for whether the partnership was perceived to be more aligned with academia than with the health service organisations. There was clear evidence that research production was prioritised over implementation in the design of the programmes, and hence they were generally perceived to be more aligned with academia. This served to reinforce the divide between the higher education institutions and the NHS service organisations involved in each CLAHRC, though the depth and shape of this divide depended on the quality of pre-existing relationships between these organisations. Each CLAHRC established a core team who carried the overall responsibility for planning and delivering the work programme agreed on by the collaborating partners. The initiative was led by a director, supported by others in the core team. The size and composition of the leadership team in each of the CLAHRCs varied and these details are also summarised in table 11.1.

Table 11.1 Background information on the three CLAHRCs

	Composition and funding	Structure	Leadership
Hazeldean CLAHRC	One university and four NHS Trusts (originally ten). Matched funding from the NHS collaborators.	Four and later three research programmes focused on people with long-term conditions and one implementation programme with a number of embedded projects focused on a range of cardiovascular conditions.	A director, deputy director and CLAHRC manager provided leadership.
Oakdown CLAHRC	Two universities, seven NHS Trusts, five Primary Care Trusts and five other organisations, including a charity. It received matched funding from these organisations.	Two research programmes and implementation programmes with four themes and a number of embedded projects in each.	Leadership provided by a core team: director, associate director, programme manager, associate programme manager, communications lead, lead for implementation, evaluation lead, research capacity lead, and patient and public involvement lead. Leadership functions were incorporated in boundary-spanning roles at a practice level.
Ashgrove CLAHRC	One university and seven partners from Acute and Primary Care Trusts, providing matched funding for the CLAHRC.	Four research themes and one implementation theme with Five overarching topics within it. Each theme had a number of embedded projects.	A director, associate director and manager worked through a CLAHRC management board and executive committee with a team structure feeding into them.

CLAHRCs had the resources to create opportunities for groups and teams across the participating partners to come together to share knowledge and expertise. Interactions were facilitated through engagement in specific projects. However, the programmatic and project design of the CLAHRCs to some extent created boundaries to knowledge sharing across different themes and topics. The design also tended to be based on separate roles and activities for the creators of research and the users of research, rather than integrating the two. The programme and role boundaries were exacerbated by the hierarchical organisation of staff within each of the CLAHRCs. Engaging researchers and practitioners outside of the core team in the work of the CLAHRC was contingent upon the incentives, benefits, and/or rewards that individuals (and the organisations they worked for) perceived they would reap from becoming involved. We return to many of these issues later in the chapter, but first we consider how the relationship between knowing and doing was conceptualised in the CLAHRCs and the types of knowledge that were privileged in their activities.

Types of Knowledge That Were Privileged

Collaboration was expected to provide both the structure and opportunity for developing a shared space (between academia and practice) in and around which knowledge production and its use could occur. As highlighted above, knowledge production was emphasised more than knowledge implementation. This, and the fact that these collaborations were tasked with narrowing the gap between research and practice, meant that it was unsurprising that research was the most prominent type of knowledge visible in the work of the CLARHCs. However, when a CLAHRC sought to involve service users in setting research priorities, other forms of knowledge were evident. For example, in Oakdown service user knowledge was incorporated in their bariatric surgery research project through open events where service user opinions were sought about research priorities.

In addition, when CLAHRCs focused their attention on the use of research-based knowledge, they began to draw on a wider range of knowledge (see Chapter 2 for an overview of different types of knowledge and ways of knowing). The approach to implementing research-based knowledge often occurred through processes of trial and error, and the use of experiential knowledge was evident. All three CLAHRCs were going through a journey of 'figuring it out'. This process was, however, often guided by what Brechin and Siddell (2000) refer to as 'theoretical knowing'. Hazeldean and Oakdown used models and frameworks to guide and support their approach to implementation. These included the 'Knowledge-to-Action' model (Graham *et al.* 2006), the 'PARIHS framework' (Kitson *et al.* 1998, 2008; Rycroft-Malone *et al.* 2002) and the Institute of Healthcare Improvement's 'Plan, Do Study, Act' approach. Nevertheless, clear and explicit links between the cited frameworks and action within the CLAHRCs were often difficult to uncover and challenging for participants to articulate.

In CLAHRCs where a service improvement approach (see for example, Bamford *et al.* 2013; McBride *et al.* 2013) was used to shape implementation activities, local empirical knowledge (particularly from audit data) was part of the knowledge mix that shaped actions. Service user knowledge was also the basis of some implementation work. For example, those at Ashgrove were implementing an online cardiac rehabilitation programme and they were relying heavily on service users to design and approve the programme.

Multiple Boundaries within the CLAHRCs

The existence of multiple boundaries was evident in our data. As indicated earlier, these boundaries were not simply the result of the 'two communities' of practitioners and academics coming together, but were also a function of a complex web of interactions between tangible and less tangible factors, including structural, professional, philosophical and geographical factors. The main boundaries are outlined below:

- Organisational boundaries—between different organisations, and between different divisions, departments and projects within and across institutions;
- Epistemic boundaries—between the different philosophical perspectives that individuals, teams and organisations have about knowledge, its provenance and its implementation;
- Semantic boundaries—between people and groups because of different understandings about meaning and language;
- Professional boundaries—between different professional groups in different contexts; and
- Geographic boundaries—as a result of the physical geography of a CLAHRC, the network of nine CLAHRCs across England, and the physical locations and dislocations between partners within each CLAHRC.

The existence of these boundaries created challenges for the operation of the CLAHRCs. One of these challenges was the way in which the CLAHRC itself was perceived. Amongst NHS partners, CLAHRCs were often viewed as 'the university' and by some as an 'academic machine'. These perceptions meant that it took effort and time to build relationships that would facilitate NHS staff involvement in CLAHRC projects and activities. CLAHRCs that needed to work across several NHS Trusts encountered additional problems in getting 'buy in' to projects, particularly in the absence of pre-existing relationships.

The physical geography of the CLAHRCs often precluded co-location and close proximity between individuals and groups. This was said to limit the potential for interaction and the development of communities of practice. Co-location of health service and higher education staff was perceived to facilitate the development of productive relationships, but this was only evident in one of the CLAHRCs we studied (Oakdown). Epistemic differences between groups were difficult to negotiate and resolve, and they were reflected in whether academics thought that engaging in CLAHRC activity would provide them with the quality outputs they needed (particularly for the research quality assessments exercises conducted by the Higher Education Funding Council for England). Motivations and the ability to engage in joint activities were also influenced by professional boundaries and associated differentials in power and authority. For example the boundary spanners (discussed further below) in Hazeldean and Ashgrove who did not have a clinical background found it difficult to work with General Practices due to this, which was seen by senior staff to result in a lack of power and authority.

The boundaries that existed within the CLAHRCs were not all negative and there were some examples which demonstrated that boundaries could also prove positive with regards to implementation work. For example, in the Chronic Kidney Disease project in Hazeldean, the organisational boundaries between individual GP Practices worked to the advantage of the CLAHRC. The CLAHRC was able to demonstrate that the project was a way of sharing information about improvement ideas and targets across GP Practices that had previously had limited interaction.

However, boundaries more often acted as barriers to success because they had to be managed or spanned for some form of productive action to take place. The resilience of some boundaries and the effort required to find a shared space for dialogue, interaction and action slowed the work programmes of the CLAHRCs. As time went on, the relationships between the component partners in each CLAHRC began to shift and this was, at least in part, due to the efforts of those with boundary-spanning roles. NHS partners began approaching members of the core CLAHRC teams to ask them to undertake implementation and improvement projects within their organisations, rather than the other way around (which had been the case earlier on in the CLAHRC lifecycle).

Boundary-Spanning Roles

The importance of boundary-spanning roles is emphasised in the literature on the implementation of research-based knowledge (McCormack *et al.* 2013, Rycroft-Malone *et al.* 2013). However, there is still much to learn about how people in these roles operate and to what effect. Each CLARHC approached the establishment of these roles differently. Box 11.1 summarises some of the features of these roles in the three CLAHRCs. In two of the CLAHRCs, Hazeldean and Oakdown, the design of the roles related to the particular theoretical framework that had been chosen to underpin and guide implementation activity. For example, in Hazeldean the role was developed around the concept of knowledge transfer and was informed by the PARIHS framework's facilitation element.

BOX 11.1 BOUNDARY-SPANNING ROLES

Ashgrove

Boundary spanners were employed in formal roles based in NHS R&D departments. Their role was to span the boundary between the Trusts and the CLAHRC core team. This involved supporting Trust staff in writing research proposals, as well as providing training sessions on finding evidence, creating guidelines and undertaking evaluations. The majority of those in these boundary-spanning roles had no NHS background and no experience of working in a similar role.

Hazeldean

Here boundary-spanning roles were part of different projects. Boundary spanners had varying backgrounds; some had clinical experience, and others did not. The latter affected their credibility with clinicians. Education and training was provided for them by one of the academics involved with the implementation of research-based knowledge, and this person had expertise in facilitation. As well as having a specific role in implementation projects, these boundary-spanning roles were seen as providing a 'foot in either camp', spanning the boundary between the academic and practice environments in the CLAHRC.

Oakdown

Some boundary spanners were employed in formal roles to work across ward settings and to support those who acted informally as boundary spanners. All had a healthcare background and some experience of implementing change or service improvement. They were able to act as a bridge between the academic and practice communities, and they were seen as clinically credible.

In all three CLAHRCs, those appointed to these boundary-spanning roles were expected to bridge the divide between academia and the NHS organisations and practitioners. They were expected to engage in activities that ranged from training in research and evaluation (e.g., Ashgrove) to facilitating implementation projects (e.g., Oakdown and Hazeldean). Where roles were more concerned with implementation, they involved the development of tools and procedures to support the use of research knowledge in practice.

It was recognised that it was necessary to have people spanning boundaries at different levels within and across CLAHRC partners. Oakdown also emphasised the importance of recognising and supporting those working in informal boundaries roles as well as those in more formal positions:

> I think what has become evident for us is the importance of boundary spanning at different levels . . . it is about the importance of boundary spanning at executive and Board level going down to middle managers and steering committee members, key clinicians in the Trust as well as middle managers and then importantly boundary spanning with frontline staff, the people whose practice we are trying to change . . .
>
> (Leadership role, Oakdown, Round 2 interview)

One of the issues for those working in boundary-spanning roles was the extent to which they were seen as credible providers of evidence, guidance and information for changing practice. In Oakdown, this was made easier by the links between the academic and the NHS partners from the outset:

> We had . . . a very sound framework for the CLAHRC before we started and those key folk [boundary spanners] contributed hugely to the writing of the application and we managed to put it together very swiftly and in terms of NHS partners because . . . key theme leads . . . they were in the NHS and they were in academia so they weren't full time university professors . . . so this little group of people were very embedded in the NHS anyway.
>
> (Leadership role Oakdown, Round 1 interview)

Likewise in Hazeldean, the boundary spanners came from a variety of backgrounds and were seen as credible messengers for the CLAHRC (particularly those who had been seconded into these roles by the NHS):

> So across the CLAHRC as a whole we've now got at least as many seconded people in knowledge transfer type roles as we have people we originally recruited [to these roles] because that does bring that much more informal knowledge of people, networks and the clinical knowledge, you know, and although there's a few of those we

recruited that are good facilitators, in view of credibility and particularly the confidence that goes with those abilities are very important I think.

(Leadership role, Hazeldean, Round 3 interview)

In contrast, in Ashgrove those in boundary-spanning roles found some aspects of their role challenging because a relationship between the academic and practice partners had not existed prior to the establishment of the CLAHRC. For those without any NHS background it was particularly difficult.

Limited engagement of clinicians in the early days of a CLAHRC led to difficulties in getting clinician buy-in as projects progressed. The involvement of clinicians from the outset of the CLAHRC (while the bids to become a CLAHRC were being written) was seen as providing credibility for subsequent activities. A lack of such involvement was a significant challenge in one implementation project in Hazeldean, and it was also problematic in Ashgrove. In the latter case, although the research leads were all clinical academics (with NHS roles), they were more engaged with their own research interests than with the implementation priorities of the NHS. A lack of clinical buy-in led some boundary spanners to feel that they were acting in a consultancy role for the NHS rather than in a partnership to support the implementation of research knowledge. Thus boundary spanners not only needed to have or develop credibility but they also needed to become embedded in the work of partner organisations:

> The fact is that although we are a co-operative, a collaborative, in many ways we are not . . . I think it is likely that CLAHRC will be seen as an external organisation in which the Trust and Clinical Commissioning Group deal. It won't be 'this is an organisation we are a part of', it won't be 'this is a club I am a part of', it will be 'this is an organisation I am aware of who does things for us because we give them money.
>
> (Leadership role, Ashgrove, Round 4 interview)

Overall, these boundary-spanning roles were seen as crucial to the work and success of the CLAHRC. They were the visible presence of the CLAHRC in the local health services and they gave the initiative credibility on the ground. This was particularly important given the general lack of understanding about CLAHRCs amongst NHS staff. There was evidence to suggest that most of those working in boundary-spanning roles developed their knowledge, skills and credibility over time. This enabled them to develop meaningful interactions with those working in different roles, and in turn bring academic, contextual and clinical knowledge to bear on implementation activity.

Boundary Objects

Objects as well as people can facilitate the spanning of boundaries. Boundary objects are described in the research use literature as vague concepts with strong cohesive properties, flexible to local needs but remaining recognisable across contexts to enable the translation of knowledge from one group to another (Star & Griesemer 1989). They therefore have a potential role in transcending the challenges generated by boundaries. Our findings indicated that boundary objects were helpful in the CLAHRCs. We were able to identify boundary objects that were both concrete and conceptual. In addition, it was possible to identify how boundary objects move from being boundary objects in theory (e.g., cited in documents such as strategies and plans) to boundary objects in use.

A range of what could be described as concrete boundary objects was evident in the language used by boundary spanners. These included, for example, disease registers, best practice guidelines and annual reports. The way in which these entities operated as boundary objects was through prompting and opening up communication, providing a common understanding or basis upon which to coordinate activity, and as reference points for sharing information and evidence. For example, a nutrition action plan developed in Oakdown stimulated communication between the clinical staff on wards and the CLAHRC boundary spanner working on the project. The nutrition plan became a boundary object that had meaning to individuals working on the ward and the ward clinical team. Less concrete objects also seemed to hold some boundary object potential, including the CLAHRC concept itself. Over time and through a process of collective sense-making the CLAHRC concept catalysed collaboration, although the potential of this concept as a boundary object was not fully realised because there remained a lack of understanding across the practice community about what a CLAHRC was.

The potential of boundary objects to have cohesive properties around which shared meaning was developed appeared to be a function of the way in which they developed and evolved. Collective generation of boundary objects through discussion and collaborative activity when developing, amending and tailoring them for use was important. The engagement of relevant stakeholders in the process resulted in a higher likelihood of these objects acquiring the desirable features of boundary objects, which led to greater potential that they would be used in practice. When developed and amended collectively, they mobilised knowledge between communities because the process involved the integration of local evidence and experiences with external evidence (such as research-based guidelines). The boundary objects became something that had meaning and resonance to researchers and practitioners, enabling them to be incorporated into practice. In contrast, where there was a lack of collective action this resulted in something that had the potential to be a boundary object, but instead of acting as a catalyst to action, it tended to be disregarded or even to work in an inhibitory way. For example, one of Hazeldean's implementation projects was designed to bridge the gap between mental and physical health. An assessment tool mentioned in documents related to this project had the potential to be a boundary object. However, it did not become a 'boundary object in use' because front-line practitioners and service users were not involved in its development.

CONCLUSION

Our discussion suggests that organisational collaboration between higher education and health services provides both the potential for, and a challenge to, connecting academic knowledge with practice. The different starting positions of partners in relation to their views about collaboration, knowledge and implementation, in combination with the quality of existing relationships, influenced how they operated in practice. Research production was prioritised over research use, and as such resources and activity were focused on doing applied research rather than facilitating its application. Research knowledge was given privileged status over other ways of knowing. This served to fuel a perception that the collaborations were there for the academy rather than for the health service. When CLAHRCs did engage in research application, knowledge transfer rather than co-production was the dominant implementation paradigm.

The division between higher education and service delivery practice was perpetuated by the way in which the collaborations structured themselves around programmes and projects, leading to siloed activity and boundaries that were challenging for individuals to cross. Some boundaries were successfully bridged by those in facilitator-type roles, and these roles were the most visible investment made in implementation activity by the collaborations. These boundary spanners created opportunities and space for sharing and learning, and they also engaged in facilitating the application of evidence through the development of tools that had the potential to acquire the properties of boundary objects. Their activities led to some positive direct impacts for service and patients. Their ability to act as effective boundary spanners was enhanced if they had previously worked in the NHS and had clinical backgrounds

CLAHRCs now seem to have become a feature of NHS England's research and practice landscape. Their potential for increasing the generation of relevant applied research that is applied in practice will continue to be of interest. The hope is that ultimately, if they are successful, they will contribute to increasing the health and well-being of the populations they serve. Future evaluations need to build on this study in order to assess the extent of their success and impact, and how this was achieved (or not).

ACKNOWLEDGEMENT AND DISCLAIMER

Project team: Jo Rycroft-Malone, Christopher Burton, Joyce Wilkinson, Gill Harvey, Brendan McCormack, Richard Baker, Sue Dopson, Ian Graham, Sophie Staniszweska, Carl Thompson, Steven Ariss, Lucy Melville, Lynne Williams.

This report presents independent research funded by the National Institute for Health Research (NIHR). The views and opinions expressed by authors in this publication are those of the authors and do not necessarily reflect those of the NHS, the NIHR, NETSCC, the HS&DR programme or the Department of Health. The verbatim quotations included in this publication are the views and opinions expressed by the interviewees and do not necessarily reflect those of the authors, those of the NHS, the NIHR, NETSCC, the HS&DR programme or the Department of Health.

SUGGESTED FURTHER READINGS

Walshe, K., & Davies, H.T.O. (2013) Health research, development & innovation in England from 1988 to 2013: From research production to knowledge mobilization. *Journal of Health Services Research & Policy.* 18(3): Suppl 1–12.
This paper provides a succinct overview of the development of health research funding and knowledge mobilisation in England. It focuses on the changing landscape of research funding and how the concepts surrounding knowledge mobilisation have evolved to reflect this landscape.
McCormack, B., Rycroft-Malone, J., De Corby, K., Hutchinson, A., Bucknall, T., Kent, B., Schultz, A., Snelgrove-Clarke, E., Stetler, C., Titler, M., Wallin, L., & Wilson, V. (2013) A realist review of interventions and strategies to promote evidence-informed healthcare: A focus on change agency. *Implementation Science.* 8: 103.
This paper focuses on the concept of change agency in healthcare and links to the boundary spanners discussed in this chapter. It provides a good review of interventions and strategies to promote research use through the medium of change agency.
Rycroft-Malone, J., Wilkinson, J., Burton, C., Andrews, G., Ariss, S., Baker, R., Dopson, S., Graham, I., Harvey, G., Martin, G., McCormack, B., Stansiewska, S., & Thompson, C. (2011) Implementing health research through academic & clinical partnerships: A realistic evaluation of the Collaborations for Leadership in Applied Health Research & Care (CLAHRC). *Implementation Science.* 6: 74.
This paper focuses on the wider evaluation of the CLAHRCs and provides further information on the study that is the focus of this chapter.

REFERENCES

Bamford, D., Rothwell, K., Tyrrell, P., & Boaden, R. (2013) Improving care for people after stroke: How change was actively facilitated. *Journal of Health Organisation & Management.* 27(5): 548–560.

Best, A., & Holmes, B.J. (2010) Systems thinking, knowledge & action: Towards better models & methods. *Evidence & Policy*. 6(2): 145–159.

Brechin, A., & Siddell, M. (2000) Evidence for practice, in R. Gomm & C. Davies (eds.), *Using evidence in health & social care*. London: SAGE, pp. 3–25.

Clinical Effectiveness Research Agenda Group (CERAG) (2008) *Implementation research agenda report*. Available: http://preview.implementationscience.com/content/supplementary/1748–5908–4–18-s1.pdf. Accessed: October 8, 2015.

Cooksey, D. (2006) *A review of UK health funding*. London: HMSO.

Davis, D. (2006) Continuing education, guideline implementation & the emerging field of transdisciplinary knowledge translation. *The Journal of Continuing Education in the Health Professions*. 26: 5–12.

Dopson, S., & Fitzgerald, L. (2005) *Knowledge to action. Evidence-based health care in context*. Oxford: Oxford University Press.

Eccles, M., Armstrong, D., Baker, R., Clearly, K., Davies, H.T.O., Davies, S., Glasziou, P., Ilott, I., Kinmonth, A.L., Leng, G., Logan, S., Marteau, T., Michie, S., Rogers, H., Rycroft-Malone, J., & Sibbald, B. (2009) An implementation research agenda. *Implementation Science*. 4: 18.

Graham, I.D., Logan, J., Harrison, M.B., Strauss, S.E., Tetroe, J., Caswell, W., & Robinson, N. (2006) Lost in translation: Time for a map? *Journal of Continuing Education in the Health Professions*. 26(1): 13–24.

Greenhalgh, T., Robert, G., MacFarlane, F., Bate, P., & Kyriakidou, O. (2004) Diffusion of innovations in service organisations: Systematic review & recommendations. *Milbank Quarterly*. 82(4): 581–629.

Ipsos MORI (2014) Available: www.ipsos-mori.com/researchpublications/researcharchive/3447/Economy-immigration-and-healthcare-are-Britons-top-three-issues-deciding-general-election-vote.aspx. Accessed: October 8, 2015.

Kitson, A., Rycroft-Malone, J., Harvey, G., McCormack, B., Seers, K., & Titchen, A. (2008) Evaluating the successful implementation of evidence into practice using the PARIHS framework: Theoretical & practical challenges. *Implementation Science*. 3: 1.

Kitson, A.L., Harvey, G., & McCormack, B. (1998) Enabling the implementation of evidence-based practice: A conceptual framework. *Quality in Health Care*. 7(3): 149–158.

McBride, A., Burley, L., Megahed, M., Feldman, C., & Deaton, C. (2014) The role of patient-held alert cards in promoting continuity of care for heart failure patients. *European Journal of Cardiovascular Nursing*. 13(1): 71–77.

McCormack, B., Rycroft-Malone, J., DeCorby, K., Hutchinson, A., Bucknall, T., Kent, B., Schultz, A., Snelgrove-Clarke, E., Stetler, C., Titler, M., Wallin, L., & Wilson, V. (2013) A realist review of interventions & strategies to promote evidence-informed healthcare: a focus on change agency. *Implementation Science*. 8: 103.

Nutley, S., Walter, I., & Davies, H.T.O. (2007) *Using evidence: How research can inform public services*. Bristol: Policy Press.

OECD Health Statistics (2014) Available: http://www.oecd.org/els/health-systems/health-data.htm. Accessed: October 8, 2015.

Pawson, R., & Tilley, N. (1997) *Realistic evaluation*. London: SAGE.

Rycroft-Malone, J., Kitson, A.L., Harvey, G., McCormack, B., Seers, K., Titchen, A., & Estabrooks, C. (2002) Ingredients for change: Revisiting a conceptual framework. *Quality & Safety in Healthcare*. 11: 174–180.

Rycroft-Malone, J., Wilkinson, J., Burton, C., Andrews, G., Ariss, S., Baker, R., Dopson, S., Graham, I., Harvey, G., Martin, G., McCormack, B., Stansiewska, S., & Thompson, C. (2011) Implementing health research through academic & clinical partnerships: A realistic evaluation of the Collaborations for Leadership in Applied Health Research & Care (CLAHRC). *Implementation Science*. 6: 74.

Rycroft-Malone, J., Wilkinson, J., Burton, C., Harvey, G., McCormack, B., Graham, I., & Stansiewska, S. (2013) Collective action around implementation in Collaborations for Leadership in Applied Health Research & Care: Towards a programme theory. *Journal of Health Services Research & Policy.* 18(3): 13–26.

Star, S.L., & Griesemer, J.R. (1989) Institutional ecology, 'translations' & boundary objects: amateurs & professionals in Berkley's museum of vertebrate zoology. *Social Studies of Science.* 19(3): 387–420.

Walshe, K., & Davies, H.T.O. (2013) Health research, development & innovation in England from 1988 to 2013: From research production to knowledge mobilization. *Journal of Health Services Research & Policy.* 18(3): Suppl 1–12.

12 Philanthropy
Knowledge, Practice and Blind Hope

Tobias Jung and Jenny Harrow

A rising sun with the motto 'Let There Be Light' is carved above the entrance of the Central Library in the Scottish town of Dunfermline, birthplace of one of the world's best-known philanthropists, Andrew Carnegie. Opened in 1883 as the first of 2,509 Carnegie Libraries built globally between 1883 and 1929, it reflects philanthropy's role as patron, purveyor, projector, mediator and stimulant of knowledge and learning, a perspective enshrined in philanthropy's origins. From the Greek 'philos' (love) and 'anthropos' (humanity), philanthropy was first used in around 460 BC by playwright Aeschylus to describe the moment when the Titan Prometheus, out of his 'philanthropos tropos', his love of humanity, offered two complementary gifts to the somewhat inept and disappointing human creatures he had created: fire, symbolising all knowledge and practical skills, and blind hope, providing optimism and empowerment to innovate.

Picking up on these two overarching themes—philanthropy's fire for knowledge and the blind hope surrounding philanthropy—our chapter draws on insights from our empirical work, conducted within the UK's ESRC Centre for Charitable Giving and Philanthropy (CGAP), and on philanthropy's wider literature, to explore the nexus between philanthropy, knowledge and practice. After a short overview of our understanding of philanthropy, the first part of the chapter outlines and discusses philanthropy's ambitions and visions for knowledge, and how these have played out since the beginnings of the twentieth century. In the second part of the chapter, we turn to philanthropy's own knowledge: what is the contemporary understanding of philanthropy, and how do foundations perceive learning, lesson drawing, and knowledge mobilisation vis-à-vis their own practices and principles? We conclude with reflections on knowledge needs in relation to philanthropy's provisions and practices.

WHAT DO WE MEAN BY PHILANTHROPY?

Now commonly perceived as the use of private resources—time, treasure, talent—for public benefit and social change, philanthropy covers a spectrum of traditions and expressions: from reciprocity and assistance in the South

African notion of *ubuntu,* via community development and humanitarian aid, to corporate philanthropy and social finance (Jung *et al.* 2016). While charity focuses on symptoms and immediate relief, philanthropy concentrates on identifying and addressing the roots of these symptoms. The most visible expression of philanthropy is the institutional form of the charitable trust or philanthropic foundation. It is through these structures that philanthropic gifts and purposes are widely, although not exclusively, offered and articulated (Anheier & Leat 2013). Consequently, throughout this chapter we use philanthropy as shorthand for the activities of philanthropic foundations.

Foundations are independent grantmaking or operating charities whose resources usually stem from private wealth. This frequently is derived from, or originates in, business ventures: pharmaceuticals as exemplified by the UK's Wellcome Trust, duty-free shops in the case of the Bermuda-registered Atlantic Philanthropies, or confiscated assets as illustrated by the German Volkswagen Stiftung. With a global surge in the number and size of philanthropic foundations since the early twentieth century, foundations have become the fastest-growing non-profit form over the last decade. Albeit fragmented and incomplete, recent statistical data indicate that within the US, 86,192 registered grantmaking foundations have a combined asset base of $715 billion and, in 2012, gave away $52 billion (Foundation Center 2015). In Europe, by comparison, foundations provide around €83–150 billion in grants each year (EESC 2010). Within the UK, the top 300 family foundations contribute £2.9 billion while making up 90% of foundations' giving (Pharoah *et al.* 2014). The latter prominently highlights philanthropy's 'long tail', a global characteristic, whereby small numbers of extremely large foundations by asset size are followed by large and larger numbers of small and smaller foundations.

Reflecting sociocultural and legal differences, foundations span a wide spectrum of functions and legal frameworks, from a very liberal tradition in the Netherlands, where foundations historically have only had rudimentary control and could pursue almost unrestricted economic activities, to the more stringent and specific demands of French foundation law (Hopt *et al.* 2006). Surrounded by an aura of mystique, a number of metaphors and analogies have been used to describe foundations: as 'giraffes', ethereal, slow-moving and aristocratic creatures that could not possibly exist (Nielsen 1972); as 'rich relations', large amounts of money are completely surrounded by people who want some (MacDonald 1956; Weissert & Knott 1995); as 'Don Quixotes in limousines', whose characters and activities combine heroic, tragic and comic features (Whitaker 1974); and as 'Pandora's Boxes', whose outward appeal and iconic properties need to be handled with care (Jung & Harrow 2015). Central to these is a recognition that foundations are paradoxical organisations: their wealth originates in self-interest, yet is supposed to be used altruistically to help those less fortunate; they have great social, economic and political power, yet this is concentrated in the hands of few, generally unelected, foundation leaders; they address public issues, yet usually do not consult the public thereon; they try to add value to society, yet often fail to explore or comprehend any change created (Fleishman 2007:48–49). As one of the most unrestricted contemporary organisational forms, foundations thereby run counter to major organisational, economic and democratic conceptions, and are largely immune from external pressures, such as market forces or popular and political will (Nielsen 1972; Anheier & Leat 2006): 'independence of funding gives the trustees the freedom to act without undue deference to the opinions and agendas of others' (Pharoah *et al.* 2014:11).

While scholars generally cluster foundations within the non-profit sector, their relative resource independence means that they do not belong into any sector (Anheier & Leat 2006). This puts foundations beyond the still-limited, and often generalised, non-profit literature on knowledge processes, knowledge development and especially knowledge sharing (see Rathi *et al.* 2014). Institutional logics underpinning organisations aiming to be 'here for good', however, support a view that foundations are 'knowledge-intensive bodies' (Capozzi *et al.* 2003:89), enabling and motivating knowledge exchange between social and public action organisations (Hurley & Green 2005). How does this play out in practice and what are the resulting opportunities and challenges?

A BURNING DESIRE: PHILANTHROPY'S FIRE FOR KNOWLEDGE

The gift of knowledge, and its potential to improve, steer and control individuals and societies, runs as a defining theme through philanthropy's rich history. This is reflected in the charters and statutes of leading philanthropic foundations: the Carnegie Corporation of New York, Carnegie's last and largest foundation, was set up to 'promote the advancement and diffusion of knowledge and understanding' (Carnegie Corporation of New York 1911); Sir Henry Wellcome's aim for his trust was the 'advancement of research in medical subjects which have, or may develop, an importance for the improvement of the physical condition of mankind' (Bembridge 1986: 343); and Rockefeller and colleagues announced that their foundation should pursue the goal of promoting 'the well-being of mankind throughout the world' by means of 'research, publication, the establishment and maintenance of charitable, benevolent, religious, missionary, and public educational activities, agencies and institutions' (Rockefeller Foundation 1913). These ideas and ideals continue to this day (see Bundesverband Deutscher Stiftungen 2013). The underlying assumption is that with sufficient systematic knowledge, pressing social issues can be practically addressed and solved (Sealander 2003).

Foundations' own perceptions of the resulting nexus of knowledge, policy and practice predates, yet mirrors, contemporary discourse about a 'three generations' perspective that shifts from linear, via relationship, towards system thinking (see Best & Holmes 2010; and Chapter 2). Within philanthropy, these phases roughly relate to three important developments during the twentieth century: the period leading up to World War II, the changed global power dynamics in the post-war years, and the ideological and political debates and challenges arising in the 1960s (Dowie 2001).

Stage 1: Gifting Knowledge and Practice

Rooted in, and reacting to, the social upheaval of the nineteenth century, the first phase started at the turn of the twentieth century. Originating in the US, it accompanied the enormous social changes brought about by large-scale industrialists, such as Carnegie and Rockefeller, and their establishing of major philanthropic foundations with previously unimaginable wealth to address and deal with these changes. Responding to 'indiscriminate giving'— giving that was impulsive, unreflective and injurious, that supported areas, objects and individuals that were unproven to be worthy—this stage focused on the production of formal knowledge to achieve real and permanent good (Carnegie 1901:22–23). The discourse surrounding this vision of 'scientific philanthropy'—whereby philanthropy both needed to use systematic and scientific principles to inform its practices and simultaneously needed to support learning, science and education—resonates with recent debates about professionalising the third sector: it envisaged that the transfer of corporate principles could turn benevolence into an effective and efficient business (Rockefeller Foundation 2015).

Within this context, the development of knowledge by universities and its spreading through libraries were considered paramount (Carnegie 1901:24–41). American philanthropists funded, founded and built colleges and universities at an enormous scale—Cornell, Hopkins, Stanford, Tufts, Vanderbilt. Scientific philanthropy's vision quickly spread from the US to other countries, such as Germany, where philanthropic resources were considered a way to obtain much-needed funding for research and education to complement government provisions (Fuchs & Hoffmann 2004). With foundations, the social sciences and 'social engineering' co-evolving during that time (Roelofs 2003), foundations perceived the social sciences as a basis for '"rationally managed" social change', at home and abroad (Berman 1983:79). As part of this, foundations played a major role in upgrading and standardising education and professional training: from social work to law and engineering (Roelofs 2003).

Stage 2: Linking Knowledge and Practice

Quickly, however, foundations realised that, despite their strengthening of scientific and technological knowledge, social problems and inequity persisted. Beginning around 1945, this led to a recasting of foundation activities and funding towards policy analysis, advocacy, and mediation between academia, professionals and government (Dowie 2001). As part of this, increasing emphasis was placed on developing links across different areas. A prominent example is the recasting of America's global role in the aftermath of World War II, whereby foundations worked closely with government, academics and professionals to develop America's own internal understanding of its place on the international stage, as well as its external expression and portrayal thereof (Müller 2012). This is vividly illustrated by the activities of the Rockefeller Foundation: it contributed to developing the Council on Foreign Relations to inform policy research; it helped to set up the Foreign Policy Association and to publish the Institute of Pacific Relations Report as essentially propaganda machines for strengthening the United States' international role; and it supported and drove the Yale Institute of International Studies as well as the Princeton Public Opinion Studies Programme geared towards understanding and shaping public opinions, and towards developing elites to represent America's newfound confidence globally (Parmar 2002).

Stage 3: Driving Knowledge and Practice

Notwithstanding some successes, working with government turned out to be difficult. Foundations realised that it might be better to take actions themselves or to fund social movements to do it for them, thereby shaping knowledge and practice directly and indirectly. This has become the defining feature of the third stage. This started in the 1960s (Dowie 2001) and, as prominently illustrated in education, continues to this day: from the intricate web of influence philanthropy has spun in the English academies programme (Ball & Junemann 2011) to philanthropy's agenda-setting in the privatisation of the Italian education system (Grimaldi & Serpieri 2013).

During this third stage, growing political and ideological chasms across the foundation world have arisen, both domestically in the US and as part of foundations' global export activities (Roelofs 2003): conservative foundations try to counteract and stem liberal foundations' prosocial activism and advocacy and vice versa (Dowie 2001); liberal foundations concerned about climate change try to advance policies and practices to prevent global warming (William & Flora Hewlett Foundation 2015) while conservative foundations have been central to successfully delaying meaningful government policies and actions by playing a major role in developing and maintaining the climate change countermovement (Brulle 2014).

Despite the change in dominant logic, the visions of, and for, knowledge inherent in the preceding two stages continue. Reflecting the argument that philanthropy's history should be perceived in geological terms, as repeating layers upon layers of developments and ideas that continue to influence and shape each other (Cunningham 2016), current activities focus on the entire spectrum of knowledge production and mobilisation: from dealing with 'formal' official and structured educational systems, to 'non-formal', voluntarily organised and provided education, as well as 'informal' learning and knowledge exchanges (Bundesverband Deutscher Stiftungen 2015:7). While the surrounding rhetoric might have moved on—'philanthropreneurship' and 'high-impact philanthropy' replacing 'scientific philanthropy'—the underlying ideas and practices prevail.

PLAYING WITH FIRE? THE DIFFICULT RELATIONSHIP BETWEEN PHILANTHROPY, KNOWLEDGE AND PRACTICE

Foundations have made major positive contributions to society. Through their quest for knowledge, they have inspired, established and strengthened new areas of research and thinking; they have helped to inform and educate the public and the professions, as well as national and international government policies and practices (Krige & Rausch 2012). While these activities have often been described in the neutralising rhetoric surrounding the advancement of knowledge and the promotion of public interest (O'Connor 2007), this has never been a neutral process. The creation, provision and distribution of knowledge through philanthropy has always had selective, normative and controlling undertones. For example, philanthropy has enabled black education to exist 'but not to flourish' (Gasman & Drezner 2008:90); reacting to the Ford Foundation's sponsorship of progressive law school clinics and poverty law curricula, the Olin Foundation played a central role in moving US law schools during the 1960s and '70s to become anchors of the conservative legal movement (Teles 2008); and contemporary management was transformed by leading US foundations through elevating its status and by conferring elite legitimacy on select management schools to incentivise others to adopt those foundations' preferred standards (Khurana 2007). Thus, in the development and distribution of knowledge, foundations can be seen as having a strong gatekeeper function (Fisher 1983). From the Rockefeller Foundation's activities in using social sciences to transform developing countries during the 1960s (Berman 1983) to the contemporary normative policy transfer activities of the Open Society Institute—hub of billionaire George Soros's network of autonomous foundations and organisations in over 60 countries—aimed towards furnishing post-socialist countries with appropriate knowledge and expertise (Stone 2010), knowledge has been seen by foundations as a provider of hegemony, as a tool that allows them to 'hasten societal development along acceptable lines' (Berman 1983:80).

Foundation funding for higher education remains a major issue in this context. Within universities themselves, as both targets for, and seekers of, philanthropic funding, and indirectly within governments, where the emphasis has been towards replacing public with philanthropic and private funding, a surprising neglect of critical reflection on which forms and directions of knowledge are, and are not, being championed by foundations is evident. On the one hand, this has allowed a slow replacing of different educational logics with neoliberal educational visions and practices (Scott *et al.* 2009); on the other, it means that foundations' own perceptions of what constitutes research, often derived from their own involvement in the natural sciences and rooted in positivist world views (see Else Kröner-Fresenius-Stiftung 2015), are being forced upon other areas, such as the social sciences and the humanities, as part of the funding process.

Most importantly, however, the implicit superiority of philanthropy over other education stakeholders remains unchallenged. Although foundations cast themselves as 'reliable partners' in, and for, research (Bundesverband Deutscher Stiftungen 2013), there is generally a very clear perspective of what such partnership entails. For example, the European Foundation Centre's (EFC) Research Forum in 2014 was emphatic that

> the division between funders who provide the money and the universities and institutes that receive it is a problem to be discussed openly. *Universities need to be helped to define the areas where they can be internationally competitive.*
>
> (EFC 2014:3—our emphasis)

In a further reminder of the nexus between knowledge transmission and power, this Forum's report also reminded its readers that

> foundations are not simply philanthropic versions of public sector funders: they can establish their own criteria, and work in novel ways to build communities and encourage risk.
>
> (EFC 2014:3)

Quite how novel foundations are in their working approaches and outcomes is, however, a contested area, as is the assertion that foundations bravely and routinely support risk-taking. Questioning their historic status as providers of innovation and challengers of social issues, the last few years have seen increasing criticism that foundations' work and support, especially in education, might be perceived as window dressing, where being seen to be doing something is more important than achieving positive outcomes (Thümler 2011); as providing hegemony and amelioration to maintain the status quo, instead of challenging or altering social order (see Fisher 1983; Herrold 2012). It is thus unsurprising that critics have raised concerns as to whether foundations are quietly supplanting democratic institutions with 'a new feudalism' (Roelofs 2007:479). As part of this, two questions warrant further exploration: who does actually benefit most from the knowledge provided by foundations, and how do such benefits express themselves?

While there have been tentative explorations into the world-making activities of Carnegie and the social, cultural, economic and symbolic capital derived from his activities (Harvey *et al.* 2011), the privileged and privileging position of philanthropy to generate and use knowledge in line with its own interests remains problematic (Guilhot 2007). Central questions need to be addressed about the gains foundations derive from their contributions to developing knowledge as they themselves invest in a variety of markets and ventures to sustain, grow or replenish their own resource bases. This is touched upon by those who have pointed to foundations' blurring of boundaries between the public, private and non-profit sectors (see Roelofs 2007), vividly illustrated in the long-standing and intricate, individual and organisational links between foundation activities in agriculture, crop research, policy advocacy on genetically modified crops, and corporate gains in the developing world (see Vidal 2010; Harmon 2013; Rockefeller Foundation 2015). As the story of philanthropy is generally told from the philanthropists' perspective rather than from the perspective of those receiving or affected by philanthropy, there is unfortunately a lack of insight and research in this area, a problem that persists across the philanthropy field more widely.

BLIND HOPE? THE NEED FOR BETTER KNOWLEDGE ON AND FOR PHILANTHROPY

With philanthropy being 'a product of social optimism and modernity' (Stauber 2010:88), one might expect foundations to focus strongly and proactively on knowledge acquisition, utilisation, sharing and exchange for social benefits. While foundations have appreciated their external role as supporters and shapers of knowledge, there has often been a failure to realise the internal importance of knowledge: that knowledge on, and for, philanthropy itself offers the basis for effective and appropriate practices in, and roles for, the field (Capozzi *et al.* 2003).

Within the literatures on organisation studies and strategy, there is widespread agreement that an understanding of organisational types is a prerequisite for defining and positioning an organisation and its processes, both theoretically and practically (see Fiss 2011). Given that foundations are an umbrella concept incorporating diverse ideas, ideals and institutional characteristics, it is, however, often hard to generalise and compare these organisations. Even when looking at a single foundation form within one country, such as UK community foundations, major local and national differences can be identified (Jung *et al.* 2013). Recognising the variety of ways in which foundations have been described, differentiated, acclaimed, criticised and understood—including categorisations around roles (e.g., grantmaking, social investment, policy advocacy), giving focus (e.g., education, health, social welfare), sources of income and power (e.g., endowed, partly endowed, single or multiple donors, individual, family, business or corporate wealth) and geographical span (e.g., national, regional, local, 'community')—a clearer mapping and typologising of foundations is urgently needed. There is, however, currently no subfield or strong organised interdisciplinary grouping focusing on the critical study of foundations (Roelofs *et al.* 2007).

This need for a stronger knowledge base on foundations as an organisational type is appreciated by the foundation world itself (Warne 2007). Alongside providing conceptual and systematic understanding, it is considered as serving a number of practical purposes: it could prevent 'outbursts of regulatory enthusiasm' (Hall 1992:242), protect 'true' foundations and their work, assist in developing more appropriate and favourable legal and fiscal operating contexts, and foster understanding about foundations' role, potential and challenges within the changing policymaking landscape (Anheier & Daley 2007; Warne 2007). Nonetheless, foundations, while happy to label themselves so as to demarcate their class and pedigree—e.g., community foundations, endowed foundations, corporate foundations—are generally reluctant to be formally grouped together. Preferring to be 'stand-alone' personae, they display a strange and stubborn aversion to unifying principles (Orosz 2007). This is illustrated in the old philanthropy sector adage that 'if you have seen one foundation, you have seen one foundation'. Whether this is attributable to the individualising approach, whereby foundations are usually named after their founder(s) or funder(s)—Bertelsmann, Bosch, Gates, Nuffield, Packard—whether, as elite, and often male, projects and accessories, an acknowledgement of similarity and overlap is difficult to accept, or whether there is indeed only a limited basis for generalisation warrants wider and more detailed examination.

Notwithstanding its activities in professionalising other areas, philanthropy itself seems to be a profession that is wanting (Stauber 2010). Despite a growing rhetoric surrounding professionalism in grantmaking, the emergence of a cadre of grantmaking professionals in the foundation world, and the recent growth in philanthropy education (see Keidan *et al.* 2014), there is a dearth of literature, theoretical or empirical, examining the roles of foundation staff and their roles vis-à-vis clients and boards. The few notable exceptions paint a complex picture. On the one hand, they point to a disjoint between foundation 'professionals' and those with direct and personal experience in, and knowledge on, the problems to be addressed (Rosenman 2010); on the other, they ascribe foundations' programme officers critical knowledge sharing or brokering roles between the different universes occupied by grantees and foundation board members (Delgado *et al.* 2001; Kohl 2008).

In line with non-profits more generally, philanthropy has traditionally suffered from 'dialectic deafness': your own organisational ideologies, commitments and practices make it difficult to hear, understand, accept and act on any criticisms of your activities (l'Anson & Pfeifer 2013:50). As part of this, the foundation world seems to mirror wider societal developments: a conflation between wealth and wisdom, the assumption that if you are, or have been, funding an area for a long time you are automatically an expert in that area (see Jung *et al.* 2014). The reluctance to engage more strongly and critically with one's own organisational situation is further aggravated by another non-profit trend: the perception that 'wasting' resources on internal costs and overheads seems unacceptable when trying to maximise 'doing good' (Capozzi *et al.* 2003). Taken together, the resulting insularity has far-reaching consequences for foundations' activities. There are indications that foundations rarely move out of their comfort zones; that their funding favours those within 'a known and comfortable universe' so that engagement with marginalised groups and causes can often be limited (Rosenman 2010:26).

However, the last years have also seen increasing efforts by foundations and philanthropists to improve accountability, transparency, grant appraisals, and wider internal and external understanding of their work (see Bill & Melinda Gates Foundation 2015; GlassPockets 2015). Yet, reports and initiatives often draw on grantees' perspectives and are commissioned, and at times written, managed and administered, by foundations themselves. Academic involvement has been limited. Even where this does happen, in a context where foundations are emerging as an increasingly important source of non-academic and academic funding, major questions about dependencies, power balances and objectivity arise (Arnove 1980; Schervish 2014). With potential stakeholders in the research process including donors, grantmakers and grantees, foundations and their professional staff and/or volunteers, trustees, the constituencies served by foundations, regulatory agencies and the researchers themselves, the area is ripe with potential and actual research dilemmas (Hall 1992). The underpinnings of philanthropy are rarely, if ever, questioned (Roelofs *et al.* 2007). All of these are further complicated by major practical challenges: a lack of reliable and longitudinal data, obstacles to research access, difficulties with attributing causality to particular foundation activities, and non-profits' conflating of overlapping ideas, such as compliance, accountability, transparency and learning (Rosenman 2010; Thümler 2011).

A final aspect that needs to be considered within this context is the question of knowledge management and knowledge ownership. Foundations' internal knowledge is rarely ever shared or made public. This is explicit in grantmaking, where confidentiality over grant application content, decision-making, and information on organisations refused funding prevails. That is, confidentiality prevails despite the potential value this might offer to applicants and/or fellow foundations, and against refused grant-seekers' reported frustration and disappointment in the lack of knowledge and feedback, urgently needed in the context of increased competition for funding (Harrow *et al.* 2011). This is a wider problem in that lessons from mistakes and failures are not shared, thereby constraining the development of more promising and informed practices (Frumkin 2006).

Within philanthropy the diversity of, and potential for, failures is both high and wide-reaching. It spans funded areas' actual or perceived under-performance against foundations' ambitions, highlighted in the Corston Independent Funders' Coalition's disquiet with the English criminal justice system (Jung *et al.* 2014); knowingly or unknowingly funding controversial organisations, prominently illustrated in the recent case of funding for the advocacy organisation CAGE by the Joseph Rowntree Charitable Trust and the Roddick Foundation (Charity Commission 2015); poor practice, high-lighted by the financial disclosure 'mistakes' made by the Bill and Hillary Rodham Clinton Foundation (Pally 2015); and questionable activities in the case of the Cup Trust which, while raising £176 million in donations and claiming £46 million in tax relief, only spent £55,000 on charitable work over a two-year period (Ricketts 2013). As such, the foundation world is rife for knowledge-sharing and lesson-drawing: its mistakes are an untapped resource (Giloth & Gewirtz 2009). Although rhetoric on this topic has been prominent (see Frumkin 2006; Giloth & Gewirtz 2009), bar few exceptions (see DP Evaluation 2012), the sharing of such knowledge remains limited. Where gleaning knowledge from philanthropic failure takes place, if done at all, it is usually only done after a long passage of time.

While the protection of internal knowledge thus seems paramount, the same cannot be said of foundations' treatment of the intellectual property they generate. Here, the opposite seems to be the case, with foundations often being blasé about what happens to, or who benefits from, the knowl-edge they have funded: research centres, universities, think tanks and other knowledge producers set up by foundations subsequently often use these resources to develop, claim, protect and benefit from the intellectual and physical outputs they produce, thereby curtailing the original provision of knowledge. With the wider move towards open access in academia, there are early indications that foundations might have woken up to this issue. This is illustrated by the Bill and Melinda Gates Foundation's (2015:np) announcement of its Open Access Policy. This is 'committed to information sharing and transparency' by allowing 'unrestricted access and reuse of all peer-reviewed published research funded, in whole or in part, by the founda-tion, including any underlying datasets'.

A similar naivety is evident in foundations' understanding of, and approach to, their own knowledge needs. Here, a strong reliance on person-ally held knowledge and verbal communication persists:

> During the many years I worked as a foundation program officer and supervised others, my staff and I were expected to know who else was funding our grantee organisations. I have never seen an internal founda-tion grant recommendation form that didn't ask for that basic piece of data. Sounds easy, right? But to this day, the primary way of gathering that information is to ask the grantee . . .
>
> (Smith 2014:np).

CONCLUDING REMARKS

Foundations are individualistic organisations operating within collective contexts. With knowledge being a 'justified personal belief that increases an individual's capacity to take effective action' (Alavi & Leidner 2001:109), foundations are a group of organisations where such beliefs may be intermingled with, or contrasted with, other evidence sources; where institutional independence as a key organising value may limit or militate against inter-organisational knowledge flows, or sanction them strongly. This autonomy and privacy may privilege informal knowledge channels and informal learning (Carliner 2013) or knowledge's formalisation for a variety of purposes. Such potentially powerful positions can enable foundations to be knowledge mentors and knowledge arbiters as well as knowledge users and seekers.

Just like any other area of philanthropic or charitable activity, philanthropic engagement with knowledge has clear underpinnings of what counts as 'deserving' and what as 'undeserving'. Within this context, foundations' power is subtle. It lies in setting the intellectual and professional parameters for knowledge and practice by deciding 'who will receive support to study what subjects in what settings' (Arnove 1980:319). Taken together, these point to similarities with the challenges experienced with organisations and their management of knowledge more broadly: reactive understanding and valuation of knowledge; hostility towards knowledge sharing; knowledge hoarding or suppression, as well as knowledge protection within organisations and their collaborators (see Manhart & Thalmann 2015). However, given that philanthropic foundations exist to promote public good, and in most states enjoy tax advantages for doing so, the question arises as to whether foundations' knowledge—internally and externally—is in fact public knowledge. With philanthropic foundations increasingly becoming a cornerstone of the private welfare state (Boesso *et al.* 2014), and in the absence of a theory of foundations and of philanthropic knowledge, the nexus between foundations and knowledge needs urgent and wider exploration, as well as intellectual and practical development. To this end, our chapter has provided a critique, not a criticism, of the area.

SUGGESTED FURTHER READINGS

Krige and Rausch's (2012) collection—although including some contributions in German and French—provides an overview of how foundations have played a central role in co-producing knowledge and shaping twentieth-century policy contexts.

Berman (1983) explores this further by pointing to the role of ideology in philanthropy's involvement in the establishment of the social sciences and in its transferring knowledge and practices internationally.

Jung *et al.* (2016) provide a comprehensive introduction to, and overview of, contemporary philanthropy's facets and expressions.

REFERENCES

Alavi, M., & Leidner, D.E. (2001) Review: Knowledge management & knowledge management systems: Conceptual foundations & research issues. *MIS Quarterly*. 25(1): 107–136.

Anheier, H.K., & Daley, S. (2007) *The politics of foundations: A comparative analysis*. London: Routledge.

Anheier, H.K., & Leat, D. (2006) *Creative philanthropy*. London: Routledge.

Anheier, H.K., & Leat, D. (2013) Philanthropic foundations: What rationales? *Social Research*. 80(2): 449–472.

Arnove, P. (1980) *Philanthropy & cultural imperialism*. Indiana: Indiana University Press.

Ball, S. & Junemann, C. (2011) Education policy & philanthropy—The changing landscape of English educational governance. *International Journal of Public Administration*. 34(10): 646–661.

Bembridge, B.A. (1986) The basic sciences & medicine, in A.R. Hall & B.A. Bembridge (eds.), *Physic & philanthropy. A history of the Wellcome Trust 1936–1986*. Cambridge: Cambridge University Press, pp. 343–387.

Berman, E.H. (1983) *The influence of the Carnegie, Ford & Rockefeller Foundations on American foreign policy: The ideology of philanthropy*. Albany: State University of New York Press.

Best, A., & Holmes, B.J. (2010) Systems thinking, knowledge & action: Towards better models & methods. *Evidence & Policy*. 6(2): 145–159.

Bill & Melinda Gates Foundation (2015) How we work. *Bill & Melinda Gates Foundation Open Access Policy*. Available: www.gatesfoundation.org/how-we-work/general-information/open-access-policy. Accessed: October 8, 2015.

Boesso, G., Cerbioni, F., & Kumar, K. (2014) What drives good philanthropy? The relationship between governance & strategy in foundations, in G. Luca, A. Hinna, & F. Monteduro (ed.), *Mechanisms, roles and consequences of governance: Emerging issues (Studies in public and non-profit governance, volume 2.)* Bradford: Emerald Group Publishing Limited, pp. 159–180.

Brulle, R.J. (2014) Institutionalizing delay: Foundation funding & the creation of US climate change counter-movement organizations. *Climatic change*. 122: 681–694.

Bundesverband Deutscher Stiftungen (2013) *Private Stiftungen als Partner der Wissenschaft*. Berlin: Bundesverband Deutscher Stiftungen.

Bundesverband Deutscher Stiftungen (2015) *Bildung ist Gemeinschaftsaufgabe. Stiftungen und ihr Beitrag zu einem kommunalen Bildungsmanagement*. Berlin: Sabine Süß.

Capozzi, M.M., Lowell, S.M., & Silverman, L. (2003) Knowledge management comes to philanthropy. *The McKinsey Quarterly*. 2. Available: http://ictkm.cgiar.org/Newsletter/McKinsey%20Quarterly.htm. Accessed: October 8, 2015.

Carliner, S. (2013) How have concepts of informal learning developed over time? *Performance Improvement*. 52(3): 5–11.

Carnegie, A. (1901) *The gospel of wealth & other timely essays*. New York: The Century Co.

Carnegie Corporation of New York (1911) Act of Incorporation. Available: www.carnegie.org/media/filer_public/0d/bc/0dbc6c21–9124–467b-b790-ba8367c7e694/ccny_governance_charter_updated_20110922.pdf. Accessed: October 8, 2015.

Charity Commission (2015) Charity Commission statement: Charities funding CAGE, 6 March. Available: www.gov.uk/government/news/charity-commission-statement-charities-funding-cage. Accessed: October 8, 2015.

Cunningham, H. (2016) The multi-layered history of western philanthropy, in T. Jung, S.D. Phillips, & J. Harrow (eds.), *The Routledge companion to philanthropy*. Routledge: London, pp. 42–71.

Delgado, L.T., Orellana-Damacela, L.E., & Zanoni, M J. (2001) *Chicago philanthropy: A profile of the grantmaking profession*. Chicago: Loyola University.

Dowie, M. (2001) *American foundations: An investigative history*. Cambridge, MA: MIT Press.

DP Evaluation (2012) A funder conundrum. Available: www.dianaprincessofwales-memorialfund.org/sites/default/files/documents/publications/A%20Funder%20 Conundrum%20-%20full%20report%20-%20Sept%2012.pdf. Accessed: October 8, 2015.

EESC (2010) INT/498 European Foundation Statute. European Economic & Social Committee Brussels, April 28.

EFC (2014) Towards a new concept of excellence in research? Report of a stakeholders' conference organized by the European Foundation Centre Research Forum, October 13–14, Warsaw, Poland.

Else Kröner-Fresenius-Stiftung (2015) Inspiration für die Zukunft: Gemeinsam zukunftsträchtige Forschungsfelder entwickeln. 71. Deutscher Stiftungstag, Karlsruhe 6. May 2015.

Fisher, D. (1983) The role of philanthropic foundations in the reproduction & production of hegemony: Rockefeller foundations & the social sciences. *Sociology*. 17(2): 206–233.

Fiss, P.C. (2011) Building better causal theories: A fuzzy set approach to typologies in organization research. *Academy of Management Journal*. 54(2): 393–420.

Fleishman, J.L. (2007) *The foundation: A great American secret*. New York: Public Affairs.

Foundation Centre (2015) Knowledge services. Available: http://foundationcenter.org/knowledgeservices. Accessed: April 6, 2015.

Frumkin, P. (2006) *Strategic giving: The art & science of philanthropy*. Chicago: University of Chicago Press.

Fuchs, E., & Hoffmann, D. (2004) Philanthropy & science in Wilhelmine Germany, in T. Adam (ed.), *Philanthropy, patronage & civil society*. Indiana: Indiana University Press, pp. 103–119.

Gasman, M., & Drezner, D. (2008) White corporate philanthropy & its support of private black colleges in the 1960s & 1970s. *International Journal of Educational Advancement*. 8: 79–92.

Giloth, R., & Gewirtz, S. (2009) Philanthropy & mistakes: An untapped resource. *Foundation Review*. 1(1): 115–124.

GlassPockets (2015) *Bringing transparency to the world of philanthropy*. Available: http://glasspockets.org. Accessed: October 8, 2015.

Grimaldi, E., & Serpieri, R. (2013) Privatising education policy-making in Italy: New governance & the reculturing of a welfarist education state. *Education Inquiry*. 4(3): 443–472.

Guilhot, N. (2007) Reforming the world: George Soros, global capitalism & the philanthropic management of the social sciences. *Critical Sociology*. 33(3): 447–477.

Hall, P.D. (1992) *Inventing the nonprofit sector & other essays on philanthropy, voluntarism, & nonprofit organisations*. Baltimore: John Hopkins University Press.

Harmon, A. (2013) Golden rice: Lifesaver? *The New York Times*, August 24.

Harrow, J., Fitzmaurice, J., McKenzie, T., & Bogdanova, M. (2011) *The art of refusal: The experiences of grantmakers & grant seekers*. London: Centre for Charity Effectiveness, Cass Business School, City University.

Harvey, C., Maclean, M., Gordon, J., & Shaw, E. (2011) Andrew Carnegie & the foundations of contemporary entrepreneurial philanthropy. *Business History*. 53(3): 425–450.

Herrold, C. (2012) Philanthropic foundations in Egypt; fueling change or safeguarding status quo? Takaful 2012, Second Annual Conference on Arab Philanthropy & Civic Engagement, Selected Research, John D. Gerhard Centre for Philanthropy & Civic Engagement, Cairo, June 10–12, 2012.

Hopt, K.J., Walz, W.R., von Hippel, T., & Then, V. (2006) *The European foundation: A new legal approach*. Cambridge: Cambridge University Press.

Hurley, T.A., & Green, C.W. (2005) Knowledge management & the nonprofit industry: A within & between approach. *Journal of Knowledge Management Practice*. 6(1).

Jung, T., & Harrow, J. (2015) New development: Philanthropy in networked governance—Treading with care. *Public Money & Management*. 35(1): 47–52.

Jung, T., Harrow, J., & Phillips, S. (2013) Developing a better understanding of community foundations in the UK's localisms. *Policy & Politics*. 41(3): 409–427.

Jung, T., Kaufmann, J., & Harrow, J. (2014) When funders do direct advocacy: An exploration of the United Kingdom's Corston Independent Funders' Coalition. *Nonprofit & Voluntary Sector Quarterly*. 43(1): 38–56.

Jung, T., Phillips, S.D., & Harrow, J. (2016) *The Routledge companion to philanthropy*. London: Routledge.

Keidan, C., Jung, T., & Pharoah, C. (2014) Philanthropy education in the United Kingdom & continental Europe: Current provision, perceptions & opportunities, Centre for Charitable Giving & Philanthropy Occasional Paper, September, Cass Business School City University London & School of Management, University of St. Andrews.

Khurana, R. (2007) *From higher aims to hired hands: The social transformation of American business schools & the unfilled promise of management as a profession*. Princeton, NJ: Princeton University Press.

Kohl, E. (2008) The program officer: Negotiating the politics of philanthropy, Institute for the Study of Societal Issues, ISSI Fellows Working Papers, Berkeley: University of California.

Krige, J., & Rausch, H. (2012) *American foundations & the coproduction of world order in the twentieth century*. Göttingen: Vandenhoeck & Ruprecht.

l'Anson, C., & G. Pfeifer (2013) A critique of humanitarian reason: Agency, power, & privilege. *Journal of Global Ethics*. 9(1): 49–63.

MacDonald, D. (1956) *The ford foundation: The men & the millions: An unauthorized biography*. New York: Reynal Publishing.

Manhart, M., & Thalmann, S. (2015) Protecting organizational knowledge: A structured literature review. *Journal of Knowledge Management*. 19(2): 190–211.

Müller, T.B. (2012) Die Macht der Menschenfreunde—Die Rockefeller Foundation, die Sozialwissenschaften und die amerikanische Außenpolitik im Kalten Krieg, in J. Krige & H. Rausch (eds.), *American foundations & the coproduction of world order in the Twentieth century*. Göttingen : Vandenhoeck & Ruprecht, pp. 146–172.

Nielsen, W.A. (1972) *The big foundations*. New York: Columbia University Press.

O'Connor, A. (2007) *Social science for what?* New York: Russell Sage Foundation.

Orosz, J.J. (2007) *Effective foundation management: 14 challenges of philanthropic leadership & how to outfox them*. Lanham, MD: AltaMira Press.

Pally, M. (2015) A commitment to honesty, transparency, & accountability. Available: www.clintonfoundation.org/blog/2015/04/26/commitment-honesty-transparency-and-accountability. Accessed: October 8, 2015.

Parmar, I. (2002) 'To relate knowledge & action': The impact of the Rockefeller Foundation on foreign policy thinking during America's rise to globalism 1939–1945. *Minerva*. 40: 235–263.

Pharoah, C., Jenkins, R., & Goddard, K. (2014) Giving trends, Top 300 foundations: 2014 Report, Association of Charitable Foundations & the Centre for Charitable Giving & Philanthropy, Cass Business School, London.

Rathi, D., M. Given, L., & Forcier, E. (2014) Inter-organisational partnerships & knowledge sharing: The perspective of non-profit organisations (NPOs). *Journal of Knowledge Management.* 18(5): 867–885.

Ricketts, A. (2013) Cup Trust scandal a 'disaster' for the sector, Charity Commission chair tells MPs, Third Sector, March 7 2013. Available: http://www.thirdsector.co.uk/cup-trust-scandal-disaster-sector-charity-commission-chair-tells-mps/finance/article/1173783. Accessed: December 22, 2015.

Rockefeller Foundation (1913) An act to incorporate The Rockefeller Foundation. Available: www.rockefellerfoundation.org/app/uploads/Rockefeller-Foundation-Charter.pdf. Accessed: October 8, 2015.

Rockefeller Foundation (2015) Research institutes. Available: http://rockefeller100.org/exhibits/show/agriculture/research-institutes. Accessed: October 8, 2015.

Roelofs, J. (2003) *Foundations & public policy.* New York: State University of New York Press.

Roelofs, J. (2007) Foundations & collaboration. *Critical Sociology.* 33(3): 479–504.

Roelofs, J., Arnove, R., & Faber, D. (2007) Note on this special issue. *Critical Sociology.* 33(3): 387–388.

Rosenman, M. (2010) *Foundations for the common good.* Washington DC: Caring to Change Project.

Schervish, P.G. (2014) High-tech donors & their impact philanthropy: The conventional, novel & strategic traits of agent-animated wealth & philanthropy, in M.L. Taylor, R.J. Strom, & D.O. Renz (eds.), *Handbook of research on entrepreneurs' engagement in philanthropy.* Cheltenham: Edward Elgar, pp. 148–182.

Scott, J., Lubienski, C., & DeBray-Pelot, E. (2009) The politics of advocacy in education. *Educational Policy.* 23(1): 3–14.

Sealander, J. (2003) Curing evils at their source: The arrival of scientific giving, in L.J. Friedman & M.D. McGarvie (eds.), *Charity, philanthropy & civil society in American history.* Cambridge: Cambridge University Press, pp. 217–239.

Smith, B. (2014) Developing a culture of knowledge management. *Stanford Social Innovation Review.* March 11.

Stauber, K. (2010) Philanthropy: Are we a profession? Should we be? *The Foundation Review.* 2(1): 87–94.

Stone, D.S. (2010) Private philanthropy or policy transfer? The transnational norms of the Open Society Institute. *Policy & Politics.* 38(2): 269–287.

Teles, S. (2008) *The rise of the conservative legal movement: The battle for control of the law.* Princeton, NJ: Princeton University Press.

Thümler, E. (2011) Foundations, schools & the state: School improvement partnerships in Germany & the United States as legitimacy-generating arrangements. *Public Management Review.* 13(8): 1095–1116.

Vidal, J. (2010) Why is the Gates foundation investing in GM giant Monsanto? Available: www.theguardian.com/global-development/poverty-matters/2010/sep/29/gates-foundation-gm-monsanto. Accessed: October 8, 2015.

Warne, J. (2007) Apples & oranges . . . and kiwis & plums—Creating a typology of foundations in Europe. *EFFECT*, Autumn: 10, European Foundation Centre.

Weissert, C.S., & Knott, J.H. (1995) Foundations' impact on policymaking: Results from a pilot study. *Health Affairs.* 14: 275–286.

Whitaker, B. (1974) *The foundations: An anatomy of philanthropy & society*. London: Eyre Methuen.

William & Flora Hewlett Foundation (2015) Philanthropy's role in fighting climate change. Available: www.hewlett.org/philanthropys-role-fighting-climate-change. Accessed: October 8, 2015.

Part C

Integrating the Insights on Knowledge and Practice and Their Implications for Action

13 Knowledge Mobilisation
Creating, Sharing and Using Knowledge

Sandra Nutley and Huw Davies

INTRODUCTION

There has long been a concern that individuals, groups and organisations do not always perform as effectively as they could. There are many possible explanations including ambiguous or conflicting goals, lack of motivation and constraining contexts. Here we focus on two other related reasons: the often slow percolation of knowledge to where it can be applied (a 'knowledge-knowing' gap); and the challenges faced in responding to new knowledge even when it is readily available (the so-called 'knowing-doing gap'). Commonly, individuals, groups and management teams may be unaware of promising developments in their field of work, and so may continue with outmoded forms of practice. This may be because such knowledge has been developed separately from the contexts in which they work and has not been shared effectively across organisational and professional boundaries. Even when new knowledge is readily available, individuals and managers may know how they could improve performance but still feel unable or disinclined to change what is actually done. Such knowledge-knowing and knowing-doing gaps have already been illustrated in Chapter 10 on environmental policy and in Chapter 11 on healthcare.

Knowledge mobilisation is concerned with the processes and activities aimed at reducing these gaps. We use it as a shorthand term for a wide range of approaches aimed at encouraging the creation, sharing and application of knowledge. These approaches are often targeted at improving the connection between knowledge and practice at an individual level, but they also need to address arrangements for building and using knowledge at an organisational level. At an even wider scale, they may recognise that organisations are embedded in systems and hence there is a need to consider the broader ecology of knowledge mobilisation.

There is a lot of debate about appropriate ways of approaching the knowledge mobilisation challenge and commentators often use different terms to differentiate between alternative perspectives on this. For example, the authors of Chapters 2 (knowledge) and 11 (healthcare) have already introduced the idea of three generations of knowledge-to-action thinking

(Best & Holmes 2010). In this schema, different terms are used to capture different assumptions about the knowledge-to-action problem and how it is best addressed:

- *Knowledge transfer*—here knowledge is seen as generalisable across contexts and the task is to improve ways of packaging and pushing this knowledge across organisational and community boundaries.
- *Knowledge exchange or interaction*—here knowledge is viewed as context-linked and the process of knowing is envisaged as a social process. The task is to develop effective interpersonal and social relationships that enable people to learn from one another, recognising that knowledge will be adapted in the process of being adopted.
- *Knowledge integration or intermediation*—here knowledge is tightly woven with local priorities, structures, cultures and contexts. The task is to understand the deeply embedded nature of knowledge and work collaboratively with groups, organisations and sectors to develop effective adaptive systems.

It is important to recognise such differences in approach. As was discussed in Chapter 2, how we think about the nature of knowledge shapes our understanding of the knowledge in (or into) practice problem and the strategies we use to improve knowledge-practice connections. Much of what is written about knowledge mobilisation assumes that it is possible and productive to analyse 'knowledge' and 'practice' as somewhat separate concepts. Hence the assumptions underpinning the content of much of this chapter are not in line with a practice theory (discussed in Chapter 3) where 'doing and knowing are one and the same' (Gherardi 2006:xii). We do, however, reflect on this at various points in the chapter and these ideas are developed further in Chapter 14 (on the co-production of knowledge and practice).

A lot of the literature exploring knowledge mobilisation is concerned with the underuse of a particular form and source of knowledge: research-based knowledge (and this is the focus of the discussions in Chapters 10 and 11 on environmental policy and healthcare respectively). However, other chapters in the book remind us that individuals and work organisations are concerned with ways of sharing insights from other ways of knowing. Chapter 7 on sensing bodies and craft work discusses the process of developing individual expertise through learning from self-experience and the experience of colleagues. Here the process of learning involves ongoing situated interaction with experts and materials. Chapter 8 considers how individuals and groups from arts and commercial backgrounds, who privilege different ways of knowing (aesthetic, analytic, commercial), share and use knowledge as part of the creative development process in an advertising agency.

The aims of this chapter, then, are to provide an overview of different ways of viewing the knowledge mobilisation challenge, and to explore their implications for developing strategies and actions to improve 'knowledge in use'. We start by outlining the view through five conceptual lenses, lenses that themselves draw from different fields of study and synthesise across various social science disciplines. Following the view from each of these perspectives, we discuss their implications for developing strategies and actions to improve knowledge mobilisation. Throughout we draw on insights from previous chapters to illustrate many of the points considered. We conclude with some reflections on the perspectives and principles discussed in the chapter and suggest areas where there is a need for further work.

THE VIEW THROUGH FIVE CONCEPTUAL LENSES

The academic literature that considers the creation, sharing and use of knowledge is widely dispersed across a range of disciplines, including philosophy, psychology, sociology, information science, organisational studies and political science. There are at least five established ways of viewing this issue. Within psychology, neuroscience and educational research, attention has mostly been paid to the process by which individuals gain new knowledge and expertise: *individual learning*. Within organisational studies, the focus has been more on the process of *organisational learning*, which can be broadly defined as the way organisations build and organise knowledge and routines, and use the broad skills of their workforce to improve organisational performance (Dodgson 1993). Remaining at an organisational level, a somewhat separate stream of literature, which has its roots in information science, uses the lens of *knowledge management* to capture the process of creating, sharing and using knowledge to enhance learning and performance in organisations (Scarborough *et al.* 1999). At a wider system level, there is a body of literature concerned with the *diffusion of innovations*, which seeks to understand the spread of ideas, technologies and practices across individuals and organisations within a sector or society. Finally, there is a growing body of work on the *mobilisation of research-based knowledge*. Although this draws on the previous four bodies of literature, we discuss it below as a fifth conceptual lens or field of enquiry. None of these five fields of enquiry offers a single, united view of the process of creating, sharing and using knowledge. Each lens acts more like a broad viewfinder than a narrow focal point, and there are multiple perspectives even within each of the five fields of enquiry.

We have elsewhere sought to distil the insights offered by these five bodies of literature, particularly in terms of how they can inform the design of strategies to promote research use (Nutley *et al.* 2002, 2004, 2007; Davies *et al.*

2015). In addition, there are many helpful overviews and reviews of each of the fields. In this section, our aim is not to provide a general summary of the insights afforded by each field; instead, we focus on two main questions:

1. How is knowledge conceptualised in each of these fields?
2. How has the process of knowledge creation, sharing and use been modelled?

Following observations in response to these two questions for each of the five lenses, we then devote a section to discussing the implications of such variations in perspective for improving the mobilisation of knowledge.

Conceptualising Knowledge across Diverse Fields

The literature on *individual learning* is primarily concerned with the acquisition, application and integration of knowledge and skills. Knowledge is conceptualised broadly as understanding, and skills are defined as the practical ability to perform tasks. Knowledge, then, is treated both as a source of learning and as an outcome of a learning process. As a source of learning, it may be found within us (via self-reflection) or outside ourselves (by using our senses to learn from the world around us). The idea of 'knowledge from outside' leans towards the idea of knowledge as an object that can be readily detached from a knower (see Chapter 2). However, many learning theories (particularly adult learning theories—see Knowles *et al.* 2005) recognise the limitations of viewing knowledge in this way because learning occurs in emotional, social and cultural contexts, which influence how individuals perceive the world around them and how they draw connections between new information and what they already know. Thus it is difficult always to retain a view of knowledge as something that is readily separable from the process of knowing, and even, in some instances, knowing as something separate from the process of doing (e.g., the skilled application of knowledge).

Both the *organisational learning* and *knowledge management* literatures are focused on the ways in which organisations create, share and apply internal knowledge. This includes both explicit and tacit forms of knowledge (Polanyi 1967; Chapter 2). The knowledge management literature tends to emphasise the leverage of knowledge as an asset (knowledge is possessed), whereas the organisational learning literature is more concerned with the social processes of knowing and their implications for action (Scarbrough and Swan 2005). The organisational learning literature, in particular, recognises the embedded nature of organisational knowledge; it is not merely the sum of knowledge held by individual organisational members but it is also embedded in organisational tools, routines and social networks (Hedberg 1981; Chapter 5—knowledge work). Here again we begin to see, in the embeddedness of routines and culturally engrained practices, the somewhat inseparability of knowing and doing.

As the name implies, the concept of an innovation rather than knowledge is central to the literature on the *diffusion of innovations*. This literature, nevertheless, offers insights into the process of mobilising knowledge (and practices) because what counts as an innovation includes ideas, practices, services and products that are perceived as new by those who adopt them. Many models of the diffusion process are suffused with the language of knowledge: tacit and explicit knowledge, pre-existing knowledge, and shared meanings (e.g., Greenhalgh *et al.* 2004:595).

Finally, although research-based knowledge sits at the heart of the literature concerned with *knowledge mobilisation,* there are many debates about the nature and privileging of research-based knowledge (Nutley *et al.* 2013). There is widespread recognition that research-based knowledge needs to be integrated with other forms of knowledge and ways of knowing in the process of being used. Several authors argue that research-based knowledge should not and cannot occupy a privileged position (Yanow 2004; Orr & Bennett 2012). Instead it sits alongside and competes with other forms of existing, structured and contextualised knowledge (e.g., professional knowledge and professional judgement). The ingrained nature of knowledge is also recognised; research-based knowledge can become embedded in the tools, protocols and routines that shape the daily work of practitioners and organisations, and it may be these tools and practices that are the focus of mobilisation activities.

Modelling Knowledge Creation, Flow and Application: Individual Learning

People have been trying to understand and model individual learning for over two thousand years. The result is much debate, some common themes but a lot of disagreement, and many theories and models of the process. Within psychology, behavioural learning theorists have argued that reinforcing desired behaviour is an effective way of developing skills (skills, of course, being a complex amalgam of knowing *about* and knowing *how*). However, cognitive learning theorists have argued that many tasks require complex thought processes and the ability to perform these tasks is not developed without paying attention to how people perceive, process and make sense of what they are experiencing. Another stream of learning theory emphasises that all learning occurs in a cultural context and involves social interactions. This is captured in the idea of socially situated learning, which sees learning as knowledge obtained from and applied to everyday situations. It not only emphasises the importance of learning from experience but also views learning as a sociocultural phenomenon, rather than as an isolated activity (Barab & Duffy 2000).

The ideas of tailoring learning processes to an individual's characteristics, as well as their social and cultural situations, is taken forward in models that seek to identify and categorise the different ways in which people learn (e.g., Kolb 1984). There are also theories which emphasise that how individuals think and feel about their own learning shapes the learning process (Crossan *et al.* 1999). Adult learning theorists have emphasised that adults learn best through doing and when the focus of that learning is of immediate use in solving a problem (Knowles *et al.* 2005).

Some of the above insights into individual learning are illustrated in box 13.1, which draws on the account in Chapter 7 (sensing bodies) of one individual's learning and development journey.

BOX 13.1 AN INDIVIDUAL LEARNING JOURNEY

Chapter 7 (sensing bodies) provides a vivid account of becoming a professional maker of pottery. The development of knowledge and skills is described and analysed as a deeply embodied and emergent process in which knowing and doing are inherently entangled. Although the authors talk about 'knowing from the inside', it is clear that knowing emerges by the maker using all of her senses to experience and learn from the social and material work of the pottery studio. In this example, learning cannot be readily analysed as a purely cognitive process; what is known is often felt rather than thought. It is much more in line with those adult learning theories that stress the importance of learning from experience, especially when the subject of that learning is of immediate use in solving a problem.

The account of the learning journey contains many examples of how progress in becoming a maker is shaped by how one feels about the process. It also exemplifies the importance of the social and cultural context of the learning environment, including opportunities to observe and get advice from other pottery makers. It goes beyond many of the existing theories and models of individual learning by emphasising the importance of the material as well as the social world. Learning occurs through interactions with materials and tools and this involves the whole body and all the senses, not just the mind.

Modelling Knowledge Creation, Flow and Application: Organisational Learning

In contrast to individual learning theories and models, the study of organisational learning is a much more recent phenomenon, which captured researchers' attention during the second half of the twentieth century. Organisational learning has been studied as both a process and a product (the how and what of organisational learning), although the emphasis tends to be on the former. It is typically viewed as a multilevel process, which needs to be analysed within and across individual, group and organisational levels (Rashman *et al.* 2009). One influential framework for analysing organisational learning states that these three levels of organisational learning are linked by four social and psychological processes: intuiting, interpreting, integrating and institutionalising (the 4Is framework—Crossan *et al.* 1999, 2011). Intuiting (the recognition of patterns in past experience that are potentially useful in the present) occurs at an individual level; interpreting (verbalising and sharing insights and ideas) is an individual- and group-level process; integrating (the collective development of shared understandings of new ideas and how to put them into action) happens at both group and organisational levels; and institutionalisation (embedding learning into the systems, structures and routines of the organisation) is an organisational level process. Organisational learning resides within and across these levels. The movement may not always be from individual to collective learning because the 4Is are connected in complex and non-linear ways (Crossan *et al.* 2011). Context is important in understanding these connections and researchers have identified a range of factors that influence organisational learning processes, including cognitive, emotional, relational, cultural and political factors.

Turning to the study of organisational learning as a product, a distinction is commonly made between different types and qualities of learning. An example is the well-cited distinction between adaptive (single-loop) and generative (double-loop) learning (Argyris & Schon 1996). This distinction taps into a tension in organisational learning between 'assimilating new learning (exploration) and using what has been learned (exploitation)' (Crossan *et al.* 2011:448).

Modelling Knowledge Creation, Flow and Application: Knowledge Management

The literature on knowledge management covers similar ground to organisational learning, but its different disciplinary origins mean that it developed largely in parallel (see Vera *et al.* 2011 for an overview of both knowledge management and organisational learning, including their areas of overlap and distinction). The knowledge management literature initially focused on the process of capturing knowledge and extracting it from its context. The associated knowledge management strategies tended to be based around carefully codifying knowledge so that it could be stored in computerised databases open to wider groupings of staff. More recently, there has been a shift towards modelling the process of accessing and applying expertise (i.e., tacit knowledge). Resulting strategies seek to develop opportunities for people to share knowledge, and the role of information and communication systems is to help people communicate knowledge, not to store it (Hansen *et al.* 1999).

Although organisational learning and knowledge management models and frameworks are firmly focused on intra-organisational learning and knowledge, there has been some interest in inter-organisational learning and knowledge flows (Haunschild & Chandler 2008; Rashman *et al.* 2009). One review of the literature identifies two inter-organisational learning processes: identification of the need and opportunity to learn from other organisations, and interaction of individuals and groups across organisational boundaries (Rashman *et al.* 2009).

Some of the above insights on organisational learning and knowledge management are illustrated in box 13.2 by applying them to the account of creative development practices in an advertising agency (Chapter 8).

BOX 13.2 ORGANISATIONAL KNOWLEDGE AND LEARNING IN AN ADVERTISING AGENCY

The account of everyday practices in an advertising agency (Chapter 8) is not on the face of it concerned with either organisational learning or knowledge management. Nevertheless, the description of five everyday practices associated with the development of advertisements sheds some light on both. We see in this account the importance of a multilevel analysis—individual, group and organisation—and there are also echoes of the 4Is framework for explaining how learning occurs within and across these levels.

Within the agency, individuals with different roles, experiences and skills work individually and in teams to define and solve clients' advertising problems. They gather, analyse and interpret a wide range of qualitative and quantitative information in the process of developing an advert. This involves both intuitive and analytical modes of thinking. Information, ideas and proposals are interpreted and judged by individuals working in project teams. They draw on the experiences they have accumulated over time in both their current organisation and in previous advertising roles. These include aesthetic understandings as well as more functional knowledge of advertising processes and products. Through multiple discussions—involving staff working in creative, strategy and producer roles and often clients too—shared understandings are developed about new ideas and promising solutions, and how to put these into action. Over time, shared understandings about the development of advertisements have become institutionalised or routinised in the five everyday practices described in Chapter 8 (kicking off the creative process, developing strategies, generating ideas, realising concepts and evaluating effects).

Modelling Knowledge Creation, Flow and Application: Diffusion of Innovations

The literature on the diffusion of innovations focuses on modelling the inter-organisational and population-level processes involved in the spread and adoption of ideas and practices. Early studies focused on the factors that explain adoption decisions: the attributes of innovations, the characteristics and behaviour of adopters, communication processes (interpersonal and mass media) and the role of intermediaries (Rogers 1995). Many of these studies focused on the adoption of innovations by individuals and this was one of the limitations of this early work (Greenhalgh *et al.* 2004). Later studies considered organisations as adopters (e.g., Van de Ven *et al.* 1999), and these studies have emphasised the influence of organisational context (both internal and external) on adopter behaviour and decisions. A key internal factor is said to be an organisation's 'absorptive capacity'—i.e., the ability to recognise, assimilate and apply new knowledge to organisational ends (Nonaka & Takeuchi 1995). Studies have also drawn on institutional theory to explain organisational choices about whether to adopt or not. These choices are influenced by institutional pressures around emerging norms, as well as the temptation to follow certain fads and fashions as part of seeking legitimacy within a field (O'Neill *et al.* 1998).

Rogers (2003) argues that there are five main stages in the innovation-decision process: knowledge about the innovation; persuasion as to its benefits or problems; acceptance or rejection of the innovation; implementation, if the innovation is accepted; and confirmation that this was the right course of action or subsequent abandonment of the innovation. Critics have argued that the process of innovation diffusion is far messier than this rational-linear model would imply (Van de Ven *et al.* 1999). The complexity of the diffusion process and the range of factors involved is illustrated by Greenhalgh *et al.*'s (2004:595) conceptual model of diffusion in service organisations, which comprises seven main components (the innovation, adoption by individuals, assimilation by the system, diffusion and dissemination, system readiness for innovation, the outer context, and implementation and routinisation), which are linked in a dynamic and iterative manner. Adopters, be they individuals or organisations, are not usually passive recipients of an innovation, and the process of adopting an innovation can involve significant adaptation, akin to a process of reinvention. Intermediaries or boundary spanners are considered to play an important role in convincing others to adopt an innovation, and they tend to have significant social ties both within and outside the organisation.

Some of the insights offered by the diffusion of innovation literature are illustrated in box 13.3 by applying them to the account (in Chapter 10) of the role of boundary organisations in environmental policy.

BOX 13.3   THE ROLE OF BOUNDARY ORGANISATIONS IN DIFFUSING IDEAS AND PRACTICE IN ENVIRONMENTAL POLICY

If we are to have hopes of 'saving the planet', a wide range of individuals, groups and organisations need to develop effective ways of improving the generation, spread and adoption of promising environmental ideas and practices. In line with this, the authors of Chapter 10 outline some of the ways in which two intermediary or boundary organisations facilitate the sharing of useful environmental knowledge and promising practices: for example, the policy updates, technical advice, tools and support that Zero Waste Scotland provides for Scottish businesses. Although the authors do not use a diffusion of innovations lens to analyse the activities of Zero Waste Scotland (ZWO) and the Centre for Research and Expertise on Water (CREW), those activities nevertheless illustrate and provide insights into some aspects of the diffusion process.

The account illustrates the complexity and messiness of the diffusion process in environmental policy. The two boundary organisations sit between science, policy and industry. This is a challenging space due to the contested nature of knowledge around environmental policy, the differing interests of the actors and organisations involved, and the shifting roles and expectations of the boundary organisations themselves. In order to mediate and negotiate connections between science, policy and industry, the boundary organisations (and those working within and through them) have needed to invest time and energy in building stakeholder and subject-specific networks. They have sought to develop credibility and relationships based on trust as far as possible.

The extent of system readiness for innovation has shaped diffusion processes and activities. For example, the historical neglect of waste management meant that ZWS initially focused on educating groups about the relative advantages of viewing waste as a resource. System incentives have also been an important factor: the varied incentive systems, diverse needs and values present within the broad arena of environmental policy have at times inhibited the generation, spread and adoption of ideas and practices.

The environmental innovations (ideas or practices), which were the focus of the activities of ZWS and CREW, developed and changed during the diffusion process. The authors use the language of co-production to capture this process and this perspective on the activities of the boundary organisations is discussed further in Chapter 14 (co-production).

Modelling Knowledge Creation, Flow and Application: Research-Based Knowledge Mobilisation

Similar to the diffusion of innovations literature, the literature on research-based knowledge mobilisation also seeks to understand and model how ideas and practices that are informed by research are (or could be) shared across inter-organisational boundaries and amongst individuals working in a particular field or sector. Such literature, which has grown enormously over the past twenty years (Davies *et al.* 2016), adds another bewildering variety of models, theories and frameworks. As noted in the introduction to this chapter, Best and Holmes (2010) have argued that one way of mapping these models and frameworks is to place them on a continuum of three generations of thinking about knowledge to action processes: linear approaches, relationship approaches and systems approaches.

There has been much criticism of linear models and the idea that research knowledge can be straightforwardly disseminated or pushed across organisational and community boundaries (Davies *et al.* 2008). Relationship models, which emphasise the importance of building social links and encouraging knowledge exchange, have gained a lot of traction, but there are criticisms that they fail to fully acknowledge the implications of conflict over what constitutes knowledge (important, given the complexity revealed throughout this book), and that they also pay insufficient attention to issues of power (Greenhalgh 2010; Greenhalgh & Wieringa 2011). There is increasing support for a systems approach in principle, particularly in terms of recognising the importance of system structure, culture and context, but there is still a lack of detailed guidance about what this would mean in practice and *for* practice. There are also differing views about the extent to which and how contextual factors can be managed or even influenced.

Early models of research-based knowledge mobilisation were built on a 'two communities' view of the challenge: that is, the requirements for 'bridging the gap' between research producers and research users. Although it is still common to distinguish between these two broad groups or communities, it is acknowledged that there are overlaps and there are also other important actors and agencies to consider, including research funders, research intermediaries and other stakeholders (Nutley *et al.* 2007). Similar to the diffusion of innovation literature, there has been a focus on the roles of intermediaries, who facilitate access to research knowledge and develop and broker networks and other connections between research producers and potential users (see Chapters 10 and 11 on environmental policy and healthcare respectively). Conceptual uncertainty remains around who should perform this brokering role and what activities should be encompassed (Knight & Lyall 2013). Often, the activities associated with research mobilisation tend to be specified at a fairly general level (Davies *et al.* 2015). For example, one framework highlights five key underlying mechanisms for research mobilisation: dissemination, interaction, social influence, facilitation, and incentives and reinforcements (Walter *et al.* 2003).

Our introduction framed the ultimate goal of knowledge mobilisation as improving individual and organisational performance, but this is only one possible goal of research application: it is often described as the direct or instrumental use of research to solve problems and shape decisions. Alternatively, the aim may be to change understanding or attitudes, which has been variously described as the conceptual, indirect or enlightenment use of research (Weiss 1995). Another way of framing the purpose of mobilisation efforts is to contrast a consensual stance (where the aim is to fine-tune practices within an existing paradigm) with a more contentious stance (where the aim is to ensure that the hidden and sometimes dysfunctional consequences of current practices are revealed). There can also be a paradigm-challenging stance—where the aim is to problematise established ways of thinking and acting, and propose and gain support for new principles of actions (Rein 1976; Weiss 1995). Thus the potential role of research goes much wider than merely improving practice.

Some of the insights offered by the literature on the mobilisation of research-based knowledge are illustrated in box 13.4 by applying them to the account in Chapter 11 of an initiative that sought to connect academic knowledge and practice in healthcare.

BOX 13.4   MOBILISING RESEARCH-BASED KNOWLEDGE IN HEALTHCARE

The Collaborations for Leadership in Applied Health Research and Care (the CLAHRCs discussed in Chapter 11) are an initiative aimed at enhancing the creation, flow and application of research-based knowledge in healthcare. Despite being established under the rubric of collaboration, the authors of Chapter 11 found that the actual operation of the CLAHRCs they studied was underpinned as much by linear, knowledge transfer models as by collaborative, relationship-based models.

The CLAHRCs were intended to act as a bridge between academic research and healthcare practice by providing an intermediary space where these 'two communities' could work together to create knowledge and apply it. However, the authors comment on how the background to the establishment of some CLAHRCs, and their early ways of working, meant that they were often perceived to be more aligned with academia than with practice. One cause (and consequence) of this was that these CLAHRCs tended to prioritise evidence production over its implementation. CLAHRCs appeared to work best as collaborative ventures when they were built upon pre-existing good working relationships between academics and practitioners.

Although it can be helpful to think of the CLAHRCs as bridging between two (academic and practice) communities, the account in Chapter 11 demonstrates that there were actually multiple boundaries to be spanned (organisational, epistemic, semantic, professional and geographic boundaries). Some individuals within each of the CLAHRCs were given formal boundary-spanning roles and there were other individuals who acted informally in this capacity. These were challenging roles and the knowledge, skills and abilities needed only developed over time—there were no quick fixes. Even then, it proved difficult for individuals with no background in healthcare practice to develop credibility as an effective boundary spanner.

Dissemination, interaction, social influence and facilitation were all evident to varying extents as underlying mechanisms for research mobilisation. However, motivation and reinforcement was an issue of concern; both academics and practitioners sometimes struggled to see what was in it for them.

Developing Strategies and Actions to Improve Knowledge Mobilisation

Having teased out some key insights into the process of knowledge mobilisation from the five bodies of literature summarised in the previous section, we now focus on the implications of these insights for developing strategies and actions to improve knowledge mobilisation. Many of the models and frameworks discussed in the previous section are descriptive and analytical. That is, they describe and analyse the processes of knowledge creation, sharing and use, but they tend not be explicit about the configurations, actions or resources needed to improve knowledge mobilisation (Davies *et al.* 2015). There are some exceptions, but these more prescriptive models do not necessarily provide a reliable guide for action as most have been subject to only limited empirical testing, and such testing, in any case, often underplays the role of context and other contingent factors.

The varied goals of knowledge mobilisation efforts, the differing types of knowledge that may be at the centre of attention, and the dynamic and complex settings within which knowledge mobilisation occurs, mean that it is unrealistic to expect a ready set of prescriptions or a menu of 'proven' knowledge mobilisation approaches. Instead, a sound conceptual understanding of the various issues at play—and their dynamic interaction—needs to be central to the design of knowledge mobilisation strategies. There are, however, five emerging principles that might be used to underpin the development of strategies and actions to improve knowledge mobilisation (see box 13.5).

BOX 13.5   FIVE EMERGING PRINCIPLES TO UNDERPIN THE DEVELOPMENT OF KNOWLEDGE MOBILISATION STRATEGIES AND PRACTICES

1. Knowledge cannot be readily separated from knowers and the settings in which they work.
2. Knowledge creation, sharing and use are naturally occurring phenomena, but a 'just let it happen' approach to knowledge mobilisation is not enough.
3. Knowledge mobilisation needs to be viewed and treated as a multilevel phenomenon involving individuals, groups, organisations and wider systems at sector or society levels.
4. It is beneficial to think in terms of building a knowledge mobilisation ecology where individuals, groups and organisations interact productively with one another and their environment.
5. Boundary-spanning people and objects play a key role in enhancing productive interactions within a knowledge mobilisation ecology.

The first principle stresses the limitations of viewing knowledge as an object that is readily separable from knowers and the settings within which they work: knowledge is embodied in individuals (personally and collectively) and embedded in work practices, structures and cultures. This suggests that strategies and actions to improve knowledge mobilisation also need to be embodied (e.g., though face-to-face dialogue and experiential learning) and embedded (e.g., through facilitating the review and development of work practices). Taken to its logical conclusion, this first principle would suggest that we should think in terms of mobilising knowledge *and* practice, and not just knowledge.

The second principle points to the need for an active approach to knowledge mobilisation. All work involves knowledge (see Chapter 5) and learning from experience and those around us is a naturally occurring phenomenon, so it might be tempting to adopt a passive approach to knowledge mobilisation—just leaving it to occur naturally. However, the introduction to this chapter comments on the limitations of a passive approach because the process of creating, sharing and use of knowledge within and across organisations is not always as effective as it could be. The consequences of this can be detrimental for organisations (e.g., inefficiency) and devastating for individuals (e.g., premature loss of life due to substandard healthcare interventions).

The third principle emphasises the importance of viewing knowledge mobilisation as a multilevel phenomenon involving individuals, groups, organisations and wider systems at sector or society levels. Knowledge mobilisation strategies and actions need to be directed at all of these levels. Reviews of the organisational learning literature (e.g., Crossan *et al.* 2011) and the research mobilisation literature (e.g., Davies *et al.* 2015) have commented that most attention to date has been paid to 'within level' strategies, particularly those aimed at individuals and groups. Strategies also need to consider broader organisational arrangements and how all parts of the systems interact with one another.

The fourth principle builds on the third and highlights the benefits of thinking in terms of a knowledge mobilisation ecology. This might involve mapping the activities of key individuals, groups and organisations involved in knowledge mobilisation (at the organisational or sector level) in order to identify how they interact with one another and their environment. The aim would be to identify activity gaps and the extent to which existing interactions are characterised by cooperation or competition (together with the implications of this). Strategies could then be aimed at addressing activity gaps and enhancing existing capacities and interactions.

The fifth and final principle draws attention to the importance of spanning boundaries, both within and across organisations, when seeking to enhance knowledge mobilisation. Strategies should consider how to develop the roles and capacities of individuals and agencies who act as intermediaries (boundary spanners; see Chapters 10 and 11 on environmental policy and healthcare respectively) and the features of things/objects that enable individuals and groups to have meaningful dialogue around issues of concern (boundary objects).

All five principles are necessarily tentative and expressed in general terms. They need to be discussed, interpreted and operationalised in specific contexts and adapted and reworked in the light of experience in those contexts. They are not a blueprint for action and they should not be accepted without critical reflection. A possible basis for such reflections is the subject of the final section of this chapter.

SOME FINAL REFLECTIONS

We noted in the second section of this chapter that none of the five conceptual lenses summarised in that section offers a single, united view of the process of creating, sharing and using knowledge. Instead there are multiple perspectives and different underpinning paradigms to be found within each of the five fields of enquiry. This inevitably leads to questions about the extent to which it is possible to synthesise ideas and findings from across these different perspectives, especially where they are based on different ontological and epistemological assumptions. Are they complementary or incommensurable? The same question can be asked about the relationship between the different perspectives offered by the authors of various chapters in this edited collection. The concluding chapter (Chapter 16) provides a fuller and more general discussion of this issue.

Here we offer some initial reflections, drawing partly on the ideas in Crossan *et al.*'s (2011) overview of the organisational learning literature, where the authors argue that lack of agreement on ontological and epistemological issues need not impede the development of a framework for understanding organisational learning. They argue that the 4I framework spans the four paradigms of social enquiry articulated by Burrell and Morgan (1979) and insights from all four paradigms add to our understanding of organisational learning processes. Similarly, we argue that drawing together insights from different paradigms of enquiry provides us with some different ways of conceptualising knowledge creation, sharing and use. It is not necessary, and probably not possible, to reconcile these different views within one agreed, overarching framework or theory. Instead, the aim should be to negotiate (but not dissolve) the tensions between them. This is likely to involve the use of differing insights depending on the questions that we pose and the challenges we face.

For all the insights available from the diverse literatures traversed in this chapter, two areas remain relatively neglected with potentially important consequences. First, much of the literature that underpins this chapter has been accused of paying insufficient attention to power, politics and conflict in organisations and society (Ferlie *et al.* 2012; Chapter 4 Power). Indeed, the same accusation might also be levelled at the content of this chapter. Second, neither the literature on the five conceptual lenses (summarised in this chapter) nor the context-specific examples of knowledge and practice (provided in Part C of this book) pay much attention to the involvement or role of clients, customers, service users and/or members of the public in creating, sharing and using knowledge. This seems an important area of neglect. Each of these deficiencies is now explored a little further in turn.

The concept of power needs to play a more central role in our understanding of knowledge mobilisation processes and challenges, and it also needs to inform mobilisation efforts within and across organisations. The optimistic tone of many (including us) when discussing the strategies and actions for improving knowledge mobilisation needs to be tempered with some harsher observations on organisational life: where knowledge and workers may be viewed as assets to be exploited, where workers may seek to protect rather than willingly share their expertise, and where occupational hierarchies may restrict knowledge mobilisation by privileging codified and embrained knowledge over social and tacit knowledge (see Chapter 5— knowledge work). There are many reasons why individuals, groups and even management teams may feel unable or disinclined to change what they do, even though they may think that this would improve performance (Pfeffer & Sutton 2000).

As discussed in Chapter 4, the concept of power (and its corollary, resistance) is often associated with negative connotations: power as coercive and repressive, and power (and resistance) as sources of conflict. However, power can also be viewed as a productive phenomenon, such as the capacity to achieve outcomes (Giddens 1984) or more neutrally as 'one person's actions structuring other people's possible actions' (Schatzki 2005:478). Chapter 4 outlines a triangular relationship between power, knowledge and practice, where there is a recursive relationship between each of these concepts (for example, knowledge facilitates the exercise of power, and power legitimises knowledge). Future work needs to build on such frameworks and draw out their implications for knowledge mobilisation.

Our final reflection concerns the relative neglect of clients, customers, service users and the like when considering when and how knowledge is created, shared and applied. The research mobilisation literature tends to cast such groups as research subjects or (perhaps) as one potential audience for research findings. The diffusion of innovation literature treats them as potential adopters, and in this guise considers their needs, motivations, values, skills, learning styles and social networks, but essentially as responders rather than initiators. In individual learning, organisational learning and knowledge management such groups are rarely considered. Across each of the lenses covered here then, clients, service users and other 'lay' actors—if they figure at all—are cast more as passive recipients than active protagonists in the knowledge mobilisation dynamic. For example, in the context-specific instances of knowledge and practice provided in this book, the authors mention that clients are involved in some of the everyday practices of the advertising agency (see box 13.2 and Chapter 8), but their involvement is not explored in any detail. This seems to be another area that is worthy of more attention in future research and practice development. If the public are considered to be the main beneficiary of the products and services provided by organisations, there is a rationale for ensuring that they have a stronger voice in the creation, sharing and use of knowledge (Davies *et al.* 2015). This issue is picked up in the next chapter, which explains how co-production can be used as lens through which knowledge and practice relationships can be viewed.

In conclusion then, we can say that much can be learned from the diverse lenses used to explore the 'knowledge-knowing' and the 'knowing-doing' gaps. Of course, these literatures do not provide fully consistent accounts: indeed, some accounts are essentially critiques of prevailing models or normative views. Moreover, there remain some weaknesses and deficiencies in the accounts (notably the treatment of power, and the sidelining of important stakeholders). Nonetheless, taken together, the diversity of views and their varied underpinnings provide many insights and point the way to new principles and actions in mobilising knowledge for improved practice.

SUGGESTED FURTHER READINGS

Selected review papers for each of the five conceptual lenses have already been highlighted in this chapter. Nutley *et al.* (2007) provides a broad overview of each of these lenses and the issues covered in this chapter.

Davies *et al.* (2015) provide a recent review of the literature on and practice of knowledge mobilisation in healthcare, education and social care.

REFERENCES

Argyris, C., & Schon, D.A. (1996) *Organizational learning II.* Reading, MA: Addison-Wesley.

Barab, S.A., & Duffy, T.M. (2000) From practice fields to communities of practice, in D.H. Jonassen & S.M. Land (eds.), *Theoretical foundations of learning environments.* Mahwah, NJ: Lawrence Erlbaum Associates, pp. 25–55.

Best, A., & Holmes, B.J. (2010) Systems thinking, knowledge & action: Towards better models & methods. *Evidence & Policy.* 6(2): 145–159.

Burrell, G., & Morgan, G. (1979) *Sociological paradigms & organizational analysis.* London: Heinemann.

Crossan, M.M., Lane, H.W., & White, R.E. (1999) An organizational learning framework: From intuition to institution. *Academy of Management Review.* 24: 522–537.

Crossan, M.M., Maurer, C.C., & White, R.E. (2011) Reflections on the 2009 AMR decade award: Do we have a theory of organizational learning? *Academy of Management Review.* 26(3): 446–460.

Davies, H.T.O., Nutley, S.M., & Walter, I. (2008) Why 'knowledge transfer' is misconceived for applied social research. *Journal of Health Services Research & Policy.* 13(3): 188–190.

Davies, H.T.O., Powell, A.E., & Nutley, S.M. (2015) Mobilising knowledge to improve UK health care: Learning from other countries & other sectors—A multi-method mapping study. *Health Services & Delivery Research.* 3(27).

Davies, H.T.O., Powell, A.E., & Nutley, S.M. (2016) Mobilizing knowledge in health care, in E. Ferlie, K. Montgomery & A.R. Pedersen (eds.), *The Oxford handbook of healthcare management.* Oxford: Oxford University Press.

Dodgson, M. (1993) Organisational learning: A review of some literatures. *Organization Studies.* 14: 375–394.

Ferlie, E., Crilly, T., Jashapara, A., & Peckham, A. (2012) Knowledge mobilisation in healthcare: A critical review of health sector & generic management literature. *Social Science & Medicine.* 74(8): 1297–1304.

Gherardi, S. (2006) *Organizational knowledge: The texture of workplace learning.* Oxford: Blackwell.

Giddens, A. (1984) *The constitution of society: Outline of the theory of structuration.* Cambridge: Polity Press.

Greenhalgh, T. (2010) What is this knowledge that we seek to 'exchange'? *The Milbank Quarterly.* 88(4): 492–499.

Greenhalgh, T., Robert, G., MacFarlane, F., Bate, P., & Kyriakidou, O. (2004) Diffusion of innovations in service organisations: Systematic review & recommendations. *Milbank Quarterly.* 82(4): 581–629.

Greenhalgh, T., & Wieringa, S. (2011) Is it time to drop the 'knowledge translation' metaphor? A critical literature review. *Journal of the Royal Society of Medicine.* 104(12): 501–509.

Hansen, M.T., Nohria, N., & Tierney, T. (1999) What's your strategy for managing knowledge? *Harvard Business Review.* March–April: 106–116.

Haunschild, P., & Chandler, D. (2008) Institutional-level learning: Learning as a source of institutional change, in C.O.R. Greenwood, K. Sahnlin, & R. Suddaby (eds.), *The SAGE handbook of organizational institutionalism*. London: SAGE, pp. 624–629.

Hedberg, B. (1981) How organizations learn & unlearn, in P. Nystrom & W. Starbuck (eds.), *Handbook of organizational design vol 1*. Oxford: Oxford University Press, pp. 3–27.

Knight, C., & Lyall, C. (2013) Knowledge brokers: The role of intermediaries in producing research impact. *Evidence & Policy*. 9(3): 309–316.

Knowles, M., Holton III, E., & Swanson, R. (2005) *The adult learner*. 6th Ed. London: Elsevier Butterworth Heinnemann.

Kolb, D.A. (1984) *Experiential Learning; Experience as the Source of Learning & Development*. Englewood Cliffs, NJ: Prentice-Hall.

Nonaka, I., & Takeuchi, H. (1995) *The knowledge-creating company*. Oxford: Oxford University Press.

Nutley, S., Powell, A., & Davies, H.T.O. (2013) *What counts as good evidence?* Provocation Paper for the Alliance for Useful Evidence. Available: http://www.alliance4usefulevidence.org/assets/What-Counts-as-Good-Evidence-WEB.pdf. Accessed: October 8, 2015.

Nutley, S.M., Davies, H.T.O., & Walter, I. (2002) *Conceptual synthesis 1: The Diffusion of Innovations*. Research Unit for Research Utilisation, University of St Andrews. Available: www.ruru.ac.uk. Accessed: October 8, 2015.

Nutley, S.M., Davies, H.T.O., & Walter, I. (2004) *Conceptual Synthesis 2: Knowledge Management*. Research Unit for Research Utilisation, University of St Andrews. Available: www.ruru.ac.uk. Accessed: October 8, 2015.

Nutley, S.M., Walter, I., & Davies, H.T.O. (2007) *Using evidence: How research can inform public services*. Bristol: Policy Press.

O'Neill, H.M., Pouder, R.W., & Buchholtz, A.K. (1998) Patterns in the diffusion of strategies across organisations: Insights from the innovation diffusion literature. *Academy of Management Review*. 23: 98–114.

Orr, K., & Bennett, M. (2012) Public administration scholarship & the politics of coproducing academic-practitioner research. *Public Administration Review*. 72(4): 487–495.

Pfeffer, J., & Sutton, R.I. (2000) *The knowing-doing gap: How smart companies turn knowledge into action*. Boston: Harvard Business School Press.

Polanyi, M. (1967) *The tacit dimension*. New York: Doubleday.

Rashman, L., Withers, E., & Hartley, J. (2009) Organizational learning & knowledge in public service organizations: A systematic review of the literature. *International Journal of Management Reviews*. 11(4): 463–494.

Rein, L. (1976) *Social science & public policy*. Harmondsworth: Penguin.

Rogers, E.M. (1995) *Diffusion of innovations*. New York: Free Press.

Rogers, E.M. (2003) *Diffusion of innovations*. 5th Ed. New York: Free Press.

Scarbrough, H., & Swan, J. (2005) Discourses of knowledge management & the learning organization: Their production & consumption, in M. Easterby-Smith & M. Lyles (eds.), *Handbook of organizational learning & knowledge management*. Oxford: Blackwell, pp. 495–512.

Scarborough, H., Swan, J., & Preston, J. (1999) *Knowledge management: A literature review*. London: Institute of Personnel & Development.

Schatzki, T.R. (2005) Peripheral vision: The sites of organizations. *Organization Studies*. 26(3): 465–484.

van de Ven, A.H., Polley, D.E., Garud, R., & Venkataraman, S. (1999) *The innovation journey*. Oxford: Oxford University Press.

Vera, D., Crossan, M., & Apaydin, M. (2011) A framework for integrating organizational learning, knowledge, capabilities, & absorptive capacity, in M. Easterby-Smith

& M. Lyles (eds.), *Handbook of organizational learning & knowledge management.* 2nd Ed. Chichester: Wiley, pp. 153–180.

Walter, I.C., Nutley, S.M., & Davies, H.T.O. (2003) *Developing a taxonomy of interventions used to increase the impact of research.* Discussion Paper 3, St Andrews: Research Unit for Research Utilisation, University of St Andrews.

Weiss, C.H. (1995) The haphazard connection: Social science & public policy. *International Journal of Educational Research.* 23(2): 137–150.

Yanow, D. (2004) Translating local knowledge at organization peripheries. *British Journal of Management.* 15(S1): S9–S25.

14 Co-producing Knowledge and Practice

Kevin Orr and Tobias Jung

In this integrative chapter, we examine how the lens of co-production helps us to make sense of the debates and discussions that play through the settings provided in the earlier chapters: craftwork, advertising, accounting, environmental policy, healthcare and philanthropy. What are the roles and limitations of knowledge co-production as a basis for understanding practices in these settings? To explore these questions, we will firstly highlight the growing importance of co-production across diverse practice arenas and policy contexts. We then consider the array of perspectives on co-production and distil the key themes and issues into an exploratory framework that forms the basis for our examination.

THE GROWING ROLE OF CO-PRODUCTION

The notion of 'co-production' has seen increasing prominence in a diffuse range of settings. It mirrors a wider socio-economic and political interest in collaboration and partnership working, and dissatisfaction with the status quo. We see examples of co-production across all sectors: from co-produced and co-funded movies to the active involvement of users in the delivery and design of their healthcare; from ideas of reflexivity and the co-creation of learning in the classroom, to the co-delivery of development aid by private sector companies and charities. Though these examples serve to illustrate how co-production has established itself as part of the everyday discourse of a broad spectrum of actors, the danger of mundane references to co-production is that the concept ceases to have any explanatory power. In other words, does its ubiquity—its very elasticity—suggest a concept under strain? We suggest that the elasticity of the concept allows the concept of co-production to be recast and renegotiated across time and place.

In relation to 'research' and 'knowledge', the interest in co-production builds on long-standing debates that point to an appreciation of how knowledge and practice stand in mutual relation. It mirrors the discourse on 'transparent' (Milofsky 2000) and 'engaged' scholarship (van de Ven 2007), the interest in 'action' and 'collaborative' research approaches (e.g., Phillips *et al.* 2013), and various forms and conceptualisations of 'knowledge mobilisation' (Phipps *et al.* 2009; Chapter 13). Essential to all of these is a recognition that engagement with, and development of, knowledge is a collective, rather than a solitary, exercise.

Knowledge co-production draws attention to the diverse knowledge- and asset-bases held by different stakeholders. It aims to bring researchers, practitioners and/or policymakers together in the quest for developing knowledge: from conceptualising and identifying appropriate research questions, to designing, carrying out and analysing research, and the presentation and dissemination of the work (Orr & Bennett 2012). The assumed advantage is that co-production offers a road to knowledge that is 'better', 'more relevant' to policy and practice, and 'more socially robust' (Hegger *et al.* 2012). Despite its intuitive appeal, co-production, and the discourse surrounding it, are by no means without their critics and challenges. Prominent concerns relate to the casting and blurring of conceptual and practical boundaries (Nutley 2010) and participants' competing agendas and vulnerabilities (Jung *et al.* 2012), as well as loyalties, politics and structural ambiguities (Orr & Bennett 2012).

The rich academic literature referring to the co-production concept encompasses the co-production of both knowledge and practice. The resulting array of definitions, assumptions and focal points is illustrated in table 14.1. This provides examples of co-production perspectives from the fields of management learning, public policy service marketing, public administration, environmental policy, education, public policy and management, urban studies, and health and social services. While other examples can be found, these areas seem especially pertinent to the focus of this book.

When looking at the definitions provided in table 14.1, and at the key concepts and their implications, it becomes apparent that there is a set of recurring thematic clusters. These relate to five issues: (1) questions of boundaries, their setting and resetting; (2) the fashioning, shaping and perception of individual and organisational identities; (3) reputational factors, such as standing, status, credibility and impressions, and how well these travel and are perceived outwith participants' respective professional domains; (4) a staged versus a fluid approach to the co-production process; and, finally, (5) agency; that is, capacity, voice, interest, power and politics. To explore these five themes and how they run through the chapters within this book, we consider the following overarching questions:

(1) How, and to what extent, does co-production feature in these different contextual accounts of knowledge and practice?
(2) What issues surrounding co-production are suggested in relation to the above themes in each setting?
(3) What insights do each of the contextual chapters offer our understanding of co-production?
(4) What are the strengths and limitations of applying a co-production lens in each case?

Table 14.1 Defining co-production: A snapshot across different academic fields

Author(s)	Field	Definition	Key concepts	Implications of the relationship between knowledge and practice
Fenwick (2012:np)	Education	"[P]rofessional services and products that are co-developed with clients or service users".	Co-development; involvement; interaction; user voice; negotiation; professionalism; identity. Visibility and invisibility. Boundaries.	Democratisation of service design and delivery. Greater representation of user voice. Ambiguity around professional accountability.
Edelenbos *et al.* (2011:675–676)	Environmental policy	"[T]he interaction process between experts, bureaucrats and stakeholders aimed at exchanging, combining and harmonizing elements like facts, interpretations, assumptions and causal relations from these different knowledge domains".	Interaction; knowledge domains; harmonisation; multiplicity of stakeholders; political interests; legitimacy.	Harmonised, integrated knowledge that is collectively agreed as supporting decision-making.
Heger *et al.* (2012:54)	Environmental policy	"[D]irect collaboration between scientists, policymakers and other societal actors in specific projects".	Multiplicity of stakeholders; identities; peer communities; temporality; intensity of relations.	Greater social accountability of public bodies and policymaking. Extension and development of peer communities. Enshrinement of local knowledge.

(Continued)

Table 14.1 (Continued)

Author(s)	Field	Definition	Key concepts	Implications of the relationship between knowledge and practice
Ottman *et al.* (2011)	Health & social services	"[A process involving] . . . individuals, communities and organisations developing the skills, knowledge, and ability to work together to develop new models".	Innovation; participatory approach; citizen empowerment; user involvement; negotiation; identities; boundaries.	Greater user voice. Enshrinement of individuals' own experiences. Enhanced legitimacy of user expertise. Potential for improvements in public services.
Antonacopoulou (2010:219)	Management learning	"[T]he transcending of boundaries between and across communities and perspectives to form productive collaborations".	Boundaries; collaboration; interaction; transcendence	Discovery of new possibilities for practice through powerful ideas.
Duijn, Rijnveld, & van Hulst (2010:227)	Public administration	"What can practitioners and researchers do alone and jointly in order to deal better with complex governance processes?"	Complexity; boundaries; identity; separation; specificity and generality; unity; action orientation.	Better grounded knowledge of local contexts. Better understanding of front-line practices and dilemmas. Informed management of complex public sector projects.
Armstrong & Alsop (2010:209)	Public policy	"[U]sers are involved throughout the research process, from agenda-setting through design, fieldwork and communication of the outcomes. In coproduction the traditional distinction between research users and research producers becomes transcended and transparent".	User involvement; multistage process; boundaries; identities; transcendence	Potential for greater economic and societal impacts.

Source	Field	Definition	Key concepts	Outcomes
Martin (2010:211)	Public policy and management	"Practitioners play an active role in commissioning, overseeing and learning from studies".	Academic independence; inclusion of stakeholders as co-researchers; utilisation; co-research; boundaries; identities.	Engaged scholarship. Addressing 'real-world' problems. Knowledge applied to practical issues.
Orr & Bennett (2012:488)	Public management	"[T]he accomplishment of research by academics and practitioners working together at each stage of the process, including conceptualization, design, fieldwork, analysis, and presentation of the work".	Interactive process; Dialogue; cooperation; multistage process; identities. Co-production agenda as a critique of existing knowledge generation practices and response to their shortcomings.	Better fieldwork access. Local knowledge applied to intellectual enquiry. Potential for relevance and impact. Political process.
Auh, Bell, McLeod, & Shih (2007:360)	Services marketing	Incorporating customers as active participants in an organisation's undertakings.	Engagement; participation; boundaries.	Customisation. Productivity. Lowering of costs. Loyalty.
O'Hare, Coaffee, & Hawkesworth (2012)	Urban studies	Closer cooperation between academic and non-academic actors: shared engagement with the 'real world'.	Boundaries between academia and wider stakeholders; barriers; trust; connectedness; permeability; inclusion.	Facilitates access of stakeholders to otherwise closed domains of knowledge. Co-researchers occupy an enhanced and privileged position at the nexus of knowledge and practice. Synergistic intertwining of production and application of knowledge.

In the next section, we use these questions to interrogate the accounts provided in Part C of the book and to explore the issues raised in each setting.

EXPLORING CO-PRODUCTION ACROSS THE BOOK'S CONTEXT-SPECIFIC CHAPTERS

Craftwork—Being One

In the first of the empirical chapters (Chapter 7—sensing bodies), the authors emphasise how, in the context of the potter's studio and becoming a maker, knowing emerges from a 'sensuous entanglement' of the social and material aspects of practice. In this reflective account, individuals are never separated; they are 'always entwined with others and things in the world'—practitioners act in ways which implicate them in a 'relational whole'. The chapter encourages us to see practising as a process of becoming knowledgeable. Co-production is also present in the creation of the text, and in particular the ways in which two of the authors (Greig and Ferraro) as academics engage in dialogues to enable Brown's reflection upon her time as an apprentice maker. They highlight how knowing and practising are co-produced inasmuch as participants learn how to act, how to speak, how to behave, how to conduct themselves, how to anticipate outcomes, how to approach tasks, how to understand the business, and the very meaning of it all, in relation to others: the novice maker is advised of extant rules and resources, of lessons learned the hard way, of shortcuts and insider knowledge. We learn of Brown's questioning of colleagues, the more experienced makers, of how to work, of how others worked, of what she should do, of her technical knowledge and the cue to tune into the subtleties of the sounds emanating from the din of the old potting wheel, or of listening to the changes in tone when tapping the lids of sealed pots. Knowledge is co-produced through dialogue and co-shaping of practice, informed by the advice of wise elders to use the senses. Over time, Brown apprehends that there are other ways to listen, see and hear—her knowing, her practising, her way of being in the world changed profoundly.

Through these interactive dialogues, and by adopting these established ways of doing, the newcomer reproduces ways of practising and gains legitimacy in the eyes of her colleagues, in a journey that hints at the politics of these processes of co-production. This immersion in practice creates affiliations, and generates values and perspectives on the world.

The chapter also provides a unique insight on the relationship between materials and the maker's body, and how knowledge emerges through the senses. The account is striking in highlighting that the materiality of the context also acts in a relation of co-production. For example, Brown tells us wryly that the clay is 'full of these rather smug little lessons', and of the importance of developing an awareness of the 'subtleties of the feedback' provided by the clay, the humidity of the air, the ferocity of heat on opening the kiln door, or through the feeling of fired pot on tongue. In this way, the authors tell us, the makers 'negotiate with all that surrounds them'.

The account underlines that knowledge is not simply a thing or a commodity to be brandished. Rather, it speaks to the very ways of being—or, as for Bourdieu, something that one is. The rich examples offered in the chapter shed light on this fascinating milieu, shattering any illusions about the work being mere 'pottering about'; it brings into sharp focus the scale, depth and nuances of the journey involved in committing to this profession, and the diverse ways of knowing and practising.

In the account, we see a co-production of mutual attunement, entwinement with the sociomaterial elements of the setting, of participation within a community of makers, in a process involving instruction, negotiation, legitimation—of becoming sensitised to new ways of knowing and open to the influence of others, both to colleagues and to the very agency of materials, sensuously experienced and interpreted by the apprentice. The strength of the co-production lens is that it highlights the multidimensional relations negotiated by the maker (materials, profession, direct colleagues, co-authors) and the thoroughly immersive interplay of knowing and doing. The weakness of the co-production lens lies in the extent to which everything is attributed to undifferentiated agency, every act a negotiation: from negotiating with the infrastructure of a room, to negotiating with the dominant traditions within a profession, or trying to carve out a niche in which a self-employed maker can ensure a living in a world of market forces. The triumph of the chapter is to show how reflecting on these micro-practices in this non-mainstream setting can speak to larger questions in our scholarly understanding of knowledge and practice.

Advertising Arena—Multiphased

Co-production provides a powerful lens for commenting on the everyday creative practices in the advertising industry (Chapter 8). In their discussion of five key practices—from initiating the creative process through to evaluating the effects of ideas or campaigns—the authors portray multidimensional processes in which different actors co-produce knowledge and co-create ideas, strategies, services and products. In the early stages, practitioners work with clients to understand, contextualise and solve problems. The authors describe a process of bridging in which strategists try to get closer to the client's situation and build up localised knowledge whilst engaging with the client to shape the development of the brief. It is clear, the authors tell us, that this process involves more than simply 'a regurgitation of all the stuff that client's brought you'. Advertising agency practitioners connect with market researchers, participants in focus groups, and academic sources as part of developing a 'gut' feeling for the consumer and/ or product. Developing a strategy is therefore a collaborative and iterative process in which the practitioners engage with a range of stakeholders and work 'hand in hand' with the client to develop a creative brief. Further co-production processes follow from this moment, the brief representing a 'jumping-off point' for the members of the creative teams. Prior to further dialogue with wider groups of colleagues, a copywriter and art director will 'bounce ideas' off each other in a process of trying to discover workable or appropriate ideas. Processes of testing then involve yet another layer of engagement with consumers whose feedback acts as a further focal point for co-influence. Directors producing content then work to a commissioned brief which, to a greater or lesser extent, relies upon their interpretation for the treatment to be realised, a process which is co-produced with those who have knowledge about budgets, and are in a position to make pragmatic judgements about scheduling, resourcing and organising. At the final stage, the process of evaluating the product, or the impact of the overall project, is negotiated with clients, each of whom may employ different criteria or methodologies with which the agency must cooperate.

This is therefore a rich context in which to trace processes of co-production and gives rise to examples in action of the themes of knowledge sharing, co-creation, bridging, engagement, generative dialogues, synthesis and melding of ideas, transformation, and working with multiple stakeholders. The authors encourage us to see this as an iterative process in which practitioners shift between different practices—working in a discontinuous process involving engaging with different co-producers. One of the ambiguities of the setting is the extent to which advertising practitioners open themselves to these processes in welcoming ways, or whether they are sceptical of the client's knowledge. In one passage it is hinted that they engage in the search for knowledge and insight in order to confirm their pre-existing gut instincts—sensuous knowledge trumps local knowledge (the views and insights of the client). It is intriguing to ponder the extent to which the creatives rail against the instrumentalities of the client, or the finance director's encroachment on their imaginative vision, or the extent to which such negotiations are seen as an enriching and pragmatic contribution to the accomplishment of a co-produced process.

Accounting—Schisms and Gaps

In Chapter 9, the authors explore whether knowledge and practice quite adds up in the accounting profession. They point to a sector characterised by gaps and separation—for example, between qualified practitioners and higher education—rather than harmonious processes of collaboration involving the co-production of knowledge. Co-production relationships are perhaps most evident in the work of the Institute of Chartered Accountants of Scotland—for example, as it seeks to commission academics to undertake 'practice-relevant' research studies, or to work with them to co-disseminate research findings amongst students or practitioners. Otherwise it seems that research-based knowledge struggles to gain much attention in the educational departments of professional accounting bodies.

The account features long-standing and ongoing legitimation struggles. A university hoping to provide particular types of accounting degrees must seek accreditation. We encounter the question of whether universities or 'on the job' training offers the best route to specialist professional knowledge. We glimpse the wider regulatory framework and the constellation of professional accounting bodies that are part of the UK landscape. The emerging picture points to a gap or schism between academic and practising accountants, with little agreement on what should be regarded as the core of accounting knowledge. There is the suggestion that university accountancy training might encourage scepticism, or at least apathy, about intellectual enquiry or the role of academics. It is a political arena in which regulators, commissioners, trainers (university staff), employers and practitioners have different views on the importance of the practical or the abstract, of enquiry and instruction, and of theory and practice. By identifying the sources of these collisions and disagreements, and the array of knowledge providers, the chapter outlines the space in which co-production might be approached by accountancy practitioners.

The charter of the Institute of Chartered Accountants of Scotland perhaps offers one route with its commitment to bring together practitioners and academics in the pursuit of problem-solving collaborations, or to broker or co-create the professional syllabus. It is therefore an account in which themes of politics, power and legitimation are to the fore. Fissures and gaps are more striking than being joined or coming together. The chapter suggests that it is a profession struggling to hold its own amongst other established professions, and within which there is competition for who should be regarded as the providers of knowledge to accountants and the wider profession, and whose voice and views should have primacy. It is a setting both lacking and ripe for co-production. The limits of co-production for understanding this context reflect the limited presence it appears to command.

Environmental Policy—Boundary Spanning

The discussion of environmental policymaking, in Chapter 10, adds further complexity to our understanding of the relationship between knowledge and practice. The authors show how the need for policymakers to engage with a range of stakeholders is well established and how there are many examples of structures in place to facilitate collaborative enquiry and practice development. The central example is of two boundary organisations, Zero Waste Scotland (ZWS) and the Centre for Research and Expertise on Water (CREW), which work at the interstices of science, policy communities and industry. The account highlights how boundary organisations implicate practitioners—boundary spanners, policymakers, scientists and so on—in ambiguous and contingent processes of continuous negotiation with other stakeholders, and how different knowledge workers (e.g., members of ZWS and CREW) have competing and shifting priorities.

ZWS is situated within a mosaic of other public bodies that have come together within the discourse of Team Scotland. ZWS acts as a conduit between policymakers and businesses, but also has a significant role in commissioning research and thereby shaping research agendas or determining the focus for the creation of new research knowledge. The account points to elements of co-production, but with ZWS very much operating at the commissioning and dissemination ends of a co-production spectrum, while the research work itself is outsourced. It also provides project support, technical advice and training, in ways that suggest a potential wider role in the co-production of practices. CREW provides clearer examples of co-production, stemming from its mission to improve the supply of research to policymakers, to steer environmental agendas across different sectors, and to promote knowledge sharing between science and policy actors. The authors suggest a demanding context for members of CREW, one in which they must translate between different language communities, read the politics of particular issues and contexts, simplify complexity, and build trust between different actors.

Together the two case organisations point to the ways in which organisational boundaries and the demarcation of roles can become fluid and blurred over time. In this way, research programmes morphed into ad hoc advisory relationships, and a delivery body became an educator and policy consultant. Exploring a world of knowledge workers operating at the interfaces between research, policy and practice, the authors highlight the politics of this setting by describing the multilateral and often asymmetrical power relationships among participants, professions and institutions. The idea of there being two (or more) 'tribes' or two (or more) 'communities' (e.g., civil servants and academics) at work in co-production is to the fore. The authors also portray this as a competitive space in which the status and legitimacy of different knowledge providers is up for grabs; where the question of what and whose knowledge counts in decision-making is inescapably political. Furthermore, in their critical account, they point to the possibility of a gap between the team-based discourse of collaboration and co-production (participative, inclusive and democratising) and the potential for boundary organisations to reinforce the very boundaries they ostensibly seek to bridge or the hierarchies they claim to wish to surmount. The context of the case—environmental policy, which seeks to address the complexity and threat of environmental catastrophe—also brings home the scale of what is at stake in this set of co-produced relationships.

Healthcare—Policy and Politics

Further developing the issues of boundaries and gaps, the discussion of knowledge and practice in healthcare, in Chapter 11, highlights a knowing-doing gap between 'two communities' involved in knowledge creation and service improvement, in which many researchers and practitioners inhabit largely separate worlds, most probably at the cost of patient experience, quality of provision and effective resource use. Such concerns have resulted in increasing calls in this arena for greater levels of collaboration in relation to the generation and use of knowledge and a bridging of the gap between knowledge and practice. In public policy terms it is perhaps the arena in which the discourse of co-production—in relation to either knowledge co-production or services co-production—has become the most prominent.

The Collaborations for Leadership in Applied Health Research (CLAHRCs) initiative, examined by the authors, is a high-profile example of this push to realise the potential of collaboration, of generating and implementing applied research knowledge through bringing together the users and producers of evidence. The account highlights the complex and politics-laden institutional landscape, featuring a multitude of professions and actors with their own interests, perspectives and practice orientations, as well as different views on what constitutes legitimate knowledge. It is an example that enshrines co-production as an important principle in the design, accomplishment and dissemination of research. The account shows how service user insights have been built into some research programmes. However, even in initiatives explicitly set up to pursue co-production and collaboration, we hear that front-line actors are worried about the creation of a further set of institutional boundaries, creating a separation between those who are part of the CLAHRC and those who are excluded. The authors draw attention to a number of other boundaries in this arena, including organisational, epistemic, semantic, professional and geographical. Their analysis highlights the importance of the work of boundary spanners, as well as the framework of incentives and rewards needed to ensure engagement in the joint endeavours. They underline that co-production involves both opportunities and opportunity costs, and if that co-production is to become taken for granted it needs effective processes of organising, boundary-spanning practices, and collaborative leadership.

Philanthropy—Dependency and Discretion

The spanning of boundaries is also an underlying issue in the chapter on philanthropy (Chapter 12). The authors show how 'the gifts' of knowledge and practice represent predominant themes throughout the history of philanthropy—a defining mission of many philanthropic enterprises has been the identification, diagnosis and tackling of societal problems through actionable knowledge and knowledgeable action. Not only have foundations played a key role in pushing the pendulum of management research from relevance to rigour and back again, but they provide a rich arena for studying the interplay between knowledge and practice given their roles as 'patron, provider, mediator and stimulant' of knowledge. However, the authors observe that philanthropic organisations are often paradoxical in the sense that they engage public issues without necessarily engaging the public; promote change but are often uninformed about its success or otherwise; and, despite exercising power and influence, stand apart from democratic institutions or other mechanisms of public accountability. The chapter therefore conveys a sense of separateness and detachment—foundations prefer to be 'stand-alone personae'—emphasising boundaries between philanthropic bodies and other actors in civil society. Indeed, the authors point to a certain defensiveness that might make dialogical exchanges with other actors either less likely or less productive, particularly in the case of those who do not share its value base or practices. The post-1945 phase of activity in the philanthropy arena involved major elements of co-production, in which foundations worked closely with governments, policymakers and academics, before there was a retreat from such partnerships towards more autonomous or independent action. The authors suggest that when partnerships have been pursued these have happened on selective bases and with profound power imbalances in the relationship. They suggest that the independence and discretion of foundations can lead to ongoing tensions between researchers, practitioners and funders. Reflecting philanthropy's distinction between 'deserving' and 'undeserving' causes, there is a sense that certain types and areas of knowledge are valued more than others. Within this context, the power exerted by foundations can run counter to the ideas and ideals of co-production. This is illustrated by examples of foundations displacing alternative visions and practices rather than complementing or co-producing them. The account suggests that the financial and political voice of foundations may make them attractive potential collaborators, but that any co-production alliance is also likely to give rise to a number of ethical and practical dilemmas for prospective partners. The fickleness of philanthropy in relation to its focal points and funding decisions raises questions about the sustainability of co-production partnerships.

CONCLUDING REMARKS

Co-production resonates with the wider sociopolitical move towards collaboration, partnerships and networks. The co-production ambition rests upon a critique of the status quo—that practices and approaches to knowledge generation which stem from traditions of separation, unqualified autonomy and insularity are inadequate or inappropriate. This criticism has led to recasting of roles and relationships in ways that mirror the inversions and reversals, which are described in Chapter 6 (identity) using the idea of medieval carnivals and the concept of 'the carnivalesque'. Those whose positions had previously been privileged—whether, for example, academics as the font of wisdom, civil servants as the source of policy advice, or clinicians as the arbiters of best practice—are now challenged by an imperative that seeks to disrupt engrained modes of operating.

The discussion in this chapter has suggested ways in which co-production can provide a useful lens through which to explore a range of settings and practices. However, when applying the lens, an important issue to consider is the conceptual ambiguity surrounding the treatment of co-production across different spheres, as set out in table 14.1. These ambiguities relate to a tendency to present every social activity from the mundane to the spectacular as, inexorably, co-produced. There are also difficulties in adopting a position that implies a boundary-less notion of co-production because it reduces the explanatory power of the concept. The conceptual ambiguity surrounding co-production may undermine its purchase and limit the extent to which it can help us to understand, or redraw, practices.

For the development of knowledge and practice, part of co-production's appeal lies in the apparent opportunity to access and exchange broader, and otherwise untapped, intellectual and physical resources. For academics and their practices, co-production addresses the growing expectation that the academy remembers its responsibilities to non-academic stakeholders and partners. It also offers one way to engage with the issue of whether research should address rigour or relevance, a question that increasingly confronts academic research. Those stressing rigour point to the distinct and potentially unbridgeable contexts occupied by researchers and practitioners. The former's responsibility is assumed to be striving for true and scientific knowledge rather than emulating the work of consultants (Kieser and Leiner 2009). Those pressing for more relevant knowledge draw attention to the implications of a disconnect between research and practice, including irrelevance and self-centred academic communities (Schultz 2010). Co-production offers a provocative basis for examining the assumptions and expectations underpinning different traditions of practice in relation to knowledge.

Resonating with the five themes in the co-production literature—boundaries, identities, standing, process and agency—this book's contextual chapters re-emphasise the fluid and complex nature of co-production practices: from direct co-learning and co-development at an individual level, to engaging with the subtle lessons and insights offered by the practices of particular settings; from open negotiations between partners, clients and funders, to the hidden agendas, politics and power plays involved in co-production. Co-production represents a concept and practice continuously in flux. It becomes recast and renegotiated: across time and place, by different players and participants. Even the language used in this chapter, where we refer to academics on the one hand and practitioners on the other, disguises that this is an artificial distinction. Academics are practitioners themselves. They are immersed in traditions and approaches to working and in the carrying off of a range of practices in their roles.

Knowing and practising are inseparable from those doing the knowing and the practising. The lessons that emerge from our critical review of the empirical chapters emphasise the importance of developing reflexive practice: embracing an examination of one's own assumptions in ways which generate openness to alternatives and to others' interests, perspectives and approaches.

SUGGESTED FURTHER READINGS

Beech, N., MacIntosh, R., Sims, D., & Antonacopoulou, E. (2011), Special Issue on *Management Practising and Knowing: Dialogues of* Theory and Practice. *Management Learning* 43(4): 373–459.
This journal special issue brings together a range of thoughtful contributors who explore academic-practitioner relationships, using a range of lenses, and with a focus on their dialogical aspects.

Orr, K., & Bennett, M. (2012) Public administration scholarship and the politics of coproducing academic–Practitioner research. *Public Administration Review.* 72(4): 487–495.
This article provides an account of the collaborations between an academic and a practitioner working together on public sector leadership research, and situates the discussion within the politics of universities and the public sector. The article was awarded the 2013 Louis Brownlow Prize by the American Society for Public Administration.

Orr, K., & Bennett, M., (2010). The Politics of Co-Produced Research. *Public Money & Management*, Special Issue on Coproduction. 30(4): 199–250.
This special issue features contributions from both academics and practitioners discussing their experience of knowledge co-production and the dilemmas, difficulties and rewards they have encountered.

REFERENCES

Antonacopoulou, E.P. (2010) Beyond co-production: Practice- relevant scholarship as a foundation for delivering impact through powerful ideas. *Public Money & Management.* 30(4): 219–226.

Armstrong, F., & Alsop, A. (2010) Debate: Co-production can contribute to research impact in the social sciences. *Public Money & Management.* 30(4): 208–210.

Auh, S., Bell, S.J., McLeod, C., & Shih, E.C.-F. (2007) Co-production & customer loyalty in financial services. *Journal of Retailing.* 83(3): 359–370.

Duijn, M., Rijnveld, M., & van Hulst, M. (2010) Meeting in the middle: joining reflection & action in complex public sector projects. *Public Money & Management.* 30(4): 227–233.

Edelenbos, J., van Buuren, A., & van Schie, N. (2011) Co-producing knowledge: Joint knowledge production between experts, bureaucrats & stakeholders in Dutch water management projects. *Environmental Science & Policy.* 14(6): 675–684.

Fenwick, T. (2012) Co-production in practice: A sociomaterial analysis. *Professions & Professionalism.* 2(2): 1–16.

Hegger, D., Lamers, M., van Zeijl-Rozema, A., & Dieperink, C. (2012) Conceptualising joint knowledge production in regional climate change adaptation projects: Success conditions & levers for action. *Environmental Science & Policy.* 18: 52–65.

Jung, T., Harrow, J., & Pharoah, C. (2012) Co-producing research: Working together or falling apart?, *CGAP Briefing Note 8*, Centre for Charitable Giving & Philanthropy, Cass Business School City University London. Available: www.cgap.org.

uk/uploads/Briefing%20Papers/CGAP%20Briefing%20Note%208%20-%20 Co-producing%20research.pdf. Accessed: October 8, 2015.

Kieser, A., & Leiner, L. (2009) Why the rigour–relevance gap in management research is unbridgeable. *Journal of Management Studies*. 46(3): 516–533.

Martin, S. (2010) Co-production of social research: Strategies for engaged scholarship. *Public Money & Management*. 30(4): 211–218.

Milofsky, C. (2000) Transparent research. *Nonprofit & Voluntary Sector Quarterly*. 29(1): 61–80.

Nutley, S. (2010) Debate: Are we all co-producers of research now? *Public Money & Management*. 30(5): 263–265.

O'Hare, P., Coaffee, J., & Hawkesworth, M. (2010) Managing sensitive relations in co- produced planning research. *Public Money & Management*. 30(4): 243–250.

Orr, K., & Bennett, M. (2012) Public administration scholarship & the politics of coproducing academic-practitioner research. *Public Administration Review*. 72(4): 487–495.

Ottman, G., Laragy, C., Allen, J., & Feldman, P. (2011) *People at centre stage: Interim report, development stage*. Melbourne: Deakin University/Uniting Community Care Options. Available: http://hdl.handle.net/10536/DRO/DU:30041066. Accessed: October 8, 2015.

Phillips, L., Kristiansen, M., Vehviläinen, M., & Gunnarsson, E. (eds.) (2013) *Knowledge and power in collaborative research: A reflexive approach*. New York: Routledge.

Phipps, D.J., Jensen, K.E., & Myers, J.G (2009) Applying social sciences research for public benefit using knowledge mobilization & social media, in A. Lopez-Varela (ed.), *Theoretical & methodological approaches to social sciences & knowledge management*. Rijeka, Croatia: InTech, pp. 167–196.

Schultz, M (2010) Reconciling pragmatism & scientific rigor. *Journal of Management Inquiry*. 19(3): 274–277.

van de Ven, A.H. (2007) *Engaged scholarship: A guide for organizational & social research*. Oxford: Oxford University Press.

15 Further Voices, Future Actions

In this chapter, we bring together five short commentaries that enrich our understanding of the core ideas concerning knowledge and practice discussed in the book, while also outlining agendas and possibilities for further action. They are written by authors whose own practice straddles universities and other arenas—including consultancy, local government, and planning—and whose interests connect with those of the Knowledge and Practice group at the University of St Andrews.

In the first of these, Stanley Blue and Elizabeth Shove comment on the implications of focusing on practices when seeking to understand knowledge and know-how. They argue that know-how has no existence independent of practices, which has implications for how we think about how knowledge travels and changes. In the second commentary, Tim Allen and Clive Grace reflect on lessons from their involvement in initiatives to improve knowledge and practice in UK local government. Their discussion is framed by a 'two communities' view of knowledge mobilisation (see Chapter 13) and they outline ways of improving connections between academic research and local government in order to inform decision-making. Duncan Maclennan, Julie Miao and Clare Moran, in the third commentary, draw on their participation in debates about the future of cities and development of 'smart cities'. They outline the benefits of adopting a learning systems perspective to rethink knowledge and practice connections within cities. The fourth and fifth commentaries discuss two areas of knowledge work: consulting, and business and management education. Mike Bennett draws on his experience as a consultant to reflect on how the relationship between consultancy knowledge and practice is approached in different organisations. He explores the everyday realities of seeking to co-produce knowledge. The chapter ends with Samuel Mansell and Charles Lovatt's reflections on the implications of knowledge and practice ideas for ethical practices in management education. They remind us of the need for critical reflection when engaging with managers and students in order to stimulate both thinking and doing. Overall, these five commentaries provide additional layers of analysis and perspective on knowledge and practice issues, and on their implications for action.

HOW SOCIAL PRACTICES GENERATE, CARRY AND REQUIRE KNOWLEDGE AND KNOW-HOW

Stanley Blue and Elizabeth Shove

This short commentary has two starting points. One is an agreement that it is possible to focus on social practices as 'the basic domain of study of the social sciences' (Giddens 1984) and the 'site of the social' (Schatzki 2002). The second is an acknowledgement that social practices entail and are constituted through the active integration of a range of elements, among them embodied skills and competence (Shove *et al.* 2012), and 'background knowledge in the form of understanding and know-how . . . and motivational knowledge' (Reckwitz 2002:249). If we take social practice as our starting point, then we need an account of knowledge and know-how that is rooted in practice.

There is already a body of useful and relevant work in something like this tradition. For example, Lave and Wenger's analysis of situated learning (1991) explores the circulation of knowledge from old hands to newcomers through the process of doing. Instead of seeing knowledge as something that exists outside practice, and that has to be acquired in advance, Lave and Wenger argue that legitimate peripheral participation in the activities of a community of practice is what enables newcomers to become old hands. They write: '. . . engaging in practice, rather than being its object, may well be a condition for the effectiveness of learning' (Lave & Wenger 93).

Others examine the routes through which embodied experiences and forms of knowing-through-doing are 'abstracted' from situations of practice, and how they are codified, packaged, stored and prepared for wider circulation. Recipe books, instruction manuals and sketch plans are outcomes of such abstraction. If it is to be of value, knowledge captured in these forms has to find its way back into practices enacted by other people and at other places and times: as Disco and van der Meulen explain, it has to be decoded, interpreted and re-enacted—in their words it has to be 'reversed' (Disco & van der Meulen 1998).

Methodologically, both these accounts take 'knowledge' as their central theme, asking questions about how it is shared and how it is de- and re-contextualised. Similarly, questions about the transferability of research 'findings' (see Chapter 11 Healthcare) are at heart questions about knowledge treated as an object that can 'circulate', or 'be transferred' between people. While Lave and Wenger and Disco and van der Meulen are interested in practice—in processes of learning and becoming, and in modes of circulation from one moment of performance to another—practices themselves are not the central topic of their analysis.

If we take practice theories seriously, a more consistent strategy would be to stick fast to the methodological suggestion that practices, as such, constitute the core objects of social enquiry. From this point of view, questions

about knowledge and know-how would not be framed in terms of how practitioners learn, nor would they focus on how knowledge travels. Instead, the
challenge would be to understand how practices constitute the knowledge
bases on which their own continued existence depends. This question is key
for getting at how practices change or extend through recruiting and losing
practitioners (Shove & Pantzar 2007).

One obvious problem is that a new practice cannot take hold unless it is
able to 'capture' recruits and carriers already capable of enacting and reproducing it. Practices can only come into being through enactment by skilled
practitioners. Hence the question: how do practices 'make' the skills/knowl-
edge they need (Disco & van der Meulen 1998)? There is unlikely to be any
one answer. Different practices will have different strategies for establishing
the knowledge bases they need. Potential techniques include the following.

- Predation: practices might leech off, or in some circumstances, completely hijack practical knowledge developed by another practice.
- Encroachment: a milder form of predation in which practices make use
  of proximal, 'boundary' overlapping practice knowledge.
- Appropriation: practices might build on sunk-knowledge embedded
  in material (inscription, infrastructure) or institutional forms (rules,
  traditions of thought, paradigms) which makes some courses of action
  easier to follow than others.
- Cultivation: practices might develop internal ladders or 'levels' of
  expertise; there might be steps or stages of progression, enabling novices to become experts within a practice; further such internal variants
  of a practice might be of a form that enables teaching/curricula to be
  built around them.
- Simplification and open access: practices might simplify themselves,
  become open access, or reduce the need for specialised know-how in
  order to increase the pool of potential recruits.

The suggestion that practices survive and thrive through producing and
re-producing the appropriately skilled activity of practitioners (which constitutes the practice) is convincing and plausible. By contrast, the related
suggestion that practices have knowledge-management strategies of their
own would strike many as odd: perhaps this pushes the agency of practice
a step too far. On the other hand, this approach provides a fresh way of
thinking about the relation between knowledge and people as the carriers of practices and as the crossing points for multiple practices (Reckwitz
2002:250).

As we know, doing develops skills in cohorts of carriers, providing them
with new knowledges and capacities and as a result enabling them to be
recruited and trained in other practices. Insofar as knowing is part of doing,
and insofar as the lives and careers of (people) are shaped by the practices
they carry, practitioners—those who do—are indeed both the containers and

the conduits of quite specific bodies of know-how, the aggregate characteristics of which define the potential for leeching, hijacking or being encroached upon by other established or emerging practices.

It follows that knowledges, being part of practices, are never fixed but always in processes of development and decay, spurting forwards in moments of exponential growth, falling into decline, being resurrected from near oblivion, or hybridised in new combinations. It also follows that developments in knowledge and knowledge-related processes of apprenticeship, or of abstraction and reversal, have no independent existence: rather, they are part of the ongoing establishment and decline of practices never in isolation but always in relation to each other, and always 'carried' by us, their variously knowing hosts.

REFERENCES

Disco, C., & van der Meulen, B. (1998) *Getting new technologies together: Studies in making sociotechnical order*. Berlin: de Gruyter.

Giddens, A. (1984) *The constitution of society: Outline of the theory of structuration*. Berkley: University of California Press.

Lave, J., & Wenger, E. (1991) *Situated learning: Legitimate peripheral participation*. Cambridge: Cambridge University Press.

Reckwitz, A. (2002) Toward a theory of social practices: A development in culturalist theorizing. *European Journal of Social Theory*. 5(2): 243–263.

Schatzki, T.R. (2002) *The site of the social: A philosophical account of the constitution of social life & change*. Pennsylvania: Pennsylvania State University Press.

Shove, E., & Pantzar, M. (2007) Recruitment & reproduction: The careers & carriers of digital photography & floorball. *Human Affairs*. 17(2): 154–167.

Shove, E., Pantzar, M., & Watson, M. (2012) *The dynamics of social practice: everyday life & how it changes*. London: SAGE.

LOCAL GOVERNMENT KNOWLEDGE AND EVIDENCE NEEDS: MAKING THE LINKS

Tim Allen and Clive Grace

UK local government and local public services face unprecedented challenges and need fresh thinking to help understand what works in redesigning services, in supporting the wider well-being of local communities, and in reshaping citizen expectations of the local state. The context is complex, with the prospect of substantial long-term financial constraints, and it is a challenge to create 'fit-for-purpose local democracy and accountability' in the face of a shifting role for the state, and the ever-present tension between what is locally driven, and what falls to central government control or direction.

Consequently, local government knowledge needs are very wide-ranging and there is an accompanying and generic requirement in ensuring that research-derived knowledge and evidence are made accessible for policy and practice (Allen *et al.* 2014). These challenges are at the heart of the case for supporting closer engagement between academic research and local government in the UK.

The Challenge

The UK has a strong research base, but engagement between local government and researchers is hit and miss. Local government has little awareness of the research undertaken by the UK's universities or the capacity to engage with it. Relatively few academics see local government as an important partner in, or potential user of, their expertise or the knowledge they generate, or they find it challenging to engage with local government. The result is that UK local government has a small and inadequate research and development capacity, which is incommensurate to the role it plays and the resources it deploys or influences.

Despite this lack of alignment, there are impressive examples of collaboration (Mortimer 2014). But engagement is inconsistent, and often depends on existing links between individual researchers and local government officers or politicians. The barriers to better and more systemic collaboration are not insuperable, but addressing them requires a change in culture and approach in both local government and research communities, and the development of some infrastructure to achieve the necessary connectivity and to facilitate communication between them.

The barriers encompass familiar challenges, and these include the potentially differential time horizons to which the two communities work. For example, new research may take time to design and deliver, yet policy and practice knowledge and evidence needs may be urgent, and local policy-makers and practitioners may lack the capacity and skills to enable them to engage with the research community. Further, in the minds of some politicians is a concern that evidence might displace political judgement about what is possible in a democratic context, matched by concerns on the part of some academics that they might be 'captured' and their research be misquoted or misused.

Nonetheless there is increasing interest in, and incentive for, academia to work with potential users of research and a growing emphasis on research impact. In practical terms this has led to investment and focus by national research funders on matters of 'impact' (the UK Research Councils, and through the UK Research Excellence Framework). Recent initiatives such as 'What Works' centres should also encourage evidence-based policy and practice and a greater emphasis in research funding on research 'impact' (RCUK 2014). Developments such as Impact Acceleration Accounts (Economic and Social Research Council 2015) will also give (some) universities greater discretion over funding for knowledge-exchange activities.

However, there are potential pitfalls for such initiatives. There is a risk that they adopt a 'supply side' approach to knowledge mobilisation based on 'push' rather than 'pull'. They may therefore not engage interactively with potential beneficiaries to define knowledge and evidence needs, and how they are best delivered—this is an issue in which 'co-production' is critical to success. They also need to engage with policy and practice beyond those already engaged—many communities of need are not yet part of the linkages that do exist and are available to be built on.

The design of research funding instruments also needs a balance that meets academic rigour and quality requirements, but also addresses the effect on many in local government when faced with complex and resource-intensive competitive processes in applying for that funding.

Towards a Solution

The approaches and infrastructure needed to achieve productive connectivity between the local government and research communities are not particularly complex or difficult to achieve.

Firstly, there is the issue of what kinds of research and researchers are needed. Evidence needs in local government policy and practice are multi-layered, ranging from 'strategic' policy challenges to specific practical issues. The former calls for engagement at senior level, because this is where leadership and direction come from both in the research world and in policy development. The latter points to the need to engage professional societies and academics who specialise in applied and practice-based research and teaching.

Secondly, 'hands-on' facilitation is very important in bringing researchers and local government together to bridge two different worlds, with different languages and imperatives. This is important to match research needs to those researchers who speak the right language and have an interest in the relevant dimension of research. Often policy and practice need access to knowledge that researchers accumulate through years of experience and research, rather than a specific study. Where new research is needed, knowledge exchange requires co-production of research agendas and problem definition as well as of the analysis that follows. In short, it requires 'embedded research'.

Hand in hand with this facilitation is the need for enabling approaches to underpin and facilitate the necessary connectivity. This means providing a facilitated modern, digital space in which researchers and local authorities are supported in linking up and being made aware of what is available in their respective domains by segmenting and matching specific needs and people to relevant and willing researchers. Technology is not a solution in itself, but rather, it provides one essential underpinning to enable successful facilitation and collaboration.

Thirdly, the exemplars of collaboration that exist demonstrate the benefits of working with and drawing on academic research. In promoting the value and use of research there is merit in highlighting examples so researchers and actual or potential customers for research can learn from others' experiences. Validated case studies are invaluable illustrations and stimulants to more effective approaches elsewhere.

Another approach is to generate rapid reviews (for example, Baars 2014; Thornton 2014, or ESRC 2015) as a cost-effective way of bringing together research on issues identified by local government as important evidence needs. Again, this involves facilitation in scoping the issues and identification of who 'needs the knowledge', and then engaging experts able to curate and communicate this knowledge to an assured standard. Key networks of councils and local government politicians, professionals and practitioners can all play a bigger role in identifying the issues that need attention and in disseminating the products. Success requires active and needy clients, and there must be active promotion of the outputs to that client audience through events and debates, for example, and the use of channels familiar to the client.

Fourthly, developing a systemic research capacity for any sector is likely to require senior leadership and sponsorship. This leadership is needed to embed organisational use of evidence and the promotion of a learning culture that seeks relevant and challenging knowledge and evidence. For example, effective use of knowledge and evidence should be a part of the peer review system that is at the heart of local government-led self-improvement. The political dimension is also very important. Local politicians who champion the use of independent research in the work of their council understand that, even where it cannot provide 'the' answer, applied research knowledge can support and strengthen local democracy by informing decision-making, service delivery, peer review, scrutiny and evaluation functions and, in doing so, provide politicians with a stronger basis for informing and challenging decisions

There is a considerable need for a long-term agenda to build effective research and development capacity to support effective and affordable local government and local public services that are fit for modern purpose. Success does not require rocket or any other science, in itself. But it does require a sustained commitment and effort to yield the substantial benefits.

REFERENCES

Allen, T., Grace, C., & Martin, S. (2014) *From analysis to action: Connecting research & local government in an age of austerity.* Report of the Local Government Knowledge Navigator, June. Available: http://www.solace.org.uk/knowledge/reports_guides/LGKN_Analysis_to_Action.pdf Accessed: September 29, 2015.

Baars, S. (2014) *The levers of local economic development*. A Local Government Knowledge Navigator Evidence Review, May. Available: http://www.solace. org.uk/knowledge/reports_guides/LGKN_NTK_ECONOMIC_GROWTH.pdf. Accessed: September 29, 2015.

Economic & Social Research Council [ESRC] (2015) *IAA FAQs: ESRC knowledge exchange*. Available: at www.esrc.ac.uk/files/funding/funding-opportunities/ impact-acceleration-accounts-faqs/. Accessed: September 29, 2015.

Mortimer, J. (2014) *Collaboration in Action: Local authorities that are making the most of research*. A Local Government Knowledge Navigator Evidence Review, June. Available: http://www.solace.org.uk/knowledge/reports_guides/LGKN_ LA_research_collaboration.pdf. Accessed: September 29, 2015.

Research Councils UK (2014) *Review of pathways to impact*. Available www. rcuk.ac.uk/RCUK-prod/assets/documents/documents/PtoIExecSummary.pdf. Accessed: September 29, 2015.

Thornton, J. (2014) *Local government in the digital age*. A local government knowledge navigator evidence review, March. Available: www.solace.org.uk/ knowledge/reports_guides/LGKN_NTK_DIGITAL_AGE.pdf. Accessed: September 29, 2015.

FULLY SMART CITIES, KNOWLEDGE AND LEARNING

Duncan Maclennan, Julie Miao and Clare Moran

Rethinking Cities

For much of the second half of the last century, cities, in academic and policy debate, were widely regarded across the OECD as places of economic decline, physical decay and social disadvantage (Maclennan 2000). Perceptions have been shifted by two developments in recent decades. The first has been wider recognition that the world is increasingly urban, and economic growth across advanced and advancing economies both drives and is underpinned by urban transformation (United Nations 2011). The second is the new prominence given in both urban theory and policy to the roles that these so-called 'agglomeration economies' have to play in raising productivity and facilitating creativity, 'buzz' and innovation (Florida 2002; Glaeser 2010; Storper 2013). The policy interest in cities has been reinforced by a growing propensity of national governments to decentralise and devolve economic and social policy autonomies to more local scales (Waite *et al.* 2013), plus the emergence of ideas and technologies related to the 'smart cities' concept.

Fully 'smart cities', in terms of successful pursuit of individual and collective goals, do not emerge simply from better engineering of technological information flows. They also imply better-informed city strategies and service delivery systems. An interest in the roles of information and knowledge in the functioning, growth and management of cities now augments older perceptions of cities as well-defined geographies of land uses, real estate structures and the transport flows that connect them.

In taking the fully smart cities agenda forward, there are many issues and questions that need to be pursued. These include an audit of how knowledge, and what knowledge, is used in city policymaking; understanding the processes and systems by which city bureaucrats and leaders learn about 'city' issues; an assessment of the structures, spaces and networks that shape effective knowledge ecologies for city governments; an assessment of how knowledge is shared with communities, voters/citizens and civil society; and examining how governance structures within cities shape their capacity to learn and innovate. This commentary sketches this emerging agenda.

Rethinking Connections: Systems Thinking

Over the last decade there has been an emerging interest in cities as systems. For example, sustainable development emphasises the importance of connections between human behaviours and ecosystem outcomes. As a consequence, policymakers at neighbourhood, city and metropolitan scales have absorbed, perhaps more than national governments, the importance of holistic approaches to complex problems, leading to new governance that connects more effectively spillovers and synergies between different policy areas (Maclennan 2013).

In the academic realms of urban theory and in the halls of government, a systems approach to cities tends to prevail, but is unevenly understood and acknowledged: systems-based arguments are often implicit rather than explicit in discussions of city development (RSA City Growth Commission 2014). For example, policy interventions may implicitly employ a systems perspective through identifying interactions between component parts of an intervention, or explicitly employ it in modelling consumer and producer behaviour. These perspectives have been important in shaping new, more comprehensive city governance approaches (Boyd & Folke 2012; Ostrom *et al.* 2012), which challenge the dominance of narrower policy frames for city development such as the 'creative' city (Florida 2002), 'skilled' city (Glaeser 2010) or 'smart' city.

Emerging policy and academic dialogue about the future of cities is increasingly informed by systems concepts such as the notion of spillovers, feedback loops, networks and inter-connectivity. In addition, the acknowledgement of disequilibrium and evolutionary processes (Martin *et al.* 2014) also recognises that systems may not be balanced and self-correcting (homeostatic) and instead are capable of rapid, non-linear changes in disruptive and difficult-to-manage ways.

City Governments As Learning Systems

There is interest in approaches to city management which involve the development of 'smart cities': cities that embed emerging information technologies in systems management and decisions. These interests are enabled by new policy autonomies for cities that have emerged at the same time as new systems of information management. The idea of smart cities has partly stemmed from tech companies seeking new markets in the wake of the global financial crisis, and partly from the emergence of 'big data'—large data sets that can be used and analysed to reveal patterns and trends—that align well with systems approaches to the city (Walport 2013).

However, for central and local government there remain tensions about the core tenets of the smart cities concept, which pulls in two directions. For some, it pulls towards a commercial driver for the radical transformation of public services, and the generation of efficiencies through novel uses of data to understand users and use in a way that makes demand on services more predictable and more easily met. Examples might be classic 'systems' issues such as the reduction of congestion or the collection of refuse. This is the angle tech and infrastructure organisations tend to pursue, and it is associated with related concepts such as big data and the internet of things; concepts that in turn generate the knowledge economy's emergent ethical issues: data security, ownership, commercialisation and privacy. For others, smart cities finally offer a mechanism for participative democracy and a means to pursue a demographically and geographically specific form of inclusive city governance, breaking down administrative and symbolic barriers between city hall and citizens. This is the angle pursued by urban theorists, academics, some policymakers, and some in local governments. Within any one government organisation—at national or local level—there will likely be individuals pulling towards these different directions or, rather, trying to maintain some pull in the direction towards democracy alongside other, perhaps dominant, forces heading towards commercialisation and digital public services. Regardless of the intentionality, the digitisation of government and public services will entail radical change within organisations (which may or may not be linked to reductions in public finances), and the need to rapidly accumulate unfamiliar practices and new categories of knowledge for those within these organisations. A narrative of core skills, innovation, learning, and transformation accompanies these changes (see for example, Government Digital Service, no date).

Effective policymaking is key to delivering better outcomes for those who live and work in cities, but this poses the key question of how city governments and city leaders learn and make decisions. The development of smart technologies fits with the image of cities as systems that are open to inflows of information, alert to innovation and capable of learning. But such settings are also riven with the politics of public choices and debates that are all too readily downplayed in the technocratic 'smart city' literature. The concept of a fully 'smart city' needs not only to view cities as learning systems that make best use of available data, but also needs to embrace the reality of conflict and differences of view on what we know, how we know it, and what this implies for future actions. The discussion of knowledge, power, boundary spanners, knowledge mobilisation and

226 Stanley Blue et al.

knowledge co-production in this volume appear to take on a special resonance in relation to rethinking cities.

REFERENCES

Boyd, E., & Folke, C. (2012) *Adapting institutions: Governance, complexity & social-ecological resilience*. Cambridge: Cambridge University Press.

Florida, R. (2002) *The rise of the creative class*. New York: Perseus.

Glaeser, E. (2010) *Agglomeration economics*. Chicago: Chicago University Press.

Government Digital Service (no date) *About Us* Available: www.gov.uk/government/organisations/government-digital-service/about. Accessed December 23, 2015

Maclennan, D. (2000) Britain's cities: A more positive view, in *Proceedings of the Lunar Society*. Birmingham: Lunar Society.

Maclennan, D. (2013) Neighbourhoods: Evolving ideas, evidence & changing policies, in D. Manley, D., van Ham, M., Bailey, N., Simpson, L., & Maclennan, D (eds.), *Neighbourhood effects or neighbourhood-based problems: A policy context*. Dordrecht: Springer, pp. 269–292.

Martin, R., Gardiner, B., & Tyler, P. (2014) *The evolving economic performance of UK cities: City growth patterns 1981–2011*. London: Government Office for Science. Available:www.gov.uk/government/uploads/system/uploads/attachment_data/file/358326/14–803-evolving-economic-performance-of-cities.pdf. Accessed: October 12, 2015.

Ostrom, E., Change, C., Pennington, M., & Tarko, V. (2012) *The future of the commons: Beyond market failure & government regulation*. London: Institute of Economic Affairs. Available: www.iea.org.uk/publications/research/the-future-of-the-commons-beyond-market-failure-and-government-regulation. Accessed: October 12, 2015.

RSA City Growth Commission (2014) *Unleashing metro growth: Final recommendations of the city growth commission*. London: RSA. Available: http://www.citygrowthcommission.com/wp-content/uploads/2014/10/City-Growth-Commission-Final-Report.pdf. Accessed: October 12, 2015.

Storper, M. (2013) *The keys to the city*. Princeton, NJ: Princeton University Press.

United Nations (2011) *World urbanization prospects*. New York: United Nations.

Waite, D., Maclennan, D., & O'Sullivan, A. (2013) Emerging city policies: Devolution, deals & disorder. *Local Economy*. 28(7–8): 770–785.

Walport, M. (2013) *Future of cities launch*. London: Government Office for Science. Available: www.gov.uk/government/speeches/future-of-cities-launch. Accessed: October 12, 2015.

IMPLICATIONS FOR CONSULTANCY PRACTICE—PUTTING KNOWLEDGE INTO PRACTICE?

Mike Bennett

The idea of putting knowledge into practice captures one simple aim of organisational consultancy and management learning: to increase capability or capacity by sharing experience and expertise to the benefit of the client. This is the preferred version of consultancy held by clients who seek consultants to bring models and to leave 'learning take aways'.

However, unfortunately not all consultants are perceived as bringing new knowledge. As a politician from one public body put it to me, consultants "steal your watch to tell you the time". While I wouldn't sign up to that caricature, perhaps his perception was not all wrong.

I will argue that while consultancy can certainly be about bringing specialist insight, it should almost always be about provoking the client to reflect critically on their own practice. Perhaps not stealing their watch, but holding up a mirror so they can see how they are reading the time from a different perspective.

The Problem of Knowledge

The concept of knowledge transfer, while limited and linear, does capture the immense value of research and innovation to the world of practice, and we see it at work in many fields, notably in science, medicine and engineering. And of course we do see the idea of putting knowledge into practice through the use of a whole range of mainstream management tools. Benchmarking, process mapping, case studies and the sharing of best practice are all ways of seeking to compare and learn from others who perform better than we do.

Ever since Taylor developed his principles of scientific management (Taylor 1911) and its philosophy of 'one best way', management and their consultants have been trying to develop knowledge about more efficient methods of working and to equip people with the skills to practice more effectively. While Taylorist principles remain relevant and do still play a role in organisational approaches to efficiency, Taylorism has been heavily criticised for under-conceptualising the role of people and context (human relations) and for its stark demarcation between managers who would bring the intellect and knowledge to design better ways of working and 'workmen' who would be selected and trained to put their betters' ideas into practice. And what happens if knowledge is partial, still developing or, indeed, hotly contested?

The notion of knowledge as difficult or impossible to access is not a postmodern fad but has been with us since Plato. As a young philosopher Plato believed in idealised forms of knowledge with which we were all born, that proper education would allow us to recover and recollect. However, in his later dialogues, for example in the *Theaetetus,* Plato explores a different account of knowledge and, with Socrates, shows the inadequacy of all available accounts of what knowledge is. By having Socrates argue us into an impasse about what is knowledge and what is knowable, Plato develops his 'aporia—pathless paths' that lead to puzzlement and open-ended questions, rather than resolution.

In management, as in consultancy, we are often working on issues which resemble open-ended questions, where there is no established operating manual based on a proven body of knowledge about the conditions or causes of success. Thus even where there is experience about what has worked in some places—i.e., how to lead, develop and motivate people, how to change organisational culture, how to build democratic organisations, how to design and implement policy that achieves its objectives—it has not always worked in all places and it is not always clear why not. In other words, our limited experience falls short of a knowledge that can universally be put into practice without reference to other factors such as the people, politics and culture of the particular context.

Often it is not a consultant's role to bring new knowledge but rather to problematise what it is to know, what knowledge about management problems might be, and then to provide the conditions for new ways of thinking about the challenges faced by the client. This version of consultancy seems to owe more to a Socratic dialogue than to a Taylorist approach. Perhaps consultancy's relationship to knowledge could be conceptualised as addressing open-ended questions, a form of aporetic reasoning, stimulating a process of dialogue and debate: collectively worrying our way towards new ways of seeing the management challenge.

The Problem of Practice

The phrase 'putting knowledge into practice' suggests not just a certainty about knowledge but also a rather static form of practice. But isn't practice itself a historical and transitory accomplishment, which consultancy has often sought to change?

Like Plato's different theories of knowledge, the idea of practice can be idealised and can be problematised. For MacIntyre (1981) practice refers to any coherent and complex form of socially established cooperative human activity through which goods internal to that form of activity are realised and where the attainment of these standards can be regarded as an end in itself. MacIntyre talks of the attainment of these standards of excellence as internal goods: that is, they are benefits to the participants over and above the outcome of the activity that are particular to each practice and which consist in carrying out the activity well (for example, the achievement or satisfaction of being a good doctor or a good teacher, as opposed to healing or teaching others). Furthermore, achievement in a practice is determined by existing culture and rules that must be learned and accepted and is therefore denied to newcomers or outsiders.

MacIntyre's account of practice is of course more complex than the summary above indicates, and he suggests what is in many ways an inspiring ideal of practice—self-correcting and perfecting over time—and one that seems relevant to the historical development of excellence in professions. But its idea of excellence—if we apply this to professional communities—is one that is entirely self-defined and sets high barriers which exclude outsiders. In one way at least this makes sense. One could argue brain surgeons are exclusively qualified to judge what counts as progress in neurosurgery. But brain surgeons exist within a broader sociopolitical, organisational context. For example, the management of neurosurgeons, the ethics and economics of neurosurgery, the organisation of neurosurgery in relation to other disciplines and other people involved in the care of their patients, and how neurosurgeons account for their actions to patients and employers are perhaps all areas in which their practice is not self-defined and must not exclude others. Indeed on these matters and others it might be important that their practice is opened up to and consults with outsiders.

The account above of MacIntyre's idealised form of a practice can appear nostalgic given the challenges and developments of recent decades. It's not just that public attitudes to professions are changing and people's experience of doctors and teachers sometimes falls short of these high standards. It's also that the idea of a closed professional community setting their own rules, impervious to the views of outsiders, seems somewhat anachronistic, protectionist and undemocratic. Through open policymaking, crowdsourcing of ideas and the use of consultants in the development of strategy and policy, we see a more porous and dynamic model of practice that is less inward-facing and more subject to outside views. It's not that professions have ceased to be important or that professions no longer set their own standards. But perhaps there is an acceptance that people external to a profession can make a contribution to the development of their practice.

Conclusion

One doesn't have to deny the existence of 'one best way' consultancies out there to argue that much contemporary consultancy is far more humble about the origins of the insights they bring and much more committed to forms of co-production with clients, their staff and service users. Yes, consultants can bring professional expertise, a broad experience, inter-organisational perspectives—and all of that could be classified as knowledge of some kind. But consultancy is not in essence about being a subject expert. It ought to be much more about stimulating critical reflection on practice and about increasing critical-thinking capacity. This is about being able to understand the strategic—organisational, policy, political—issue, formulate the challenge and the open-ended questions (the aporia), and stimulate thinking about how to change, how to reframe the challenge so the impasse can be overcome.

REFERENCES

MacIntyre, A. (1981) *After Virtue*. London: Duckworth.
Taylor, F.W. (1911) *Scientific management, comprising Shop management, The principles of scientific management & Testimony before the special house committee*. New York: Harper & Row.

ETHICAL PRACTICE IN MANAGEMENT EDUCATION

Samuel Mansell and Charles Lovatt

Management education in general, and the MBA degree in particular, have been the target of an influential critique in recent years. For many students and employers, the master of business administration (MBA) is the hall-marked standard of management education. Accredited MBA programmes are widely taught across North America, Europe and the Asia-Pacific. However, according to a number of leading management academics, crystallised in the pedagogy of the MBA are dangerous assumptions about management knowledge and its appropriate mode of explanation (Mintzberg 2004; Ghoshal 2005; Freeman *et al.* 2010). In particular, it is argued that business schools undermine the capacity of management students to identify and respond to *ethical* considerations. To the extent that the critics offer an accurate characterisation of business education, this book offers an alternative perspective on the nature of organisational knowledge and its link to practice. We briefly review the critics' arguments before reflecting upon how a responsible approach to the teaching of management might be shaped by the insights in this book.

What is the epistemology that subverts managerial ethics? According to some critics, it is that management is a science and can be explained only with models appropriate to the physical sciences. For Ghoshal (2005:79): "Management theories at present are overwhelmingly causal or functional in their modes of explanation" and any perspective which does not yield "sharp, testable propositions" (2005:81) is simply ignored. Similarly, Mintzberg believes that MBA education misrepresents the real world of strategy by encouraging the false confidence of self-assured and arrogant analyses of case studies, with the exclusion of competent knowledge (Mintzberg 2004:74). This, Mintzberg continues, leads to the corruption of managerial practice.

The fundamental mistake in using the 'scientific model' (Ghoshal 2005:76) is that it leaves no scope for ethical *choice* on the part of managers: we have "replaced all notions of human intentionality with a firm belief in causal determinism for explaining all aspects of corporate performance . . ." (2005:77). A manager, in this deterministic account, does not "have to make difficult value judgements, she/he simply follows a quasi-mathematical model . . ." (Hühn 2014:537). Following Ghoshal, Freeman *et al.* (2010:70) conclude: "If we treat the world of business as discovered, not created, we absolve managers of their responsibility for its structure".

This book offers a wealth of alternatives to the 'scientific' model of organisational knowledge. Furthermore, it draws examples from a variety of management contexts not limited to the for-profit sector. The authors of Chapter 2 (knowledge) observe that while the natural sciences "seem to have converged in their understanding about what counts as knowledge . . .

nothing like such agreement is seen" when discussing the social world (p. 17). Management knowledge is often *tacit* and *contextually specific;* it is embedded in the culture of an organisation and therefore irreducible to purely abstract and causal modes of explanation. The review of the conceptual terrain, in Chapter 2, distinguishes 'content-based subject matter' (knowing *that* or knowing *about*) from 'skills-based capability' (knowing *how* and with what effect); the latter is often "exhibited in the demonstration of skills, and thereby inseparable from the knower" (p. 19). The mainstream of management education, according to its critics, has focused exclusively on 'knowing *that*' or 'knowing *about*'.

The inescapable relevance of contextual knowledge is evident in the chapter on everyday practices at an advertising agency (Chapter 8). Advertising practitioners are said to be "working in discontinuity" to address their clients' needs, constantly shifting between a range of practices (including developing strategies, generating ideas and realising concepts—p. 112). Likewise, in Chapter 10 we find that environmental policy draws together 'expert, professional, tacit and experiential knowledge' and cannot rely on a "neutral package of 'facts'" (p. 140). A similar observation can be found in the chapter on academic knowledge in healthcare (Chapter 11): "When CLAHRCs focused their attention on the use of research-based knowledge . . . the approach to implementing research-based knowledge often occurred through processes of trial and error, and the use of experiential knowledge was evident" (p. 150).

Contextual specificity has the practical consequence that organisational politics and power dynamics shape the mobilisation of knowledge. In Chapter 10 (p. 140) we find that in the "crafting of knowledge for environmental policy" by boundary organisations such as CREW and ZWS, "packages of facts and evidence may be contested or actively ignored through strategies of denial, dismissal, diversion or displacement". These same organisations may 'reify certain ways of knowing that exclude others in order to legitimate their own roles and positions . . .' (p. 141). Furthermore, in healthcare (Chapter 11) the diverse expectations of research users shape what is considered to be credible knowledge. For example, "boundary spanners . . . who did not have a clinical background found it difficult to work with General Practices" because of a perceived "lack of power and authority" (p. 152). The authors of Chapter 11 also highlight numerous 'structural, professional, philosophical, and geographical factors' which result in 'multiple boundaries' between communities of academics and practitioners working together (p. 151). These findings bring into question the implicit separation of 'scientific' management knowledge from its practical context, and the universal applicability claimed on its behalf, in business school education.

Much of the critique of business schools focuses upon false assurances of certainty rooted in the discipline of management science. The result is deepening but ever narrower knowledge 'about' managerial work. Meanwhile, in the 'real world' of management there are many calls for broader under-standing and less granular knowledge. Gillian Tett's (2015) newly published *The Silo Effect* is one such call, with examples drawn from the fields of healthcare, banking and technology. She argues that siloed structures inhibit innovation and hinder strategic understanding. Similarly, if we teach stu-dents from within siloed paradigms, then we fail to prepare them for the diverse range of practices they must work across. Further, siloed teaching leads to the separated inculcation of ethics. In other words, students may feel absolved from taking a moral perspective on management when 'ethics' is consigned to a stand-alone module.

The broader perspectives in this book suggest that the role of business and management schools is not to equip students with the analytical tools to deduce the 'right' answer in any scenario. Instead, it is to integrate the vari-ous strands of knowing *about* management with an understanding of the *effect* and the consequences of management, while noting the wide variety of settings in which people are managed and organised (see also Parker *et al.* 2014). Teaching is, as Freire (1985) pointed out, a political act, and there are moral judgements in selecting what to teach, what not to teach and how it should be taught. The choices teachers make in curriculum design have ethical consequences in shaping students' *Weltanschauung*. Our pedagogy moulds their view of the world, their internal paradigm and the way they will engage with the power dynamics of the workplace.

In conclusion, we suggest that 'knowledge' forms a contextual map of managerial terrain that is navigated through the moral compass of critical reflection. Moreover, despite the institutional rigidities with which we are familiar in UK higher education (curriculum design, quality assurance, credit value, etc.), to some extent there is an element of *co-creation* in the learn-ing experience. As teachers, we are not mobilising 'our' knowledge into the minds of students; rather we see knowing as a process of co-production with students (see Chapter 14). This suggests that to teach responsible enterprise is to adopt a *relational* understanding of teaching and a reflexive approach to teaching practice; such an approach can itself be seen as a 'responsible enterprise'.

REFERENCES

Freeman, R., Harrison, J., Wicks, A., Parmar, B., & de Colle, S. (2010) *Stakeholder theory: The state of the art*. Cambridge: Cambridge University Press.

Freire, P. (1985) The politics of education: Culture, power, & liberation (D. Macedo, trans.). South Hadley, MA: Bergin & Garvey.

Ghoshal, S. (2005) Bad management theories are destroying good management prac-tices. *Academy of Management Learning & Education*. 4(1): 75–91.

Hühn, M. (2014) You reap what you sow: How MBA programs undermine ethics. *Journal of Business Ethics*. 121(4): 527–541.

Mintzberg, H. (2004) *Managers not MBAs: A hard look at the soft practice of managing & management development*. Harlow: Pearson Education Ltd.

Parker, M., Cheney, G., Fournier, V., & Land, C. (2014) *The Routledge companion to alternative organisation*. London: Routledge.

Tett, G. (2015) *The silo effect: Why putting everything in its place isn't such a bright idea*. New York: Simon & Schuster.

16 Concluding Reflections
Exploring and Mapping the Knowledge and Practice Terrain

Sandra Nutley, Rod Bain, Bonnie Hacking, Clare Moran, Kevin Orr and Shona Russell

INTRODUCTION

In writing this book our aim has been to contribute to a continuing conversation about knowledge and practice. To sum up our contribution to this conversation thus far, after setting the scene in Chapter 1 (introduction), we have explored the conceptual terrain and some of the key debates about knowledge and practice in Part A. We have then provided context-specific examples of ways of understanding the relationship between knowledge and practice in Part B. And in Part C, we have considered different approaches to improving the creation, sharing and use of knowledge, while also providing some initial reflections on their implications for actions. What emerges are the rich and varied ways in which we can understand both knowledge and practice and how they relate to one another.

We could leave it at that. However, as explained in Chapter 1, this writing project has been a learning journey for the authors and for the broader community of people involved. It therefore seems appropriate to share some further thoughts and reflections on our expedition and our emerging map of the knowledge and practice terrain. In offering these reflections, we are not attempting to provide some notion of the final word. We do not wish to foreclose discussion of other ways of interpreting the key messages to emerge from previous chapters. We hope and anticipate readers will also be drawing and sharing their own conclusions.

This chapter continues by reiterating our diverse points of departure and what we hoped to provide for ourselves and others by embarking on this expedition—issues introduced in Chapter 1. We then turn to consider our intermediate points of arrival: in particular our emerging conceptual map of the knowledge and practice terrain, which identifies the key domains and 'fault lines' within this arena plus their implications. This is followed by some reflections on how we got to this point: our own knowledge and practice in producing the book, and our approach to moving between and across the fault lines and perspectives depicted in the conceptual map. Finally, we consider future directions of travel for ourselves and others: domains and fault lines that could be explored; ideas and values to carry with us, and some things we should probably leave behind.

POINTS OF DEPARTURE

This was a collective writing project, which brought together people who shared a common interest in broadening and deepening their understanding of knowledge and practice. Despite this shared interest, there were diverse points of departure for our individual engagement in the project, including different career histories, disciplinary backgrounds, and areas of research and practice. There were also differences in epistemological positions and methodological choices, the balance between explanatory, normative and critical stances, and attitudes to and experience of applied research and engaged scholarship. It was clear from the outset that we approached, examined, enacted and explained knowledge and practice issues in various ways and in diverse settings.

There were, however, limits to both the diversity of our learning community and our ambitions for the journey ahead. We were all primarily concerned with studying knowledge and practice in and between organisations, albeit these included public, private and not-for-profit organisations of varying scales and scopes. We were all based in the UK and this is reflected in the choice of settings investigated in Part B. Although many participants had experience of other national contexts, our focus was on ways of understanding knowledge and practice in organisations and societies shaped by a Western intellectual tradition. We recognised there would be additional insights to be gained from studying these issues in other settings and societies but this was a boundary we did not plan to cross on this occasion. Nevertheless, through our UK focus we were joining wider international debates and conversations about knowledge and practice.

PROVISIONAL POINTS OF ARRIVAL

We did not begin with a guiding map of the knowledge and practice terrain or a clear idea of where we would arrive at the end of the project. We did, however, decide early on that we would share the results of our learning with others in the form of an edited collection. Discussing the shape of this book helped to structure our expedition and specific events organised around the component parts of the book provided convenient staging posts along the way.

The individual chapters within this book go a long way towards capturing our provisional points of arrival for the concepts we reviewed in Part A and the context-specific examples we considered in Part B. In Part C of the book, we began the process of looking across the chapters with the specific aim of considering the implications of our investigations for understanding (and improving) the creation, sharing and use of knowledge. As part of this we considered (in Chapter 14) whether the concept of co-producing knowledge and practice provides a useful way of integrating the insights from the context-specific chapters. We found it a helpful lens for viewing the relationship between knowledge and practice, but it is just one way of viewing this relationship. To more fully capture and map the conceptual landscape covered by the book, we need to think more broadly. The results of this broader analysis are depicted in our emerging conceptual map of the knowledge and practice terrain (figure 16.1).

AN EMERGING CONCEPTUAL MAP OF THE KNOWLEDGE AND PRACTICE TERRAIN

Our map of this terrain centres on two dimensions or 'fault lines' emerging first in the conceptual chapters on knowledge (Chapter 2) and practice (Chapter 3), and then revisited and discussed in subsequent chapters. The first of these fault lines (shown on the vertical axis in figure 16.1) concerns the conceptualisation of knowledge and practice. At the top end of this axis, knowledge is seen as a product or thing, separate from practice. In terms of Cartesian dualism (see Chapter 3), mind/thinking and body/action are separated and practice becomes defined as the opposite of theory or simply what people do. At the bottom end of this fault line, knowing is viewed as a process, wherein knowing and doing are intertwined. A fracture point in conceptualisation occurs somewhere between the two ends of this dimension, but we find many authors (in this book and beyond) cluster around the middle. For example, they may recognise the importance of viewing knowing as a process but nevertheless still frame much of their discussion in terms of a gap between knowledge and practice. For this reason it is not always easy to see which side of this conceptual divide is ultimately driving their thinking and actions.

The second fault line or dimension (the horizontal axis) concerns the unit or level of analysis used to study knowledge and practice. At the left-hand side of this dimension is the study of knowledge and practice at different levels of granularity: micro, meso and macro levels. The micro level typically involves considering the knowledge and practice of individuals and/ or groups. At the meso level the focus is on the knowledge and practice of larger collectives, particularly organisations. At the macro level the focal point moves to wider systems, inter-organisational relationships and institutions. The wider level may include, for example, a sector-by-sector analysis of knowledge and practice, or an analysis of national policymaking. At the right-hand side of the horizontal dimension we find the 'flat ontology' of practice theory (see Chapter 3), where the unit of analysis is

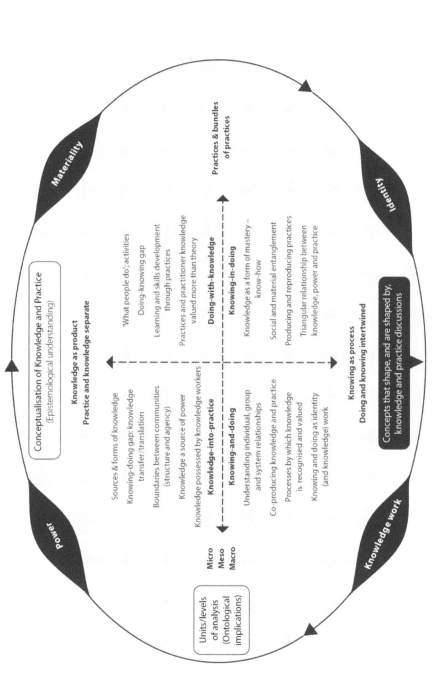

Figure 16.1 An emerging conceptual map of the knowledge and practice terrain

Materiality

Identity

Knowledge work

Power

Conceptualisation of Knowledge and Practice
(Epistemological understanding)

Units/levels of analysis
(Ontological implications)

Micro
Meso
Macro

Knowledge as product
Practice and knowledge separate

'What people do': activities
Doing-knowing gap
Learning and skills development through practices
Practices and practitioner knowledge valued more than theory

Doing-with-knowledge
Knowing-in-doing

Knowledge as a form of mastery – know-how
Social and material entanglement
Producing and reproducing practices
Triangular relationship between knowledge, power and practice

Practices & bundles of practices

Sources & forms of knowledge
Knowing-doing gap: knowledge transfer/translation
Boundaries between communities (structure and agency)
Knowledge a source of power
Knowledge possessed by knowledge workers

Knowledge-into-practice
Knowing-and-doing

Understanding individual, group and system relationships
Co-producing knowledge and practice
Processes by which knowledge is recognised and valued
Knowing and doing as identity (and knowledge) work

Knowing as process
Doing and knowing intertwined

Concepts that shape, and are shaped by, knowledge and practice discussions practices and bundles of these. The perspectives of the majority of authors in this book cluster towards the left-hand side of this horizontal dimension, but three of the conceptual chapters—Chapters 3 (practice), 4 (power) and 6 (identity)—highlight some of the benefits of adopting a practice-theory ontology. Two of the context-specific chapters—Chapters 7 (sensing bodies) and 8 (advertising)—also demonstrate the insights provided by adopting this perspective. In addition, the commentary by Blue and Shove in Chapter 15 teases out the implications of practice theory for developing know-how.

The placement of these two dimensions at right angles to one another produces a figure that demarcates four perspectives or domains of thought on knowledge and practice. The characterisation of each of these domains (below) captures the main debates in the field as examined by this book. The figure is not intended to depict a desirable progression between the domains; rather it indicates the differences between them. And it is, of course, only one way of mapping the terrain. Like all maps, it is selective in what is captured, but we offer it as a potentially helpful guide.

FOUR DOMAINS OF THOUGHT ON KNOWLEDGE AND PRACTICE

The summary text provided for each domain in figure 16.1 indicates how knowledge and practice *tend to* be approached and characterised by those adopting the assumptions and unit of analysis associated with the domain. We use the phrase *tend to* advisedly because the boundaries between the domains are porous and there is some crossover in the language and images used in each. Nevertheless, the tendencies are sufficient to enable us to characterise the enquiry focus, types of explanation, and recommendations associated with each.

In the top left-hand domain, labelled *knowledge-into-practice,* knowledge is viewed as somewhat separate from practice and the knowledge-practice relationship is often considered as a problem to be addressed: a knowing-doing gap (see Chapter 13 on knowledge mobilisation). Different sources and forms of knowledge are recognised (as outlined in Chapter 2). However, the varying interests, needs and preoccupations of different epistemic and practice communities (Haas 1992) often mean the value they place on different forms and sources of knowledge varies. In this way, boundaries develop between interest groups and communities and this hampers the process of knowledge sharing and practice development. Boundary spanners are envisaged as key agents in enabling knowledge to flow across these structures and communities (see Chapter 10 on environmental policy and Chapter 11 on healthcare). A relationship between knowledge and power is frequently recognised. Power tends to be viewed as a resource: those who have greater power in a system influence which forms and sources of knowledge have greater voice and traction (see Chapter 9 on accounting). Knowledge is also viewed as a source of power. In line with this, knowledge workers (Chapter 5), from this perspective, have greater status due to their possession of a valued resource.

In the bottom left-hand domain, labelled *knowing-and-doing,* the separation between knowledge and practice is less evident, and is fully dissolved at the bottom margin. There may still be recognition of different forms of knowledge, but these are more likely to be viewed as intertwined strands. The focus is less on different forms of knowledge than on the processes by which individuals and groups come to know how to do things, and the processes that lead to certain ways of knowing and doing becoming recognised and valued. This involves understanding relationships between individuals and groups. It also involves an appreciation of the dynamics of complex systems (Best and Holmes 2010). The concept of co-production (Chapter 14) is sometimes used to describe the basis and politics of intertwining relationships, but it is also used in a normative sense to indicate what are envisaged to be more effective ways of approaching the development of knowing and doing. The concepts of knowledge work and identity work intersect with these process explanations. Within the *knowing-and-doing* domain both knowledge and identity work are viewed as processes representing how people act in the workplace and why this is the case (see Chapter 5 on knowledge work and Chapter 6 on identity).

In the top right-hand domain, labelled *doing-with-knowledge,* the focus is on empirically grounded descriptions of what people do—the activities they undertake. The extent to which knowing and doing are viewed as separate activities within this domain varies across studies. As noted in Chapter 3 (practice), one branch of empirical work adopting a practice-focused approach has tended to study the detail of practices, unmediated by *a priori* theoretical frameworks. Such an approach does not feature strongly in this book and the closest example we provide is the study of advertising agency practices (Chapter 8). A focus on practices as the unit of analysis is associated with the idea that learning, knowing and skills are developed through practices. Theorised knowledge may be viewed as somewhat disconnected from what happens in practice (a doing-knowing gap) leading to a disregard for much academic research (as discussed in Chapter 9 on accounting).

An examination of what people do is also at the forefront of the approach represented in the bottom right-hand domain, labelled *knowing-in-doing.* Here practice theorising features more strongly than in *doing-with-knowledge.* With this come particular assumptions about the intertwined nature of knowing and doing. The importance of the material as well as the social world is emphasised, and both of these are viewed as inseparably entangled. The focus in this domain is on explaining the production and reproduction of practices, with the promise of greater insights into continuity and change, and the development of know-how. Chapter 7 (sensing bodies) provides a good example of this approach. The perspective represented by this domain is challenging because it suggests that "practices survive and thrive through producing and re-producing the appropriately skilled activity of practitioners" rather than vice versa (Blue and Shove, Chapter 15, p. 218). That is, practices rather than people have agency.

RELATED SOCIAL SCIENCE CONCEPTS

The social science concepts intersecting most directly with discussions of knowledge and practice are depicted in the outer circle of figure 16.1. We have only highlighted those concepts that feature strongly in the analyses presented in this book; other analyses are likely to reveal a wider range of intersecting concepts. As already indicated, the way these concepts are interpreted and expressed in each domain varies. This is illustrated by focusing on just one of the concepts: power. The approach to power in the *knowledge-into-practice* domain is more likely to adopt a resource-based and coercive view of that power. In contrast, in the *knowing-and-doing* and *knowing-in-doing* domains the focus is more likely to be on the productive capacity of power and power as doing (see Chapter 4 on power). In the *doing-with-knowledge* domain, the view of power may emphasise its productive capacity, but power may also be viewed as something that is possessed and exercised coercively (as in the jurisdictional disputes reported in Chapter 9 on accounting).

Not only do these related social science concepts shape approaches and explanations in each of the domains, but the discussion of these concepts in the context of knowledge and practice also influences debates about the concepts themselves. For example, Chapter 4 (power) illustrates the way in which a practice-theory perspective, *knowing-in-doing,* can help to refine our conceptualisation of power. Similarly, Chapter 6 (identity) discusses the way in which the same perspective offers new ways of thinking about identity and identity work.

The concepts are depicted in figure 16.1 as somewhat separate and removed from discussions of knowledge and practice. However, in some analyses, particularly those adopting perspectives towards the bottom of the figure, concepts such as power and identity are seen as intrinsic to understanding knowledge and practice. Given the emergent nature of figure 16.1, it would be interesting to see what other concepts and connections might emerge as key from different portfolios of knowledge and practice explorations.

ENQUIRY GOALS AND METHODS

Different analytical goals can influence the nature of the approach taken in each domain. The chapters in this book have varying emphases on explanation, critical assessment, and more normative judgements about what needs to change in relation to knowledge and practice. Although there is a risk of overgeneralising, we note (based on the examples in the book) that those operating from within the *doing-with-knowledge* and *knowing-in-doing* domains tend to focus on description and explanation (e.g., Chapters 7 and 8 on sensing bodies and advertising respectively), whereas those operating from the *knowledge-into-practice* and *knowing-and-doing* domains have a greater tendency to critically assess (e.g., Chapter 12 on philanthropy) and provide more normative judgements (e.g., Chapter 11 on healthcare and Chapter 13 on knowledge mobilisation). These differences in analytical goals are linked to the breadth of possibilities offered by different ontologies—the horizontal dimension of figure 16.1.

A combination of analytical goals and ontological perspectives influences the range of enquiry methods used by researchers operating with or across the domains. Empirical studies reflecting the two domains on the right-hand side of the figure tend to adopt broadly ethnographic methods. In contrast, a wider mix of research methods is more evident in studies conducted within the domains on the left-hand side. These include case studies, surveys, and experimental methods, as well as more observational methods.

COMPLEMENTARY OR INCOMMENSURATE PERSPECTIVES

We have used the phrase 'fault lines' to characterise the two dimensions depicted in figure 16.1 because they capture different ontological and epistemological perspectives on knowledge and practice. This raises the question of whether the domains in figure 16.1 represent 'incommensurable paradigms' that provide alternative rather than complementary world views (see Burrell & Morgan 1979). Our use of dotted lines to portray the boundaries between the domains suggests there is some fluidity across the boundaries: some sharing of ideas. However, at their heart, the domains represent different philosophical positions that cannot be simply disregarded or fully dissolved. Accordingly, we do not consider it feasible to arrive at an integrated 'grand theory' of knowledge and practice, one that pays due attention to the assumptions and concerns of all domains. This does not mean researchers or other practitioners necessarily need to confine themselves to investigations (or other practices) that are shaped by the perspectives of only one domain. On the contrary, they may profitably choose to offer multiple perspectives on the same phenomenon or act differently in different situations.

One of our guiding principles in this project has been to value the insights offered by different perspectives, even when these do not readily fit with our own approaches to understanding knowledge and practice. However, reflecting on the conclusions drawn in each of the chapters, we realise they tend to cluster towards the bottom two-thirds of the diagram in figure 16.1. Hence our instinct to promote the equal value of all perspectives needs to be qualified by the realisation that, in practice, we are somewhat sceptical of drawing a sharp distinction between knowledge and practice. Although many of the chapters still use the language of knowledge *and* practice, what they actually say is not far out of line with the ideas of knowing as a process and the intertwined nature of doing and knowing *(knowing-and-doing* and *knowing-in-doing).* In terms of the unit of analysis, the perspectives taken in this book cluster more towards the left-hand side of the figure, but our learning community could, nevertheless, see the merits of focusing more on practices *(doing-with-knowledge* and *knowing-in-doing).* The fact that empirical studies adopting these perspectives are not exemplified more frequently within the book may just reflect happenstance and the composition of our learning community at the time the book was produced.

While we have argued that it is not possible to disregard or fully dissolve the differences between the four domains in our conceptual map, this does not rule out the potential for productive dialogue across these boundaries. We next discuss how this was achieved during the process of developing and writing this book.

REFLECTIONS ON THE LEARNING JOURNEY

As already indicated, our aim has been to stimulate open and constructive dialogue between people with different work roles, experiences and perspectives. We did not strive to achieve an overarching consensus about the nature of knowledge and practice, but we did want to appreciate more fully points of difference and commonality. In some senses, our intentions around working together could be characterised as 'agonistic' (Mouffe 2013), reflecting an approach where conflicting views are valued and the aim is to foster 'diverging and converging interactions in a way that recognises opportunities for collaboration, without losing sight of diverse interests and frames' (Frame & Brown 2008, 234).

But how could we achieve this? What would be a productive way of working and learning together? We were not entirely sure at the outset, but over time we established some norms and principles for working together. These included a norm of constructive rather than confrontational dialogue. Chapter authors were not expected to defend or justify their draft chapters, but instead take on the role of active listeners when their chapters were being discussed. There was an expectation of constructive feedback, underpinned by principles of respect, equality of voice and a duty of care towards others. There was a strong sense of the need to value the process of working together as much as the intended product—this book. There was a preference for conducting much of this interaction through face-to-face dialogue rather than relying mainly on written communication, because it was felt to be more generative and satisfying for participants.

These ways of working together emerged and developed during a schedule of retreats, workshops and seminars organised to plan, develop and review chapters, and to reflect on their relationship to one another. This process involved extensive and repeated peer reviews of all chapters, which developed a sense of collective responsibility for the shape and quality of the overall book.

Members of our group had differing levels of involvement in these activities. Some dipped in and out, but a substantial core of people participated throughout the process. The sense of being part of a learning community was felt most strongly by core members, indicating the benefits of sustained interaction when seeking to build a community. There were costs of working in these ways, particularly in terms of the amount of time devoted to learning together. The need to maintain an open mind and suspend judgement was also not without its stresses and strains. Nevertheless, it was an energising and rewarding learning process that developed individual and collective understandings, and our writing, reviewing and editing skills at the same time.

FUTURE DIRECTIONS OF TRAVEL

Although the publication of this book is an important landmark for us, this is not the end of our individual or collective travels. We are also not alone in our explorations: there are many fellow travellers out there, and our choice of citations and suggestions for further reading, in each of the chapters, gives some indication of the many people who are inspiring our own academic practices. A key question is in what directions future explorations should be heading. There are many possibilities and we reflect on some of these.

We hope others will join us in seeking to extend, revise and refine our conceptual map of the knowledge and practice terrain (figure 16.1). This will undoubtedly involve extending the examination of related concepts. It is also likely to involve further analysis of how existing and additional concepts intersect with and provide new insights into knowledge and practice. The domains lying at the centre of our conceptual map should also be debated, refined and challenged, particularly in the light of a wider range of context-specific empirical studies.

There is a need for continuing exploration of knowledge and practice in disciplines and in settings other than those related to work and organisations. There is also potentially much to be gained from developing a richer understanding of knowledge and practice in other societies, particularly those not steeped in a Western intellectual tradition, for instance by drawing on and collaborating with social anthropologists. While extending the scope of our empirical gaze, we need to consider how insights from such studies can inform our understanding of knowledge and practice in organisations.

In undertaking future explorations in this terrain, we would recommend that there are some values and practices to 'pack' for the journey: valuing and respecting difference; suspending judgement; opening up rather than closing down conversations; including a diversity of voices; and ensuring equality of voice. There are also some things that we should probably leave behind: rigid baggage and frameworks from the past that overly constrain where we can travel in the future and our means of getting there. We may also wish to jettison unrealistic expectations of quick journeys with clear and tangible outcomes.

Finally, before heading off in different directions, we should reflect on why we are doing so. There are potentially many reasons why researchers and other practitioners are interested in the relationship between knowledge and practice. At least three underpinning motives are evident across the chapters of this book. First, for some authors the underpinning motive is to enhance understanding in order to improve opportunities and processes for learning and development (at individual, group and organisational levels), which in turn has the potential to improve performance. Second, other authors are primarily driven by a desire to better understand and challenge evident inequalities of voice, opportunities, resources and rewards in organisations and societies. Finally, some authors seek to develop and enrich our understanding of continuity and change (at organisational and societal levels), which in turn can help us to challenge the status quo. These motives are not mutually exclusive and they are all important. For this and many other reasons we wish you well on your future travels and we hope to hear from you, in some form or another, along the way.

REFERENCES

Best, A., & Holmes, B.J. (2010) Systems thinking, knowledge & action: Towards better models & methods. *Evidence & Policy.* 6(2): 145–159.

Burrell, G., & Morgan, G. (1979) *Sociological paradigms & organizational analysis.* London: Heinemann.

Frame, B., & Brown, J. (2008) Developing post-normal technologies for sustainability. *Ecological Economics.* 65: 225–241.

Haas, P.M. (1992) Epistemic communities & international policy coordination. *International Organization.* 46(1): 1–35.

Mouffe, C. (2013) *Agonistics: Thinking the world politically.* London: Verso.

Mapping a way

Index

For Product Safety Concerns and Information please contact our EU
representative GPSR@taylorandfrancis.com
Taylor & Francis Verlag GmbH, Kaufingerstraße 24, 80331 München, Germany